The Devil's Box

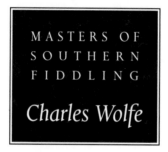

MASTERS OF
SOUTHERN
FIDDLING

Charles Wolfe

Foreword by Mark O'Connor

The Country Music Foundation Press & Vanderbilt University Press
NASHVILLE

First paperback edition 1998
First digital edition 2009

Printed on acid-free paper
Manufactured in the United States of America

Library of Congress Cataloging-in-Publication Data

Wolfe, Charles K.
The devil's box : masters of southern fiddling / Charles Wolfe;
foreword by Mark O'Connor. — 1st ed.
    p. cm.
Includes bibliographical references and index.
    ISBN 13: 978-0-8265-1324-3 (paper: alk. paper)
    ISBN 10: 0-8265-1324-7 (paper: alk. paper)
        1. Fiddling—History and criticism. 2. Fiddlers—Southern
States—Biography. 3. Fiddle tunes—History and criticism.
I. Title.
ML3551.7.S68W65   1997
787.2'1642'09—dc21
96-51254

To Bill Harrison,

Publisher of *The Devil's Box*,

and to

Stephen Davis,

Editor of *The Devil's Box*,

for their years of

encouragement and devotion to

old-time fiddling

Contents

Foreword

I<small>T IS WITH GREAT DELIGHT THAT</small> I <small>FIND</small> *The Devil's Box* taking its place in the history of American fiddling as one of the finest chronicles of this uniquely American art form. Charles Wolfe is a widely respected country-music historian and a friend and colleague in music, supremely qualified to explore the influences, history, and connections represented in fiddle music. With *The Devil's Box*, he has ensured that the Southern fiddle tradition is revealed as an undeniable influence in the history of American music. I can think of no one more qualified to explore the subject of fiddling or who could handle this task with greater care or skill. His book has much to teach us about America's musical heritage and about the possibilities open to imaginative musicians.

Opening these pages for the first time to read of the musical journeys of my heroes, I found myself continually reminded of those fiddlers who have cleared the paths for modern fiddlers like me. I found myself reminded of the debt I owe not only my own teachers but their teachers as well.

After all, fiddling is a tradition carried on by teachers, whether formally or informally. I am who I am today largely because of what I was taught and the legacy that was passed to me. In my work as an adjunct professor at Vanderbilt University's Blair School of Music, I strive to hand down the music with the same care that was used when it was given to me.

From quite an early age, I was fortunate to have had the chance to meet and play with some of the greatest fiddlers who ever laid bow to string. Hearing the stories they told about their heroes (the fiddlers in this book) held great fascination for me. How could they not become my heroes too?

As a contest fiddler, I grew up hearing about the legends of these Southern fiddlers from the older folks around me. My teacher, Benny Thomasson, was friends with Eck Robertson in Texas, and what a legacy they—along with Bob Wills, Clark Kessinger, and others—have left us. Benny's father and uncle were both great fiddlers and composed one of the most beautiful waltzes to ease off a Texas fiddle, "Midnight on the Water." Benny taught me this gem in 1974, and I still play it in concerts and recitals to this day.

As much as I grilled Benny about the old days, he never told me about the Thomasson Brothers recording their music at a 1920s session in Texas—which was something I learned from this book. Could they possibly have recorded "Midnight on the Water" at that session? Could a Thomasson Brothers recording of that classic tune still exist in a box of old things in an attic somewhere in Texas? I get chills just thinking about that.

To be sure, *The Devil's Box* chronicles the careers of the first fiddlers to record in America. But in a larger sense Charles Wolfe has documented the legacy of all fiddlers. Not only have fiddlers learned from the music of these performers, but we can discover great insight from the hard-traveled paths they took, whether they were session musicians, contest fiddlers, recording artists, or composers.

As I read *The Devil's Box*, not only did I learn more about the great fiddlers who preceded us, I also learned a great deal about myself. We fiddlers and fiddling enthusiasts of today are very much connected to these men from the past. It's as if the same blood runs through our veins and a similar spirit enters the body as the bow is lifted to strike the tune. It is uncanny how the careers of modern-day fiddlers relate to those of the pioneers covered in the pages of this book.

Tommy Jackson, for example, the first country session fiddling king and one of the true Nashville Cats of the forties and fifties, kept fiddling alive in Nashville as rock & roll threatened to obliterate country and bluegrass. In the eighties, I faced a similar problem when fiddling was nearly dead in Nashville because of an influx of pop musicians and producers as well as the introduction of the synthesizer.

Atlanta's Clayton McMichen spent a lifetime trying to fight against the hillbilly image of country stringbands and old-time fiddlers with his forays into jazz. I too lived in Atlanta, playing fiddle with a jazz fusion group called the Dixie Dregs. I have always felt the hillbilly stigma, and my work in the jazz and classical settings is due, in part, to a belief that the fiddle can rise above any pigeonhole.

Clark Kessinger says he was a natural musician, a self-taught country fiddler who was a fierce competitor in fiddling contests. But he also knew and studied the records of classical greats Kreisler, Szigeti, and Heifetz. I have always described my music education in much the same way and have played with, and for, the three classical greats of this era: Stern, Perlman, and Zuckerman. Kessinger, in 1971, made his last record for the Rounder label (Rounder 004) and passed away on June 4, 1975. I made my first record in 1974 for Rounder (Rounder 044), and within a week after Kessinger's passing I won the Grand Master's Fiddling championship at the age of thirteen.

Reading the studies of the fiddlers in these pages makes me wish I had been able to make better contact with these older heroes when they were still with us. Fortunately, Charles Wolfe brings to life each of these pioneering fiddlers with such vividness and clarity that their stories, and their music, will not soon be forgotten.

Every year, when I host an instructional camp for fiddlers just west of Nashville, I take one evening to observe my own personal tradition. Out there in the woods I walk up to a lake where one can hear a multitude of natural sounds along with the strains of fiddle music filtering up from the camp. When in the distance I hear the sound of a freight train headed for Nashville, I can't help but think that it must be the same railway line that Fiddlin' Arthur Smith of the Grand Ole Opry used to work for. Thanks to Charles Wolfe's book, we know what Smith was probably going to do when he got to town.

I hope we can all keep the memories of these greats with us as we continue to explore the myriad possibilities of the fiddle. No right-thinking person would dare challenge our devotion to this passion—or our appreciation of its storied history. After all, fiddlin' is serious business.

"*Don't you give up that fiddle, boy!*" That's a timeless phrase I must have heard again and again over the years. It lives on today, though now you would often be obliged to substitute "girl," as fiddling knows no gender boundaries in the 1990s.

The lore of the fiddle continues, moving this way and that like a well-rosined bow. *"Hey, did you hear 'bout the time when Uncle Eck went up against a young Ben Thomasson down in Texas? Tied ten times! . . . Nobody could play a waltz better than Kessinger, no siree! . . . Did you know that the tune 'Martha Campbell' came from Kentucky? Or was it Tennessee? . . . Nope, my friend's grand-dad wrote 'Black Mountain Rag,' and that's a fact! . . . Could you play 'Hell Amongst the Yearlings' and pull that long bow across it one more time?"*

Yahoo! Get after it, son—and daughter! Catch you on the Internet, or at camp, or at Vanderbilt . . . or just down the road.

Mark O'Connor
Nashville

Acknowledgments

A number of people have helped me with individual essays, and I have tried to express my gratitude to them in the "Sources" notes of the specific essays. However, there are also people who have been invaluable sources of encouragement and knowledge for this book as a whole, and during the twenty-five years I have been researching and writing about Southern fiddling and old-time music. These include Bill Harrison, whose knowledge of Southern fiddling is exceeded only by his generosity in sharing it; and Steve Davis, who for years has carved time out from a busy schedule to edit *The Devil's Box*, and to share with me tapes, records, and opinions. Another source of wisdom and encouragement has been John Hartford, one of the country's most ardent students of fiddling traditions, and one of the most creative at finding ways to keep these traditions alive. I am also indebted to Charlie Seemann and Richard Blaustein for their advice and suggestions, as well as Paul Wells, of the Center for Popular Music. I have drawn upon discography research by the late Gus Meade, as well as the forthcoming country music discography compiled by Tony Russell and Bob Pinson.

In addition, I have benefited much from discussions and advice over the years from Paul Ritscher, Mike Seeger, Alan Jabbour, Eddie Stubbs, W. K. McNeil, Gene Wiggins, Curly Fox, Reuben Powell, Ivan Tribe, George Custer, Jim Griffith, and Lepingwell Freeze. I am grateful to the staff of the Country Music Foundation: Bob Pinson, Paul Kingsbury, and Chris Skinker for their advice as the book developed, and to Charles Backus of Vanderbilt University Press for his enthusiasm and encouragement in developing this book.

I owe a very special debt to my wife, Mary Dean, who assisted me with many of the interviews for this book, and to my daughters, Stacey Wolfe and Cindy Wolfe Beatty, for their help. For help in preparing the manuscript, I must thank Susan Gay and Betty Nokes. And finally, but by no means least, I am grateful to the country's best-known contemporary fiddler, Mark O'Connor, for his eloquent foreword to the book.

The Commercial Fiddling Tradition

I can hear them dance, like a foggy song,
Through the deepest one of my slumbers,
The fiddle squeaking the boots along
And my father calling the numbers.
> —Stephen Vincent Benet

Now you play pretty good fiddle, boy,
But give the devil his due;
I'll bet a fiddle of gold against your soul,
'Cause I think I'm better than you.
> —Charlie Daniels

THEY CALLED THE INSTRUMENT "THE DEVIL S BOX" because some thought it was sinful to play one. Sometimes in recent years, people would be tearing down old log cabins to get at the logs and they would find hidden in the wall an old beat-up fiddle. At first they puzzled about this, but then people explained that the man who lived there was once a fine old-time fiddler, but that in later years he had gotten religion. In his zeal, he became convinced that he must turn his back on his old life, and especially that devil's instrument, the fiddle. After all, the fiddle was for good times and strong drink. Look at the old tunes; you gave the fiddler a "dram," and you heard tunes like "Devil's Dream" and "Devil in the Woodpile," "Hell Among the Yearlings" and "Hell Broke Loose in Georgia," "Hell and Scissors" and "Hell Bound for Alabama." And didn't one take the rattles of a serpent—the rattlesnake—and put them in the fiddle to improve the tone? The evidence was strong, and many newly saved fiddlers took their instruments and smashed them against the wall. But others, unable to part with the heirlooms they had devoted so much of their lives to, quietly dropped them behind the walls of their cabins and kept quiet, hoping perhaps that some day in the future, in a kinder and more tolerant age, someone would find them and let them be heard again.

One such age started in the 1920s, when the new mass media of radio and phonograph records were beginning to revolutionize American music. In 1922 a brash young Texas fiddler named Eck Robertson appeared at the New York offices of the Victor Talking Machine Company and recorded "Sallie Gooden." In 1923, a middle-aged Georgia millhand named John Carson climbed the stairs to a temporary studio in Atlanta, and recorded for the General Phonograph Company a tune he had been playing at fiddler's contests for years, "The Old Hen Cackled and the Rooster Is Going to Crow." Both were important firsts, and today historians credit them with being the first two recordings in a new genre that would eventually be called country music.

For the next two decades as the new music struggled to emerge from its regional bounds and overcome the stereotypes imposed on it, the fiddle became a key instrument in its image. The guitarist was an accompanist, keeping rhythm and backing singers; the banjoist, in those pre-bluegrass days, was a comedian. Only the fiddler was a really serious instrumentalist, the one who kicked off the tune, played the melody, took the breaks, drove the band. It was always assumed that the fiddle was the hardest of the folk instruments to play and that the fiddler was the most serious artist in the classic Southern stringband. After all, the classic virtuosos of the time, such as Szigeti and Kreisler, never singled out the singing of the Carter Family or Jimmie Rodgers, or the banjo playing of Uncle Dave Macon; they heaped their praise on Clark Kessinger and Eck Robertson—fiddlers. Southern music contests included categories for guitar, banjo, and harmonica, but they were, in the end, *fiddling* contests. The big money was always in the various fiddle categories, and there were always more fiddle entries than in any other categories. The big stars, the ones who could draw the crowds, were fiddlers that had made records or been heard on radio. In the 1930s, when promoters like Larry Sunbrock sponsored traveling fiddling contests that attracted thousands of fans, the big champion fiddlers stalked the land like western gunfighters—playing a town at a time, balancing their skills with their reputations, always wondering when they would have to face down some young kid who thought he was better.

Newcomers to this world often asked if there was a difference between a fiddle and a violin. One answer is that the word "fiddle" has always been associated with the folk or the working class, whereas "violin" has implied formal training, usually in the European manner. Yet "fiddle" is an venerable word, which *The Oxford English Dictionary* finds in use as early as 1205, and in the classic *Piers Plowman* in 1377. It is hard to tell just what kind of instrument these medieval uses refer to, but they often seem associated with the dance (one reference explains a "fiddler" is "one to whose music others dance"), and have a contemptuous tone to them. But the instruments themselves have no real difference; good fiddlers sought out the best older violins they could afford. Lesser musicians would experiment with adjusting the soundpost and even add steel strings to make the tone louder and more easily heard at country dances.

Unlike the world of acoustic guitars and banjos, for whom the commercial companies like Martin and Gibson have set nationwide standards for manufacturing, the world of fiddles has an older and much murkier sense of pedigree. Many of the fiddlers from the 1920s preferred nineteenth-century European instruments. A favorite type was a Stainer, made over several generations by a German family. These were "fat" instruments, with a higher arch and belly, and country fiddlers liked them because they were louder than average. Another familiar type were copies of the classic Stradivarius, imitating the classic design even down to the label or inscription. During the nineteenth century, hundreds of these imitation Strads made their way into America, and even though they were counterfeits, many were not bad instruments. Bob Wills, for example, had such a copy as one of his main instruments. Fiddlin' John Carson played an old family fiddle that his grandfather had brought over from Ireland in the 1840s. For years, Grand Ole Opry star Roy Acuff introduced his fiddler, Howdy Forrester, as playing a Stradivarius, though in fact what Forrester was playing was a Guarnerius. It was an impressive violin by any standards, one that Acuff had purchased from a classical violinist in Buffalo, New York. Acuff himself had learned to play fiddle in his twenties on a Hoff violin.

All of which is not to say that there was no domestic or folk tradition of fiddle-making. While museums love to show instruments made from cigar boxes and ones made from gourds and even things like automobile mufflers, a serious tradition of Southern fiddle-makers has existed for generations. Gordon Tanner, son of famed leader of the string-band called the Skillet Lickers, spent much of his career in his Georgia fiddle shop. Ernie Hodges, profiled in these pages, for years maintained a fiddle shop and repair shop near Atlanta, servicing members of the Atlanta symphony and members of country square-dance bands.

While the instruments themselves are not all that different from the older European models, many fiddlers do experiment with unusual ways of tuning the strings. A favorite is what many call "cross tuning," usually E–A–E–A, to get a bagpipe-like drone effect. Other techniques include raising one or two of the strings with matchsticks so as to play triple stops (hitting three strings at once). In the 1960s Nashville studio fiddler Tommy Jackson actually invented a capo (or clamp) to go across the neck of the fiddle in order to play in a higher position. Other makers, like their European counterparts, experimented with different woods and varnishes, seeking the distinctive tone. Howdy Forrester was fond of noting, however, that the true secret to tone in country music was the bow, and that someone with a good, well-strung bow could make do on a mediocre instrument.

* * *

In spite of the zeal of preachers, fiddling had been for generations a hallmark of Southern culture, lore, and politics. Thomas Jefferson was a fiddler, and one who thought enough of the fiddle tunes he ran across to write them down in his notebooks. The legendary Davy Crockett was a skilled fiddler and buck dancer, and his song "Col. Crockett's Reel," collected as early as 1839, is still played today in West Virginia under the name "The Route." Civil War photos show dozens of soldiers holding their fiddles proudly, and diaries and letters are full of references to fiddle tunes and how they originated. In the 1880s voters in Tennessee were treated to the spectacle of two brothers, Alf and Bob Taylor, running against each other for the governor's chair. This was unusual enough, but each brother was an accomplished fiddler, and each took his fiddle on the campaign trail with him. Illustrated newspapers of the day featured pictures of them playing against each other on the platform. (Alf helped popularize a tune called "The Fox Chase" and even made recordings in the 1920s.)

In the 1920s Henry Ford, who for some Americans had more moral authority than many politicians, became concerned about the moral threat posed by jazz, by flappers who bobbed their hair, and by the Red scare. The solution to much of this, he reasoned, was to reawaken the old traditional values by reawakening traditional American music and dance. In a famous issue of his magazine *The Dearborn Independent*, he ran a cover showing a white-bearded fiddler dozing in a chair while smartly-dressed couples at a dance are shouting at him to wake him up and play some old square-dance music. Ford began running not only stories about the benefits of fiddle music but also diagrams showing how to do dances like the Virginia reel. He started his own record company to record fiddle tunes for square dances. Worried that there were many fiddlers out there who had been pushed into retirement by the popularity of the fox trot and the Charleston, Ford decided to flush them out by staging a series of fiddling contests at Ford dealerships across the South and Midwest. The result was a flurry of popular interest in fiddlers and fiddling contests in 1925 and 1926, with front-page stories in newspapers and even newsreel footage in theaters. Many of the fiddlers in Ford's contests, such as Tennessee's Uncle Bunt Stephens and Uncle Jimmy Thompson, did get their music on records and on the radio. And though the South had been having grassroots fiddling competitions long before and long after Ford came on the scene, the Ford campaign gave fiddlers a new sense of respectability—a moral vindication and even a political validation.

Fiddlers continued to play a part in Southern politics. In the 1930s Huey Long of Louisiana hired Will Gilmer's stringband, the Leake County Revelers, to play for his campaign and reinforce his image of a grassroots populist. In the 1940s Grand Ole Opry star Roy Acuff, originally a fiddler himself, ran for governor in Tennessee. In the 1960s Albert Gore Sr., the father of the later vice president, took his fiddle with him and played "Soldier's Joy" to crowds on his run for the Senate. In the 1970s, Robert Byrd, the senator from West Virginia and Senate majority leader, appeared at bluegrass festivals, on the Grand Ole Opry stage, and in the recording studio playing his fiddle. Many of his tunes were ones he had learned while growing up in West Virginia and during his early days as a local politician when he was known as "Fiddlin' Bob Byrd."

While fiddlers existed in virtually every county of the South, it was in the era from 1925 to 1955 that some of them became regionally and even nationally known. Records, radio, and sophisticated touring and promotion methods created a generation of fiddling "stars"—musicians whose styles and repertoires became popular throughout the South. Men like Uncle Jimmy Thompson, the "founder" of the Grand Ole Opry, and Eck Robertson, the popularizer of Texas-style contest fiddling, became legends in their time. Clayton McMichen and Arthur Smith sold thousands of records and became as well known in the South as the big-band leaders of the swing era. People like Slim Miller, who was also known as a comedian, and Doc Roberts, who played on as many vocal records as fiddle records, showed how fiddlers could adapt to newer forms of entertainment and still preserve their integrity as musicians. Fiddlin' John Carson and Gid Tanner were willing to play the rube to sell their music, but others, like Clark Kessinger, refused to compromise. Indeed, Kessinger became known as a "fiddler's fiddler," selling nothing but dazzling musicianship.

The Devil's Box is an interlocking series of studies of fiddlers from this golden age. These are musicians whose access to mass media at a crucial time in the development of Southern music gave them unparalleled power and influence on later generations of fiddlers. Their styles and tunes are heard yet today in a variety of settings: on breaks of hit records by George Jones, Alison Krauss, Randy Travis, Garth Brooks, Vince Gill; on the stages of dozens of fiddle contests, from the Grand Masters in Nashville to the venerable stage at Galax; in bluegrass festivals and records; and even on the stage of symphony orchestras, where artists like the McClain Family and Mark O'Connor have sought to merge the older fiddling styles with modern formal music. Some of this influence has been handed down already through generations: Clark Kessinger's tunes were passed to Benny Thomasson and through him to Mark O'Connor; Bob Wills's style has been passed through Merle Haggard to younger groups like Asleep at the Wheel; the sound of Arthur Smith is heard in the music of Ralph Blizard and to a younger generation yet unsung.

During the first decade of country records, fiddling constituted a major part of the commercial releases. Frank Walker, the man who founded Columbia's "Old Familiar Tunes" series, considered fiddle tunes one of the four major categories of his product. Though there were no individual fiddle records that approached the million-selling status of "The Wreck of the Old 97" or the half-million status of Jimmie Rodgers, as a genre the records sold steadily and widely. In their search for new recording stars, the seven major companies routinely toured the South, setting up field sessions and temporary studios in hotel rooms from Louisville to San Antonio. They managed to capture an impressive cross section of Southern fiddling. Between 1922 (when Victor first recorded Eck Robertson) and 1942 (when the American musicians' union went on national strike, and country music began to feature newer, electric instruments), the main commercial companies released sides by some 300 Southern fiddlers. Many of them did only a handful of sides—two or four—and dropped back into obscurity, to spend the rest of their lives playing for local dances or contests. At some time in the future, this vast, virtually unexplored body of music needs to be systematically studied to gain some insight into what varieties of Southern fiddle music are represented.

In other cases, the companies recorded a few fiddle players extensively. Table 1 (below) lists the number of records released by the most-recorded of these fiddlers. The chart is based on the number of records made, not on the number actually sold. (Sales figures for these early days are hard to come by; fairly complete figures exist only for Columbia and Victor, and scattered figures for Gennett.)

TABLE 1

Clayton McMichen*	Col., Decca et al 1924–39	175 sides
John Carson	Col., Bluebird 1923–34	170 sides
Doc Roberts*	Gennett, ARC 1925–34	80 sides
Kessinger Bros.	Brunswick, Vocalion	70 sides
Willie Narmour	Okeh, Bluebird	50 sides
Bob Wills**	Bluebird, ARC	49 sides
Stripling Bros.	Brunswick, ARC	46 sides
Cliff Gross***	ARC, 1933–38	43 sides
Arthur Smith****	Bluebird et. al.	30 sides

*excludes vocal sides
** excludes sides not featuring fiddle
*** includes selected sides done with Light Crust Doughboys
**** excludes sides done under name of Delmore Brothers, and those sides done after World War II.

Each one of these artists—as well as others chronicled here—dealt with his fame, his art, and his image differently. None set out with the deliberate intent to forge a career in music. Like similar artists in blues, country, and gospel music during these early years, each began with a simple love of the music and had to improvise ways to turn this into a viable career. The different methods these fiddlers used to accomplish this is part of the theme of this book.

By no means should this book be seen as a complete history of Southern fiddling, or a complete documentary of Southern fiddlers. Some important names are missing. Fiddlin' John Carson himself is not discussed at length, because he is already the subject of an excellent biography, Gene Wiggins's *Fiddlin' Georgia Crazy* (1987). The fine Alabama team, the Stripling Brothers, is also discussed in Joyce Cauthen's *With Fiddle and Well-Rosined Bow* (1989). Willie Narmour, the fascinating Mississippi fiddler, well deserves a chapter to himself; his repertoire and style, exemplified in tunes like "Charleston # 1" and "Carroll County Blues," are perhaps the most unusual and distinctive of all the fiddlers discussed here. But Narmour died in 1961, long before anyone was interested in interviewing him, and what is really known about him and his music could be fitted onto one page. The definitive Cajun fiddler Dennis McGee, known for his breathtaking fiddle duets with Sadie Courville and later Ernest Frugé, deserves a chapter here, but to place him in the proper cultural context of Cajun music would require far more than a mere chapter. Curly Fox and Tommy Magness deserve more space than they get in my discussion of "The Black Mountain Rag." The stories of Cliff Gross, Howdy Forrester, Erwin Rouse, and Dale Potter need yet to be told as well.

By the same token, a complete history of fiddling in the South would include the great traditional fiddlers who, for various reasons, did not commercially record or forge a career in radio. These would include the legendary West Virginia artist Ed Haley, who influenced people as diverse as Clark Kessinger and Georgia Slim Rutland, and whose work survives only as a series of home recordings; the Mississippian W. E. Claunch, whose work is preserved on a series of small discs for the Library of Congress; the brilliant Kentuckian W. M. Stepp, whose masterpiece "Glory in the Meeting House" was preserved only on a fragile Library of Congress disc; the influential Georgia long bow master Joe Lee, or west Tennessee's Grady Stringer, or east Tennessee's

Charlie Acuff. None of these ever won the widespread popularity of a McMichen or Smith—many of them refused to record commercially, suspicious that their music would be stolen or bowdlerized—but they influenced an impressive number of key fiddlers on a one-on-one basis.

More recently, such a complete history would also include the bluegrass fiddlers that came to prominence after World War II: Chubby Wise, Benny Sims, Benny Martin, Paul Warren, Buck Ryan, Vassar Clements, Gordon Terry, Red Taylor, Bobby Hicks, Kenny Baker, and others. It would include women performers, starting with Samantha Bumgarner, leader of one of the first stringbands to record; Lilly May Ledford, of the Coon Creek Girls; Ramona Jones, whose long partnership with husband Grandpa Jones has sometimes overshadowed her own considerable skills; and extending up to recent award-winning stars like Alison Krauss and Laurie Lewis. It would also include the new generation of versatile soloists like John Hartford and Mark O'Connor, who are taking the older traditions into new frontiers. A complete history would include tributes to all of these, but that is another book for another time.

* * *

Since 1969, many fiddlers across the South have kept in touch through a quarterly publication that has leant its name to this book: *The Devil's Box*. Originating as a newsletter for the Tennessee Valley Old-Time Fiddlers' Association, *The Devil's Box* contains news of upcoming contests, record and tape reviews, transcribed fiddle tunes, news about fiddlers and old-time musicians, and articles about fiddlers, both famous and obscure. For much of that time, the journal has been the responsibility of two men: Bill Harrison, of Madison, Alabama, who has been the publisher and subscription manager; and Steve Davis, of Emporia, Kansas, who has been the editor and scrounger of articles. Today it is read by music fans throughout the world, and has been named to a Library of Congress select list of publications about fiddling. It has become a powerful forum for discussions about fiddling and where it is going (and where it has been), and Messrs. Harrison and Davis remain as devoted as ever to their mission. (Subscriptions and further information may be gotten from *The Devil's Box*, 305 Stella Drive, Madison, Alabama 35758.)

Many of the essays in this collection first appeared in *The Devil's Box*, and most of the others have been inspired by it. The long pieces on Arthur Smith, Tommy Jackson, and Uncle Jimmy Thompson first appeared as special issues of the journal. Some, such as the one about Clayton McMichen, have been substantially expanded from the versions that appeared in the *Box*. "The Recordings of Eck Robertson" first appeared in *The Journal of Country Music* and is reproduced here by permission. "Kessinger," "Mr. Grayson's Train," and "Doc Roberts: Behind the Masks" appear in print for the first time.

I

The Pioneers

The Oldest Recorded
Fiddling Styles

O F THE PIONEERING PHONOGRAPH RECORDS MADE BY various fiddlers in the 1920s, which represents the most archaic or oldest style? It has been known for some years that a number of old fiddlers who recorded in the mid to late 1920s had roots well back into the nineteenth century, but how far back? And how accurately do the records represent their music? What is the relationship between the date of the recording and the age of the fiddler? Did fiddlers who recorded after the 1920s, and were possibly exposed to radio and records, "contaminate" their styles by listening to these mass media? On the other hand, did younger fiddlers in some cases more accurately and carefully preserve a style that was much older than their physical ages?

To begin with, it is important to note that many of the best-known fiddlers from the 1920s and 1930s were in fact quite young when they made their most famous records and won their reputations. Some, like Lowe Stokes and Curly Fox, were mere teenagers when they first gained fame, and others were only in their twenties: Clayton McMichen was twenty-five when he first recorded, and Doc Roberts was only twenty-eight. Clark Kessinger was thirty-two when he first cut records. Many of the really successful stars of old-time music were, in fact, brash young men who could readily adopt their styles and repertoires to the demands of the new age's commercialism and media. Even Eck Robertson, who is generally hailed as the first Southern fiddler to record (he did so in 1922, a year before Fiddlin' John Carson), was only thirty-four when he went into the studio to do his great "Sallie Gooden." And there is evidence that he was elaborating from a fancy, personal "contest" style rather than a pure traditional style. However, a handful of senior citizens did get into the studios in the early years, and it is to these musicians we must first look for the purest and most archaic styles preserved.

Unfortunately, the very quality that interests us about these musicians—their strong ties with nineteenth-century music—worked against them in the studios and in the new commercial world. Many of them only made two to four recordings, unable or unwilling to make the changes the record company executives wanted in the rapidly developing world of commercial old-time music. Very few of them preserved any substantial part of their repertoires, and some of these— as we shall see—were compromised by demands the company made on the fiddlers. After the initial success of Fiddlin' John Carson in 1923–25, very few of the companies were willing to record unaccompanied fiddle performances such as Eck Robertson's "Sallie Gooden." The few unaccompanied fiddle pieces that were recorded were often done because the fiddler was also a singer or comedian, such as in the case of John Carson or Henry Bandy. Furthermore, few of these records by older fiddlers were very popular. Jilson Setters's Victor records sold only between 5,000 and 10,000 copies each, and Uncle Jimmy Thompson's sole 1926 side sold barely 9,000 copies. Other recordings, such as those on the Broadway label by Dedrick Harris, are so rare that even an accurate discography, much less music analysis, is well nigh impossible.

Because of this record company attitude, a number of fiddlers went into the studios to have custom records made, paying for the discs out of their own pockets and hoping to sell enough back home to make it all worthwhile. (These records, for all their incredible rarity, are at least honest; the fiddlers themselves were footing the bills, and they played the tunes they wanted, the way they wanted.) Jess Young, for instance, did two such solos at his first 1925 session (along with several band pieces, which were issued), and while they were pressed and printed for Young, no copies appear to be extant. RCA Victor files also show that in mid-1925 a fiddler named John W. Daniel, from Shreveport, Louisiana, recorded four sides which were probably custom jobs (he was the first Louisiana fiddler, or country artist at all, to record). Even more alluring is a citation from the Victor files of August 14, 1925, when a fiddler named Ted Markle, from Winsboro, Texas, appeared in New York to make three recordings, all of which bear fascinating titles:

BVE 100 33312-3   Reel of Old Time Tunes
BVE 96 33313-3   Long Horn Pipes
BVE 96 33314-1   Indian Dance

There are dozens of other similar hints of unknown or unrecovered early recordings as well. The world of cylinder discography has scarcely been explored by old-time music and folk music scholars, and doubtless there are other pre-1920 cylinders like the ones allegedly made in 1899 by Art Haines, a Texas fiddler who later played with Bob Wills.

Thus any list of the "oldest" fiddling styles on record must necessarily be labeled "tentative." Nonetheless, I have compiled a table of these fiddlers (see table 2). One could organize such a table in one of several ways: simple chronology of earliest recording, in which case Robertson's recordings done in July 20, 1922, would be first; age of fiddler at initial recording; or birth date of fiddler. I have chosen to structure the table here by the last method, putting birth date of fiddler as the most important concern.

Surprisingly, the much-ballyhooed Uncle Jimmy Thompson comes out on top of this list, with a birth date of 1848. Uncle Jimmy, who is widely credited with being the old fiddler who "started" the Grand Old Opry in 1925 (see chapter 3 for more on Thompson), was learning his recorded version of "Flying Clouds" as early as 1860, when he was seventeen. Uncle Jimmy left us a total of four recordings, and on all of them he betrays his age a little; we also have extensive repertoire lists of Thompson's songs. On all the recordings, Uncle Jimmy is accompanied on the piano by his niece, a formally trained musician, and we have no way of knowing how this might have affected his playing. (He often played solo in his personal appearances.)

One of the oldest fiddlers to record is missing from this table. This is Henry C. Gilliland, the fiddler who accompanied Eck Robertson in 1922. Gilliland was about the same age as Uncle Jimmy, being born in Texas or the Indian Territory about 1848. He was a Confederate veteran, a former Indian fighter, and a former justice of the peace. He liked to entertain at the various Confederate reunions around the country, and in 1922, when he was seventy-four, he met young Eck Robertson at such a gathering in Virginia. The pair traveled to New York to see a

Table 2 *Early Fiddle Studies Preserved On Record*

Name	Birth date	Home	Date Recorded	Age when rec.	No. sides	Company
Uncle Jimmy Thompson	1848	Wilson Co TN	1926, 1930	76	2/2	Colum./Voc.
Blind Joe Mangrum	1853	Paducah KY	1928	75	2*	Victor
Uncle Am Stuart	1856	Morristown TN	1924	68	14	Vocalion
Blind Bill Day ("Jilson Setters")	1860	Rowan Co KY	1928 (LC1937)	68 (77)	10	Victor (LC)
Emmett Lundy	1864	Grayson Co VA	1925 (LC1941)	61 (87)	2 (ca. 25)	Okeh (LC)
Fiddlin' John Carson	1868	Fannin Co GA	1923 et al.	56	2 et al.	Okeh
Dedrick Harris	1868(?)	Asheville NC	1924, 1925	56	4/1	Broadway/Okeh
Fiddlin' Cowan Powers	1870(?)	Dungannon VA	1924 et al.	54	17 et al.	Victor/Okeh
Jim Booker	1872	Jessamine Co KY	1927	55	5 plus	Gennett
Henry Bandy	1876	Petroleum KY	1928	52	4 (uniss.)	Gennett***
Morrison Twins	1876	Searcy AR	1930	53	2	Victor
Carter Brothers: George	1869	Monroe Co MS	1928	64	13 (3 uniss.)	Okeh/Vocalion
Andrew	1878			60		
Ahas Gray	1881	Carroll Co GA	1924	43	2**	Okeh
W. B. Houchens	1884	Anderson Co KY	1922	38	12 plus	Gennett
Eck Robertson	1887	Amarillo TX	1922 et al.	34	15****	Victor

* Other unissued sides have survived, making total of 4

** Recorded in 1930 with band headed by John Dilleshaw (Seven Foot Dilly)

*** 4 Gennett sides originally issued, not released until 1981

**** Recent search of Victor vaults confirms none of unissued parts survive friend of Gilliland's and made their two historic recordings on June 30, 1922; they did fiddle duets of two chestnuts, "Arkansas Traveler" and "Turkey in the Straw." The problem is that Gilliland did not record any solo numbers and that he played second to Eck's lead in the duets. Thus, it is impossible for us to really evaluate what his fiddling might have sounded like. He is thus omitted from the list.

Blind Joe Mangrum, from Paducah, Kentucky, is probably the second oldest fiddler to record. He won fame late in life by placing high in the same national Henry Ford–sponsored contest that won Uncle Jimmy Thompson so much fame. (Indeed, Mangrum and Thompson competed head-to-head at a regional contest in Louisville in 1926.) Mangrum's two sole released records for Victor show him accompanied by an accordion player—which was an accurate reflection of his personal appearances—and playing two breakdowns, "Bill Cheatam" and "Bacon and Cabbage," with a surprisingly pure tone and precision. (The Victor record only sold 4,300 when it was issued in 1929). Mangrum loved to show off his tone in waltzes and even light classical pieces, and was always disappointed when personnel at the Grand Ole Opry, on which he appeared regularly until the mid-1930s, discouraged him from playing these. Recently two test pressings of Mangrum waltzes have surfaced, and they do display a haunting, mellow sound unlike anything else in early recorded fiddle music.

The two oldest fiddlers to leave any substantial repertoire were Uncle Am Stuart, from Morristown, Tennessee, and Blind Bill Day, from Kentucky. Stuart left us some fourteen sides, done in June 1924 in New York, and Day (using his stage name Jilson Setters) left us ten 1928 sides for Victor, as well as some less interesting Library of Congress discs done in 1937. Unfortunately, both bodies of work are in some way compromised or "contaminated." Stuart was allowed to cut four unaccompanied sides ("Billie in the Low Ground," "Dixie - with Variations," "Waggoner," and "Grey Eagle") before being saddled with a New York studio musician who added vocals and a stiff tenor banjo to the remaining recordings. (This studio man was none other than Gene Austin, who would later become famous for singing "My Blue Heaven.") Stuart had almost certainly never played with Austin before, and the results of the collaboration are interesting, but hardly authentic. Day, for his part, was not allowed to record any sides solo, but was assigned a studio guitarist, Carson Robison, for a back-up man. Robison, well known as a singer and composer in early country music, does a superb job of backing Day, to be sure, but other evidence suggests that Day was more accustomed to performing solo.

Probably the largest and purest recorded repertoire of these early fiddlers is that left by Fiddlin' Cowan Powers of Virginia. On August 18, 1924, Powers brought his fiddle and his family stringband into Room No. 2 of the Victor studios in New York and began recording "Brown's Dream." During the next two days, Powers and his band (ukelele, banjo, guitar, mandolin) went through seventeen selections for the primitive Victor acoustic horn, with only minimal interference. (The ubiquitous Carson Robison was brought on to sing on two of the cuts.) The Powers recordings—some of which were never released—were among the first full stringband sides ever made, and some of them were popular enough that a few years later Victor had Ernest Stoneman make cover versions of them in the new electric process. (For more on Powers and his family band, see chapter 4.)

A few notes are in order about certain other fiddlers listed here. Jim Booker is notable in that he is one of the few black fiddlers to record, as well as one of the older fiddlers to record. He recorded as a member of Taylor's Kentucky Boys and as the Booker Orchestra in 1927, and may well have appeared incognito on other sides. (The sides by Taylor's Kentucky Boys, incidentally, done in 1927, form the first integrated recording sessions in American music history; jazz could not claim an integrated session until 1931.) Ahas Gray (A. A. Gray) is noteworthy in that he was one of the few older fiddlers allowed to record *solo*. The same is true of Dedrick Harris, a legendary fiddler from Asheville about whom too little is known, but who was an influence on Cherokee fiddler Manco Sneed. Harris recorded one solo ("Grey Eagle") for the rare Broadway label in New York in December 1924, and a second ("Cackling Hen") for Okeh in 1925. Finally, it is ironic that Eck Robertson, always listed first in fiddle record history, shows up *last* on this list, showing us that many older fiddling styles *followed* him into the studio.

If we assume that most non-professional fiddlers begin developing style and repertory by the time they are fifteen and that most have found their style by the time they are thirty (a hypothesis that surely needs testing), then we can assume that any fiddler born before 1870 almost certainly was a product of nineteenth century folk fiddling styles and repertoires. In this case, we then have eight candidates who might well have preserved nineteenth century styles and songs on record: Thompson, Mangrum, Stuart, Day, Lundy, Carson, Harris, and Powers. While each musician would need far more study to determine how "pure" each recorded repertoire is, it might be useful to list the songs that each recorded at their initial session. I have done this in table 3.

Table 3 Discography of Oldest Recorded Fiddling Styles

I. Uncle Jimmy Thompson

Nov. 1, 1926	Karo	Columbia
Atlanta	Billy Wilson	
April 4, 1930	Lynchburg	Vocalion
Knoxville	Uncle Jimmy's Favorite	
	Fiddling Pieces (Flying Clouds, Leather Britches)	

Reissues: Karo and Billy Wilson on County LP 542.
Lynchburg and Pieces on Hilltop JM-6022, Sears SPS-114

II. Blind Joe Mangrum

October 6, 1928	Mammoth Cave Waltz (uniss)	Victor
Nashville	Rose Waltz (uniss)	
	Bacon and Cabbage	
	Bill Cheetham (sic)	
	Cradle Song (uniss)	

Reissue: Bill Cheatam on County LP 542.

III. Uncle Am Stuart

June, 1924	Billie in the Low Ground	Vocalion
New York	Old Liza Jane	
	Sally Gooden	
	Dixie - with Variations	
	Waggoner	
	Grey Eagle	
	Cumberland Gap	
	Sourwood Mountain	
	Leather Breeches	
	Forki Deer	
	Nigger in the Woodpile	
	Old Granny Rattle-Trap	

George Boker
Rye Straw or The Unfortunate Dog

Reissues: none.

IV. Blind Bill Day (Jilson Setters)

Feb. 27, 1928   Forked Deer   Victor
New York   Marthie Campbell
                     The Wild Waggoner
                     Billy in the Lowlands
                     The Wild Horse or Stoney Point
                     Black-Eyed Susie
                     Grand Hornpipe
                     Little Boy Working on the Road
                     Way up on Clinch Mountain (Drunken Hiccough)
                     The Arkansas Traveler

Reissues: Billy in the Lowground and Forky Deer on Vetco 102.
            Stoney Point on Rounder 1033 (forthcoming).
NOTE: This artist recorded later for the Library of Congress.

V. Emmett Lundy

May 27, 1925   Piney Woods Gal   Okeh
New York   The Long-Eared Mule
                     (fiddle-harmonica duets w. E. Stoneman)

Reissue: Piney Woods Girl is on County LP 535.
NOTE: This artist recorded for the Library of Congress in 1941; 25 of these
            sides can be found on String LP 802, and three others on County 535.

VI. Fiddlin' John Carson

(Carson's extensive discography of over 170 songs is listed in JEMF Quarterly No.
36, winter 1974.)
Reissue: Rounder LP 1003.

VII. Dedrick Harris

Dec. 1924   The Grey Eagle (solo)   Broadway
New York   Bucking Mule (with Ernest Helton)

Whip the Devil Around the Stump
(with Ernest Helton)
Lone and Sad (vocal by Harris: no fiddle)

Aug. 1925	The Cackling Hen	Okeh
Asheville	(prob. other uniss sides)	

Reissues: none.

VIII. Fiddlin' Cowan Powers

Chapter 4 is a detailed account of Powers's career and includes a summary of this complex discography.

Reissue: Patty on the Turnpike is on County 525.

Finally, a bit of sobering perspective. For those truly interested in what nineteenth century fiddling sounded like, a look at the recorded history of Scots-Irish fiddling is instructive. Whereas no significant American fiddlers from the South apparently recorded before 1920, the Scotch master J. Scott Skinner was recording commercially as early as 1899. Skinner, referred to as "The Strathspey King," was born in Banchory in 1843, five years before Uncle Jimmy Thompson, and was appearing in contests by 1863. By February 1910, Skinner had already recorded over thirty tunes for major record companies in Great Britain, tunes of a style and repertoire well fixed by the time of the Civil War. Skinner too was one of Henry Ford's fiddlers, coming to America in 1926 to compete in one of Ford's international fiddle contests. No one seems to remember whether he brought any of his records.

The Recordings of Eck Robertson

MOST HISTORIANS NOW GIVE CREDIT TO LEGENDARY
Texas fiddler Eck Robertson (1887–1975) for making country
music's first commercial recordings. He did this at the New
York Victor studios in June 1922, over a year before Fiddlin' John Carson made his first recordings, and over five years before Jimmie
Rodgers first entered a studio. Unlike many of his contemporaries, Eck
Robertson lived well into the modern era and even appeared at a number of folk festivals. In spite of this, his career has not been well documented.

Robertson was important not only because he was a pioneering
recording artist, but also because he was a key figure in the development of the Texas fiddle style—the style that has come to dominate
most modern contest fiddling. Neither of these concerns has been
especially well addressed in the various writings about Robertson, or in
the handful of published interviews with him. Recent years, though,
have seen important new developments on this front. In 1991 County
Records issued an LP drawn from field tapes done at Robertson's home
back in 1963 by John Cohen, Mike Seeger, and Tracy Schwarz—the New
Lost City Ramblers. Included with the album was a large illustrated
booklet containing the most detailed and authoritative account so far
of Robertson's life and long career. Written by folklorists Blanton
Owen and Tom Carter, the booklet is based on materials loaned by the
Robertson family, as well as a number of excellent interviews done in
the 1960s by Mike Seeger. (This set, available only on LP, is *Eck Robertson: Famous Cowboy Fiddler*, County 202.) More recently, the Country
Music Foundation has acquired more material about the Robertson

saga, including Robertson's old scrapbooks, as well as documents from the original Victor files. This new data is especially revealing about the relationship between Robertson and the Victor company. It, along with the other new material and with new research into the roots of Texas fiddle music, makes it feasible to try to look more deeply at how this "first" country recording star went about his work, and how Eck Robertson sought to forge a career in the fledgling country music industry.

The natural starting point is that day when Eck Robertson and his friend Henry Gilliland appeared at the Victor studio in New York and asked for an audition. It is one of the classic stories of country music history: both men traveling from a Confederate reunion in Virginia, appearing in New York in their Confederate uniforms, and playing for astonished executives. Yet the ultimate source for this account seems to be a 1924 Victor catalogue publicity blurb for Victor release 18956—"Arkansas Traveler" (a fiddle duet with Robertson and Gilliland) and "Sallie Gooden" (a solo by Robertson). It reads:

> When we first saw these two artists, it was at our own Victor door, in the garb of Western plainsmen. They told us they could play the fiddle, and asked a hearing. As we knew several thousand persons who could play the fiddle, more or less, we were not especially impressed, but we asked them to begin. After the second number or so, we engaged them to make records of the old American country dances.

It is noteworthy that this account described the attire not specifically as Confederate uniforms, but merely as "the garb of Western plains-men"—garb that appears in the famous picture of Robertson in the cat-alogue—the picture where the flag is hanging from his fiddle neck, and where the dress is certainly more cowboy than Confederate. More curious, though, is the question of what motivated these men to want to put their music on record and to travel far up to New York to try to do so. There is also the question of what moved Victor to accept the challenge, and to give them a chance. In addition, to what extent did Robertson's cowboy image play a role in his getting to record, and exactly how did the recordings take place? Fortunately, some of the material in the Robertson scrapbooks and the original Victor files sheds some light on this.

If we assume the Robertson scrapbooks served the function that most performer scrapbooks do, we can surmise that they were designed to reflect the professional, public career of the artist. What is surprising in the Robertson case is that they do not start in June 1922—suggesting that Robertson had had a public career before he went to New York. One of the earliest pictures is dated 1907, and shows Robertson and his new wife, Nettie, posed with their instruments. In interviews Robertson recalled that he had decided to make a living with music when he was sixteen, and that by 1906 he and his wife were traveling around performing fiddle and piano music at silent movie houses. Often he did this dressed in a cowboy outfit, and it was probably around this time that he began billing himself as "the cowboy fiddler." Other clippings describe his rise to fame in the fiddle contest circuit, and by 1919 he was starting to attend the Old Confederate Soldiers' Reunions, held annually at various cities across the South. Many of the other fiddlers he met at these were, like his friend Henry Gilliland, genuine Confederate veterans; Robertson, though, got in as a son of a veteran. By 1921, he had met the famed Tennessee governor and fiddler Alf Taylor, and was invited to perform with him on stage at one of the reunions. (Curiously, John Carson, Robertson's rival to the claim of first country recording artist, also knew Taylor.)

Thus it was not surprising to find Robertson being invited to the annual 1922 Reunion held in Richmond, Virginia. This would become a crucial event in his decision to go to New York to record, but so far little printed documentation about the event has surfaced. Early in Robertson's notebook, though, is a yellowed, crumbling newspaper from the *Richmond News Leader* of June 21, 1922. In a banner headline story, the paper recounts details of the Confederate reunion, and features two photos of Robertson and his friend Henry Gilliland. (Gilliland was a former Indian fighter and justice of the peace from Altus, Oklahoma, but it is not clear whether Robertson met him at Richmond or had known him from earlier contests and reunions.) In one photo, Robertson and Gilliland are shown fiddling together, in standard suits, hatless; the caption notes that they turned the lobby of the Jefferson Hotel into a "barn dance." A second photo shows the pair playing on the sidewalk outside the hotel while General Jack Hale and a friend did an "old-time 'shake-down' and 'buck and wing.'" Other accounts mention that the pair played for the opening session of some

4,000, and it is easy to imagine fans and friends encouraging them to go up to put their wonderful music on record.

Just a few weeks before the Richmond trip, however, another incident occurred that might well have inspired Robertson to try to record. Since he was a child, Robertson had been living in the town of Vernon, Texas, and by the early 1920s he had been traveling and performing with two other locals under the informal name, the Vernon Fiddlers. The other fiddlers were Lewis Franklin and Dr. A. P. Howard, both well known on the contest circuit, and both later to play important roles in Texas fiddle history. By April 1922, the fame of the trio had spread far enough that a newsreel crew from Fox came to town to film them. "Representatives of Fox News Service Comes to Vernon For Express Purpose of Getting Close-Ups of Vernon Musicians In Action—Will Herald Throughout United States," read the headline in the *Vernon Record*. The "representative" focused on the three fiddlers as they were "attired in cowboy garb of bright hues," playing "two well-known fiddling tunes," on the doorstep of the Howard home. The cameraman had traveled by car from Ft. Worth expressly to get the trio before the camera and in hopes of "getting something different." He also concentrated on the trio's rare instruments: Howard owned a "Nicolaus Amatus" valued at $20,000, and a Stradivarius priced at $25,000; Franklin owned a Cordovara "made partly by a Norwegian"; Robertson could boast of a Stainer some "200 years old" which had "a wonderful tone."

To date, no prints of this film have surfaced, though a still photo showing the cameraman and the three fiddlers survives in the Robertson notebook. Whether it was really shown "over the country" or not is also not known. Obviously, any 1922 film would have been silent, but the whole experience might well have whetted Robertson's interest in the mass media. One can imagine him feeling that if he was good enough for a nationwide newsreel, he was also good enough for a commercial sound recording. Such a scenario, at least, might explain why a Southern fiddler might suddenly be motivated to try something no other fiddler from his area had tried, and something none of the commercial record companies had really thought of.

Once Robertson had the motivation to record, the next question was why he chose to try Victor. Here the answer seems to have been serendipity. Gilliland happened to have a contact at Victor—a lawyer named Martin W. Littleton who did occasional work for the company.

He invited the two fiddlers to stay with him after they got to New York (about June 28), gave them a tour of the city, and introduced them to the people up at the Victor studio. Robertson recalled the audition vividly, forty years later. "You couldn't fool that man that was running the shop then in the Victor office. . . . But when he come at me, he just come into the room just in a hurry with a long piece of paper with names on it. He done that on purpose, you see, thought he'd get rid of me just like he had all the rest of them. He said, 'Young man, get your fiddle out and start off on a tune.' Said, 'I can tell that quick whether I can use you or not.' Well, I just said to him right back, just as honest as I could, I said, 'Mister, I've come a long way to get an audition with you. Maybe I better wait and come back some other time.'" But the manager insisted Robertson play on the spot, so he started out on "Sallie Gooden." "Well, I didn't get to play half of 'Sallie Gooden'; he just throwed up his hands and stopped me. Said, 'By Ned, that's fine!' . . . Said, 'Come back in the morning at nine o'clock and we'll make a test record.'"

At this point, the assumption has always been that Gilliland and Robertson returned on Friday, June 30, to record two duets ("Arkansas Traveler" and "Turkey in the Straw"), and that Robertson returned the following day to record two more records by himself. The implication has been that the Victor folk were dubious about this strange music, and were cautiously testing the waters. There is some truth to this: on the original sheets in the company's recording book, someone typed the notation: "FIRST RECORDING—RECORDS TO BE LISTED IN BLACK LABEL CLASS." Since the performances were officially described as "violin duets," the company did not want them mistakenly released in their Red Seal classical series. But other information on the sheets implies that the Victor A&R people were far more interested in Robertson's music than previously thought. They recorded not just two, but four, duets with Gilliland that first day; and the following day, they recorded from Robertson not just the four released sides, but an additional two sides that remained in the vaults. In other words, this first session yielded ten sides, not the six previously thought.

The two unissued duet sides are both common enough tunes: "Forked Deer" and "Apple Blossom." The latter would be re-recorded by Robertson in 1929, but it too would not be released. One curious aspect of the recording ledger is the name "Joe Terry" listed as though he were the composer of "Apple Blossom."

Given Robertson's willingness to credit fiddlers he learned tunes from, this might well be the name of an older Texas player who originated or taught Robertson the tune. Robertson's solos—some of which were accompanied by staff pianist Nat Shilkret, an experienced arranger who later helped do arrangements for Jimmie Rodgers—also harbor some curiosities. One is a medley of two tunes called "General Logan—Reel" and "Dominion Hornpipe," accompanied by Shilkret but never issued. The latter may be a version of a song found in the "Fiddler's Bible," *1,000 Fiddle Tunes*, a printed collection dating from the mid-nineteenth century which many fiddlers knew and learned from. No record has thus far been found of "General Logan," but it might well have a printed source too or an association with a Confederate reunion. The other unissued solo was "Brilliancy and Cheatum," which might have been an early version of Robertson's "Brilliancy Medley" that he would redo in 1929.

Recording the tunes was one thing; releasing them to the public was something else. Victor 18956, which paired one duet side with Robertson's solo of "Sallie Gooden," was technically released on September 1, 1922, two months after the session. According to Peter Feldman, however, the release was not widely circulated until April 1923. The other two records were issued in 1923 and 1924, and all three were featured in a 1924 Victor catalogue supplement, *Old Time Fiddlin' Tunes*. There seems no way to determine how well the three discs sold, but "Sallie Gooden" certainly got wide circulation and eventually became what Bill C. Malone has called "one of the most justly famous renditions in country music." Malone also notes that in late March 1923, Robertson performed the two tunes on this first disc over radio station WBAP in Ft. Worth, possibly becoming the first country musician to plug his records on the air.

All in all, it was a promising start, and with a little luck, Robertson should have had the long recording career that other pioneers like Fiddlin' John Carson and Henry Whitter had. But for some reason, he didn't. As the country recording industry blossomed in the mid-1920s, it somehow by-passed Robertson and many other Texas fiddlers. In 1929, Robertson's old friend Dr. J. B. Cranfill (see below) would comment on the incredible popularity of the records by Fiddlin' John Carson: "I have some of this fiddler's records and there are dozens of fiddlers in Texas that can beat him eight times over, but this singing stuff,

with which he accompanies his fiddling, carries him through." Cranfill's implication is that "real" fiddlers—ones from Texas—didn't
believe in polluting their fiddling by singing along like Carson did. If
so, this may give some clue as to why the Texas fiddlers were slighted
by the recording companies. Still, there were a number of fiddlers
who did manage to follow Robertson's lead and get at least a sample
of their work on disc. But for some reason, Robertson did not—he sat
on the sidelines for a full seven years before he made another move
to record.

By the time Eck Robertson took steps to record again for Victor in
October 1929, he had witnessed a veritable parade of recording crews
into the Dallas-Ft. Worth area. Though they sought out and recorded a
rich variety of music, from blues to gospel, from piano jazz to Mexican
stringbands, they also put onto disc many of the fiddlers Robertson
knew and competed against in local contests. And while Texas fiddling
was not recorded as extensively as north Georgia or Virginia fiddling,
the extent of the documentation is more impressive than many fans
and historians have assumed. The list includes:

W. B. Chenoweth (Okeh, 1924–1927), a novelty fiddler who liked to bill
   himself as "The Texas Fiddling Wampus Cat," and who wound up
   doing three released sides for Okeh, and a pair for Paramount;
Capt. M. J. Bonner (Victor, 1925), apparently a genuine Confederate veteran who had won fame for his pioneer radio broadcasts over
   WBAP (Ft. Worth) and who recorded, with a harp-guitar accompaniment, one of the first versions of the Texas contest favorite
   "Dusty Miller";
Daniel Williams (Columbia 1927, Brunswick 1928, and later), the fiddler
   for the popular stringband the East Texas Serenaders, who recorded "Sweetest Flower" and "Combination Rag" at the initial Columbia session;
W. N. "Nat" Bird (Brunswick, 1929), a Dallas contest fiddler who
   recorded a "Hornpipe Medley" and "Medley of Old Fiddlers
   Favorites" for Brunswick;
Hugh Roden (Okeh, June 1929), another contest regular who supposedly could "play the violin in 52 different positions" and who
   recorded both under his own name and with his stringband, the
   Texas Nighthawks;

A. L. "Red" Steeley (Brunswick, October 1929), from the Arlington area, who with his friend J. W. Graham had a Ft. Worth radio show where they were billed as "The Red Headed Fiddlers;" their seminal versions of "Cheat'em" and "Texas Quickstep" were recorded just days before Robertson's 1929 session;

Oscar Harper (Okeh, 1928), a barber from nearby Terrell who was another formidable contest opponent and who was an associate of Prince Albert Hunt; later he would record an influential version of "Beaumont Rag," but in 1928 he was best known for his recording of "Kelly Waltz";

Prince Albert Hunt (Okeh, March and June 1929), the colorful medicine show fiddler best known for his "Blues in the Bottle," just a couple of years away from a tragic and sudden death;

Samuel Morgan Peacock (Vocalion, October 1928 and March 1929), another barber, from Cleburne, who was one of the first to play on Ft. Worth radio; under the name Smith's Garage Fiddle Band, he was first to record several Texas contest favorites, including "Beaumont Rag";

Robert Cook (Vocalion, October 1928), a Dallas player who often appears in contest write-ups and who recorded an interesting pair of fiddle tune medleys.

In addition to these, there were several other area fiddlers who recorded commercially, but would never see any of their work released. These include Forrest Copeland (Brunswick, 1929), who did "Brilliancy" and "Killie-Cranky"; Captain McKinney (Okeh, 1929), who did four sides, including "Soap Suds Over the Fence" and "Kiss Waltz"; a group identified as the Thomasson Brothers (Okeh, 1929), who were probably the father and uncle of Benny Thomasson (the father of modern contest fiddling) and who did versions of "Scolding Wife" and "Star Waltz"; and a very young Bob Wills (Brunswick, November 1929), who did "Gulf Coast Blues" and "Wills Breakdown."

Though Eck Robertson was aware that some of the best of the older fiddlers, like Lefty Franklin and Matt Brown (supposedly the originator of "Done Gone"), never had an interest in recording, he was very much aware that many of his own generation were following his lead into the recording studio. Had he counted them up, he would have found that since he had made his trip to the Victor studio in 1922, no fewer

than fourteen of his central Texas fiddlers had managed to get recorded. Within a few months, some would make even more records, and
new faces would join their ranks: the Humphries Brother (Okeh), the
Lewis Brothers (Victor), Jim Pate (Victor), and the team of Ervin
Solomon and Joe Hughes (Victor). Brunswick, Okeh, and Victor were
the companies that seemed especially keen on coming to Dallas to capture some of the amazing music that the deep-rooted contest tradition
had generated.

But there were other reasons for Robertson suddenly wanting to
record again in 1929. One was that Victor had let the 1922 releases go
out of print—not because of their musical value, but because they were
done in the old acoustic method. Since 1927 the company had been
using the new electric "orthophonic" system developed by Western
Electric, and in some cases had even re-recorded some of their acoustic
best-sellers in the new process. There is no evidence that they had
approached Robertson about doing this, but once he wrote them, they
certainly jumped at the chance to record him again. Additionally,
Robertson was starting to work his family into his act, and to try to
book out on the concert and vaudeville circuit. While solo records
were nice, he was also anxious to have samples of his family band to
sell at these dates.

Ralph Peer, the legendary Victor A&R man who discovered Jimmie
Rodgers, the Carter Family, and a host of other first generation country
acts, was still traveling the South in 1929, still searching for new Carter
Families and new Jimmie Rodgerses, still corralling song copyrights for
his Southern Music Publishing Company. He would make two trips to
Texas in the latter half of 1929: a trip that started in El Paso around July
8, going onto San Antonio, and eventually getting to Dallas around
August 8; and a later one in September that would start in Memphis,
eventually arriving in Dallas on October 9. On July 6, after Peer had
already arrived at the Hotel Hussman in El Paso, Robertson found out
about him and wrote a letter explaining his earlier work for Victor and
asking about the chances of making some new records. Peer replied,
inviting him to come to San Antonio on the twentieth of July, or, if
more convenient, to the session in Dallas around the first of August.
Robertson at this time was living in Borger, way up in the Panhandle,
north of Amarillo, some 350 miles from Dallas. Either location Peer
offered meant quite a trip, but Robertson eventually settled on Dallas.

What was more interesting was Peer's attitude toward the session and the tunes for it. He wrote Robertson on July 8: "I have no idea as to how much you received on your former contract with Victor and will appreciate it if you will write me what you got and what you expect now for your work. If you do not ask for enough, I will tell you so just as fast as though you ask for too much. If we are going to record you, we will have to put you under a new contract and this should all be understood before you start gallivanting around the country." There was apparently no interest by the company in having Robertson re-record his old acoustic pieces, at least for now. Peer *was* interested, as he always was, in new, copyrightable material. "What ideas have you as to the selections to be recorded?" he wrote Robertson. "We want stuff that hasn't been done before or, if the piece has been done before, we want it arranged so fancy that we can give it a new name. I think you will understand the importance of having new stuff to hand out in this day of intense competition."

As it turned out, Peer was finding more talent than he had expected and was running behind schedule; he had written to Robertson that he hoped to be into Dallas "about the 25th" of July, but didn't actually get there until the first week in August, and did not start recording until August 8. This jammed his schedule, and gave him only five days of recording time; some of this had to be allotted to his biggest star at the time, Jimmie Rodgers, who had recently taken up residence at Kerrville. Rodgers did his sides, as did a parade of blues singers, gospel groups, and cowboy performers like Arthur Miles and the Cartwright Brothers. That left Robertson and his family band to record on the last day of the session, August 12.

In addition to Eck on fiddle, the Robertson family band consisted of Eck's wife Nettie on standard guitar, his young son Dueron (who was sometimes billed as "Eck, Jr.") on tenor banjo, his grown daughter Daphne on tenor guitar. Another daughter, Marguerite, performed with the group as a tap dancer, but did not record. This gave the this new group of recordings a texture quite different from the 1922 ones, the best of which were unaccompanied fiddle pieces. These newer ones had more of a classic stringband sound, with three rhythm instruments propelling Robertson's fiddle on "Texas Wagoner," taken at a blistering tempo, and "There's a Brown-Skin Girl Down the Road Somewhere," which is generally credited to Robertson's old contest nemesis Lefty Franklin. These were followed by "Amarillo Waltz," a distinctive piece with unusual chord progressions, and one that Robertson claimed authorship of; and "Brown Kelly Waltz" recorded in two parts, which probably came from Matt Brown, the originator of "Done Gone." In fact, Robertson claimed composer credit for all four tunes, and assigned copyrights on to Peer's Southern Music Publishing Company, Inc. The first two were issued back-to-back on November 22, 1929, and eventually sold almost 8,000 copies—not bad for a fiddle record of that time. "Amarillo Waltz" would not be released until a year later, September 19, 1930, and would sell only 2,600 copies. "Brown Kelly Waltz" would be held up until December 1930, and would sell most of its copies when it was reissued on Bluebird and Montgomery Ward labels. Blanton Owen, in his study of the Robertson Family repertoire, has noted that "Brown Kelly" and "Amarillo" were among the most performed numbers at live shows.

It seems apparent, though, that Peer was impressed with Robertson's music—as well he might, since the fiddler was at the peak of his abilities. The trouble was, Peer was out of time; Robertson and his group managed to do these four (actually five) masters in two hours of the last afternoon the Victor unit was in Dallas, and the popular radio singer Peg Moreland still had to do his records. One can imagine Ralph Peer reluctantly having to postpone future records by the Robertsons. One recent Robertson biographer has said that these records were "the last commercial recordings made by Eck Robertson" (notes to *Famous Cowboy Fiddler*, p. 5), but the Victor session sheets clearly show that there was a final, separate Victor session held in October—probably because Peer ran out of time on the August session.

Peer must have known that he would return to Dallas for more recording later that fall, in October, and probably told Robertson to be prepared to do more sides. In fact, none of Robertson's August records would even be issued before October, and Victor would have no way of telling how they might sell. That Peer committed the Robertsons to a second session "blind" was a testimony to his faith in the group. And, when October came, and the Victor field crew rolled into the Jefferson Hotel, Robertson was one of the first artists on their schedule—recording the second day of the session, October 10, 1929, exactly three weeks before the stock market crash. The record business, though, still looked good; this was reflected by the huge number of artists that Victor had scheduled to record on this trip. Nearly thirty acts were were set, including Rodgers, as well as a bevy of local fiddlers, stringbands, and blues singers. Peer explained to a local newspaper writer that the company was "going to have a special catalogue of old fiddle music and fiddlers prepared which will be ready for the public within a reasonably short time." The reason was because, Peer explained, "this folklore music is enjoying bewilderingly large sales in countless areas of the United States," outselling formal Victor artists like Fritz Kreisler and John McCormack.

The newspaper writer, in fact, left us a detailed account of this important session; he was Dr. J. B. Cranfill, a local fiddler and historian who actually recorded as a second fiddler on four of Robertson's records. Cranfill (1858–1942) was an actual medical doctor, a native of Parker County, Texas, distantly related to Daniel Boone, and a well-known Baptist preacher and local writer. Throughout his several autobiographical books are references to Texas fiddling history, and he wrote numerous articles about fiddle history for the *Dallas Times Herald*. (For a more detailed account of Cranfill and his chronicles, see my earlier articles about him in *The Devil's Box*, Winter 1983 and Spring 1984.) Preserved in the Robertson scrapbook is an article from the *Dallas Times Herald*, November 10, 1929, entitled "I Have Made a Record," a lengthy and witty account of Peer's visit—one of the very few first-person descriptions of an early field recording session.

The recordings were done in the ballroom of the hotel, inside of which Peer and his engineers "erected another room entirely of canvass." While the recording was in progress, "all the windows were down for the reason that this recording mike is so sensitive that if a cricket would chirp outside while we were recording, his noise would tangle up with ours and the auditors would think we were playing cricket." There were wires, he noted, "connecting this mike with the recording instrument in another room hidden so far away that nobody can see it and to which no human being was admitted except the recording artist and his staff." When the engineer touched a buzzer, they were to get ready to play; thirty seconds later, he gave two short buzzes, and this meant they were to start playing.

The way the band was grouped around the microphone was rather simple, and reflected a technique that wouldn't really change much in the next fifteen years. Cranfill explains:

> Big Eck and I stood facing the mike and toeing the mark as we played our fiddles. He stood on one side of the mike toeing the mark—and it's awfully hard to get Eck to toe a mark of any kind—and I on the other side toeing another mark. Then the accompanists were 'ranged around us, positioned at proper distances from the mike, which is a very sensitive instrument, and the recording artist [i.e., engineer], like the photographer, after having us all properly placed, took a good look at us, told us to "look pleasant" and went to rearrange his recording machine.

It took from 2:30 to 5:30 in the afternoon of October 10 to get the first two fiddle duets recorded—"Great Big Taters," a common Texas tune, and one the Victor files identified as "Run Nigger Run," a favorite from Georgia which had made its way to the Southwest. One explanation for the length of the session is found in Cranfill's memoir. At the end of the first take of "Great Big Tater," Robertson broke a string. ("I didn't say a word and it wouldn't be right to say what Eck said.") Cranfill fished out a new E string and gave it to his partner; soon they were off on the second take. As they were finishing that, though, Cranfill recounted: "I hit my F string with the little hickey on the end of my fiddle bow and, behold another test fell dead on the mike." The third try was a charm, though, and soon the band was listening to a playback through "the reproducer."

After supper the band recorded "Apple Blossom," another venerable favorite and one of the unissued pieces Robertson had recorded at his first 1922 session with Henry Gilliland, and something called "My Frog Ain't Got No Blues," which might have featured Robertson singing. Neither side would ever be released. Difficulties continued the following day, October 11. The entire morning, three and a half hours, was taken up with getting a decent take on one cut—something Robertson called "Brilliancy Medley." This was a dizzying amalgam of several fiddle tunes, none of them really common: "Drunken Billygoat," "Wake Up Susan," "Old Billy Wilson," and "Bill Cheatum." (Curiously, "Billy Wilson" was known and recorded by Uncle Jimmy Thompson, the legendary "founder" of the Grand Ole Opry, who himself often traveled to Texas to compete in contests; it is very possible that he and Robertson competed against each other in the early 1920s.) This turned out to be one of Robertson's best-known pieces; it sold over 2,600 copies when it was released in September 1930, and years later was included in Harry Smith's famous 1952 Folkways *Anthology of American Folk Music*.

The afternoon session, though, yielded nothing Victor thought releasable. There was another novelty number featuring Robertson on the guitar and on vocals, "My Experience on the Ranch," and remakes of two of his 1922 sides, "The Arkansas Traveler" and "Sally Goodin." It was a sign of the times that earlier no one thought anything about Robertson's recording these without guitar accompaniment; now both were done with guitar backing. Robertson had taken seriously, though, Peer's admonition to find new or unusual songs; there is nothing in the annals of old-time music with titles like "My Frog Ain't Got No Blues" or "My Experience on the Ranch." And the final entry from the session, done that night after supper, was the strange ballad, "The Island Unknown," sung by Robertson and his wife, to his fiddle and her guitar. This was no common folk ballad; it appears to be of Irish origin, and to tell a version of the Robinson Crusoe story. It does not appear in Blanton Owen's repertoire list of Robertson's music except as from this recording; nor is there much evidence that it was a regular part of his live shows. But there are a couple of other odd pieces to the puzzle in the Robertson papers. On December 10, two months after the recording of the song, Robertson suddenly wrote to Peer in New York wanting to make sure that his name appeared as composer on the record label. A man named Gilmore from Southern Music answered, explaining, rather lamely, that "as it is a big title they did not want to crowd your name on the label twice"; he assured Robertson that "we know you are the composer" and that you will get royalties. Robertson had signed the standard contract with Peer giving him rights to the song on October 19, in exchange for 45/100 cents on each Victor record sold, 2¢ a copy on each piece of sheet music, and "25 percent of any other mechanical royalties." Why, then, would he feel obliged to write again about his label credits? As it turned out, the record was not issued until December 1929, and was deleted from the Victor catalogue in 1931, after selling some 3,600 copies, and earning less than one hundred dollars in artist and composer royalties.

At the August session, Robertson had signed a contract to do six selections for the flat rate of $50 for "each master record" approved. Now, at this October session, he was able to negotiate an advance against royalties, and was able to pay his accompanists $5 each for each selection on which they played. Robertson himself got a sum of $200, which he described as a "50% advance" on his share of the payments. It was a good piece of negotiating, and reflects the fact that Robertson was far from an itinerant rancher who fiddled for the fun of it; he was very much aware of the potential for commercializing his music, and aggressive about pursuing it. Unfortunately, this final Victor session was not really commercially successful by any definitions—of the ten sides recorded, only five were released, and of the ones that were issued, none sold more than 3,500 copies. Nor did they stay in print long; "The Island Unknown" was deleted in 1931, the "Great Big Taters"/ "Run Nigger Run" coupling in 1932. The "Brilliancy Medley" lasted in the catalogue until 1935 (as did the earlier "Texas Wagoner"/ "There's a Brown Skin Girl"). But both Robertson and Peer were convinced that the hard times were just temporary, and that more Robertson records were in the future. On July 16, 1930, Victor (now the Victor Division of RCA Victor) exercised their option on Robertson's 1929 contract, extending it for a full year. Hopeful, Robertson wrote back agreeing and offering to extend it yet another year beyond that. Even more revealing is the fact that in September 1931 Robertson wrote to Peer asking for an advance against future royalties. Surprisingly Peer agreed and sent a money order for $100 to Borger. Apparently Peer had plans to record Robertson again on his upcoming February 1932 trip to Dallas to get more Jimmie Rodgers material, but for some reason this did not happen. The Depression continued to deepen, field trips were cut back, and Peer himself was reducing his involvement with the recording end of things. As a result, none of the plans ever materialized.

Throughout the 1930s, Robertson continued to wait, as an "exclusive Victor artist," to hear from New York; he was always careful to bill himself and his family as "Victor artists." He got from the T. E. Swann company in Dallas wholesale copies of his records to sell at contests and shows as long as they were available. But by the end of the decade, things were changing; Robertson had moved to Panhandle, Texas; his daughter Daphne (who played tenor guitar on the Victor records) died of pneumonia in 1931; and "little Eck" (Dueron) was now twenty-one (he would be killed in the war in 1944). Nettie had to stay home to care for a new batch of children that had come along, and "the Robertson Family" was on the verge of disbanding. Robertson decided to make one last try with Victor. In February 1939 he wrote the company asking why he hadn't been receiving any royalties. The people there now barely knew Peer and couldn't even find a copy of Robertson's old contract. They responded that all the Robertson records were out of print. In October 1940 Robertson tried to remedy this by writing to a "Mr. Early," suggesting that he might record again. The letter was passed onto young Steve Sholes (later to become one of the founders of the Nashville Sound), who said: "We appreciate very much your interest in suggesting that we make some recordings of your fiddle playing. However, just at this moment, we are not in need of this type of music nor do we plan a recording expedition to Dallas before next spring." He concluded by reminding Robertson that "it is now impossible to make phonograph records by any instrumental musician who does not belong to the American Federation of Musicians."

Robertson was not as hidebound in his playing and repertoire as Sholes seemed to believe. Various set lists preserved in the Robertson collection, lists that date from this period (the late 1930s) contain more popular and western swing tunes than "pure" fiddle tunes. This list (reproduced in full in the brochure notes to County LP 202) not only includes predictable pop western favorites like "El Rancho Grande," "The Last Roundup," "I'm an Old Cowhand," and "Tie Me to Your Apron Strings Again," but also out-and-out pop swing era hits like "Dipsy Doodle," "Beer Barrel Polka," "Three Little Fishes," and even the Kate Smith theme "When the Moon Comes Over the Mountain." While Robertson undoubtedly preferred the old, complex fiddle contest tunes, he was certainly able and willing to expand his repertoire in order to keep working and doing shows.

In fact, it was one such show that led to the last and most mysterious lot of Robertson's commercial recordings. For years it had been rumored that Robertson had recorded for the Sellers transcription studios in Dallas—a studio that had earlier done transcriptions for groups like the Callahan Brothers and the Chuck Wagon Gang. These were discs designed strictly for airplay on regional stations in the Southwest and formed but one of a number of enterprises operated by J. E. Sellers from his office at 912 Commerce Street in Dallas. This time it was the recording company who came to Robertson. In August 1940, Sellers saw Robertson perform at the Dallas Sportatorium (at a contest) and wrote him: "I might be able to use you in some transcription work. . . . On account of the distance you live from here, it would probably be advisable to just have you come in for a couple of days and record something like 100 to 125 of your better numbers, one right after the other, until you become tired and need a rest. In other words, we would turn them out as quickly as possible, and we would furnish a band to work with you so as to make a full background." Sellers would pay Robertson the sum of $1 a side, with the understanding "that I might use these ten-inch records for dubbing into programs later in case I should have need for them." Apparently, then, the recordings would not be the larger twelve- or sixteen-inch discs with four or five songs on a side, but singles like the commercial 78s Robertson had done already.

Robertson, who apparently had already broken up his family band by now, jumped at the chance. During the week of September 20, 1940, Robertson traveled to Dallas and began recording. Receipts show that he was paid $100 on September 27 for recording one-hundred musical selections, with the understanding that "no processing of these records will be done for any purpose, but they may be dubbed for use in the United States and Mexico."

We, unfortunately, have no lists of these selections, nor have any of the discs themselves surfaced—neither the original ten-inch masters, nor any larger transcriptions onto which they were dubbed. It is a shame, for they might have constituted the largest and best sampling preserved of Robertson's music: he was only fifty-three in 1940, the prime of his life, and a formidable and mature fiddler. We do know that Sellers was pleased with Robertson's work, for a few years later, in February 1944, he wrote him again offering him a staff position with a new station he was staffing in Corpus Christi. The salary was $25 a week for daytime programs only. It is unclear whether Robertson ever took the job, or whether he made any other radio recordings while there. Until and if someone locates some of the Sellers discs, we have no way of knowing what this master fiddler and key figure in country music sounded like during this crucial period in his career.

Fortunately, Eck Robertson was recorded in later years by folk-lorists and fans, and at least some of his huge and complex repertoire was preserved. His relationship with the commercial recording industry, though, was in many ways a series of misfortunes, poor timing, and missed opportunities. He had all the skills, versatility, commercial appeal, and personality to become a major recording figure in the 1920s and 1930s, but he did not. His role in the history of country music is secure enough, but the old image of him and the Victor company stumbling blindly into the idea of recording country music is simply wrong. It was not a lucky accident that Robertson came to the Victor studio, nor a happenstance that the company recorded him to get rid of him. Robertson wanted to record as part of his ongoing interest in using the media to build a career, and the Victor A&R men knew from the first that he was a skilled artist who would be an interesting addition to their roster. The fact that neither party could properly follow up on these initial impulses was bad for the country record industry, and personally frustrating for its first star.

Sources

The majority of information here comes from Eck Robertson's personal collection of correspondence, photographs, and clippings now archived at the Country Music Foundation. It was donated to them in 1992 by Beulah Davis, of Battle Mountain, Nevada, the fiddler's sole surviving daughter. Other sources include the brochure notes to County 201 LP written by Blanton Owen and Tom Carter, as well as Earl Spielman's "An Interview with Eck Robertson," *JEMF Quarterly*, No. 28 (Winter 1972), 179–187. An earlier piece is John Cohen's "Fiddlin' Eck Robertson" in *Sing Out!*, 14, No. 2 (April–May, 1964), 55–59. The material on other early Texas fiddlers who recorded in the 1920s is drawn from the author's files.

Across the Amerikee:
The Story of Uncle Jimmy Thompson

TRADITIONALLY THE HISTORY OF THE GRAND OLE Opry has been traced to November 28, 1925, when the show's founder, George D. Hay, unleashed upon America the music and personality of then seventy-seven-year-old Uncle Jimmy Thompson. The famous publicity photo of Thompson sitting before the WSM microphone with Hay standing and interviewing him has become an icon of country music; for years it was used as the emblem for the official program for the Grand Masters' Fiddling Contest at Opryland. Yet the picture we have of Thompson is, like that icon, curiously one-dimensional. We see a stocky, white-bearded man dressed in a conservative black suit sitting before a large carbon microphone, fiddling away with a sort of detached amusement. We see him playing for hours on end during those first formative months of what will become the Opry, but then virtually dropping out of sight. Reading the traditional histories, it almost seems that Thompson did not exist prior to November 1925 or after April 1926. But he obviously did, and obviously saw the Opry as part of a long and full life that ranged from the Civil War to the Texas frontier. There was a man behind the legend; as late as the 1970s there were still people around who remembered him, who shared a jug with him, who heard him tell jokes, and who listened to him "bring cussing to the land." To these people, Uncle Jimmy Thompson was not a remote figure. To them he was a friend or neighbor, an independent, self-reliant, outspoken, hard-living, rough-talking nineteenth-century man of the land. It is a reality far more interesting than the Grand Ole Opry publicity.

In 1975 the Tennessee Valley Old-Time Fiddlers' Association discovered that Thompson was resting in an unmarked grave in his home town of Laguardo, Tennessee. They soon began a drive to raise funds to place a suitable marker on the site, but quickly found that even such basic data as the birth and death dates for Thompson were not known. Bill Harrison, one of the founders of the TVOTFA, began looking into the matter. He made several trips to Laguardo to locate the grave and to see if there were any people around who could talk about Thompson. To his amazement, Harrison found several in the area, including a former riverboat captain who showed him where Thompson's homestead was. He shared this with other researchers, including myself, and soon more data was rolling in. A major breakthrough occurred when, alerted by a casual comment of a colleague, I managed to locate Mrs. Katherine Thompson, Uncle Jimmy's daughter-in-law and closest survivor; Mrs. Thompson still plays the banjo a little and spent many evenings making music with Uncle Jimmy. The ceremonies at Laguardo brought out even more informants, and soon we had information about Thompson running out our ears. The following is a distillation of all this, and the clearest account we have been able to piece together of Uncle Jimmy Thompson's fabulous life and times.

Uncle Jimmy was born James Donald Thompson near Baxter, in Smith County, about halfway between Nashville and Knoxville in northern Tennessee. He had at least two brothers, neither of whom distinguished himself musically. However, Lee, who eventually settled around Cookeville, Tennessee, was the father of Eva Thompson Jones, Thompson's well-known niece who accompanied him on WSM. Little is known about the history of the Thompson family itself, though the line probably sprang from Scottish origins.

When he was a boy, Thompson's family moved to Texas shortly before the Civil War. The family must have been fond of Texas, for both of Thompson's brothers stayed there after the war, and Thompson himself returned there several times. Jimmy was too young for the Civil War, but by the time he was seventeen (1860), had begun mastering fiddle tunes like "Flying Clouds," which would remain one of his favorites. The young man continued to learn tunes, some from men who had fought in the Civil War, others from fiddlers whose repertoires might well have stretched back to Revolutionary America. Thompson recalled later that on August 4, 1866, he learned a "fine quadrille," the old minstrel show number "Lynchburg" (also known as "Lynchburg Town").

Though he primarily farmed for a living, the young man Jimmy Thompson traveled widely in his youth and eventually returned to his native Smith County, Tennessee. There, in the 1880s, he married Mahalia Elizabeth Montgomery, of Smith County. The union resulted in two sons and two daughters: Jess (born 1886), Willie Lee (born 1896), Sally (who eventually married and moved to Montana), and Fanny, who died in infancy. (All the children are now deceased.) But about 1902 Thompson took his family back to Texas and settled around the Bonham area, northeast of Dallas and close to the Oklahoma line. He continued to farm but was beginning to play more and more in public on his fiddle.

In 1907 Thompson participated in the famous eight-day marathon contest he so vividly described to Judge Hay the night of his first broadcast. The contest was held in Dallas, and Thompson won "the nation's championship in his class against nearly one hundred contestants" (*Nashville Tennessean*, June 13, 1925). (The actual figure given by Thompson later was eighty-six.) Information is lacking about who participated in this contest, but the fact that Jimmy won indicates that he had absorbed a good deal of the Texas "long-bow" style during his various stays there. (His style, which has been described as "fancy," is in distinct contrast to the older, heavier styles of traditional Southeastern fiddlers, like Fiddlin' John Carson or Gid Tanner; it has much more in common with the Southwestern stylings of Eck Robertson.)

About 1912, Thompson now sixty-four and with most of his family grown, returned to Tennessee and bought a farm near Hendersonville in north central Tennessee. His wife was dying of cancer, and perhaps she wanted to go back to her native Tennessee before she died. Soon after they returned, she died and was buried in Smith County.

By this time Eva Thompson, Uncle Jimmy's niece, was starting to teach music in rural Tennessee schools. As a young girl, Eva was fond of classical and semi-classical music (and the turn-of-the-century parlor music that passed for such). She used to accompany her father into Nashville when he came to sell stock, just to watch the touring shows that played there. Later Eva was to study at Ward Belmont College, then as now one of Nashville's more prestigious musical schools, and later recalled going by horse and buggy to give music lessons. (Most of the biographical material on Eva Thompson Jones comes from Don Cummings's pamphlet, *The Birth of the Grand Ole Opry*. Mrs. Jones talked to Cummings before she died, and her remarks are reflected in the book.) In 1915 Eva was teaching in Sumner County, and was indirectly responsible for introducing Thompson to his future daughter-in-law, Katherine Womack.

Katherine, who was Thompson's closest living relative, recalled the night she met him:

> It was at a school entertainment up here at Number One in Sumner County—that's the way I met my husband. Eva was teaching music there, and she knew I played a banjo, so they sent home and got my banjo, and he come down to play for us, Uncle Jimmy did, and I played with him. And he was just tickled to death to find a woman playing a banjo. So we really had a big time down there at the school. He went home and told his son about it, and that's how I met my husband.

Katherine's husband was Willie Lee, Thompson's youngest child, and after they were married both she and her husband played with Uncle Jimmy on an informal basis. Willie Lee played guitar, Katherine banjo. On one of two later occasions they joined Thompson on the radio. He was especially fond of Katherine and liked to listen to her sing and play the banjo on some of his favorite numbers like "Red Wing," "The Preacher and the Bear," and "Rainbow."

About 1916 when he was sixty-eight years old, Thompson decided to remarry. He chose Ella Manners, from nearby Wilson County, Tennessee, an older woman who soon became known as "Aunt Ella." It was after this that Thompson moved down to Wilson County, near Laguardo, and bought a house formerly occupied by an old physician. Both he and Aunt Ella were to live at Laguardo for the rest of their lives.

From all accounts Aunt Ella was just as high-spirited as Uncle Jimmy. She loved to buck dance, and she loved her dram of white lightening as much as her husband. Neighbors in Laguardo recall often visiting the pair and watching Aunt Ella buck dance in a long white dress while Uncle Jimmy played solo fiddle. Occasionally Ella and Jimmy would travel around the middle Tennessee area playing for fairs and outings, pulling up in their truck, unrolling a special rug for Ella to dance on, and performing an impromptu show. They would then pass the hat and collect quarters and dollars from the audience. One neighbor recalls a fiddling session at the Thompsons' house when both Uncle Jimmy and Aunt Ella had a little too much bootleg. "Aunt Ella finally fell flat on her face, and Uncle Jimmy, fiddling all the time, glanced down at her and remarked, 'Watch it, now Ella, you done gone and spoiled it thar.'" Another neighbor repeats stories about Uncle Jimmy and Aunt Ella chasing each other around their old house, each with a loaded gun, firing playfully into the air.

It is not clear just how much "paraprofessional" entertaining Thompson did before his fame on the radio, but it seems obvious that he enjoyed at least a regional reputation as a fiddler before his WSM days. Some friends have said that he traveled quite widely, both with Eva Thompson Jones and Aunt Ella, and staged shows across Tennessee in the days after World War I. Jim Thompson (no relation), a former neighbor of Uncle Jimmy's, says that Thompson began to do shows to make a living when he began to get too old to farm.

"Before he played on the Opry, he was mainly a farmer, till his age got the best of him. And while he was a farmer he had fiddled, so he just quit trying to work on account of his age and went to playin' the fiddle. And he'd get right smart o' donations when he'd go around to these different places playing. That's how they lived. They'd put on these little shows."

Thompson had a rather unique means of transportation for getting around to these shows. He had taken a little Ford sedan, built a truck bed onto it in 1922, and constructed a little house on the back. It was a rough prototype of the modern-day camper, but it caused quite a stir in the 1920s. Katherine Thompson remembers:

> He had furnished it; it was real amusin' to all of us. He had a floor covering on there of matting, and he had the inside all fixed up and had a cot in there. Had a water bucket, a dipper, washpan, towel, even a little wood stove, so he could spend the night travelin' if he wanted to.

Thompson and occasionally Aunt Ella would travel in this camper and seldom be out any expenses on their trips. Thompson was very proud of the little truck, and all of his friends have their favorite stories about the way he cared for the truck. Grandson Fred Thompson remembers that Uncle Jimmy always wiped the truck off with motor oil, and refused to let anybody touch the truck body. "He was afraid that the salt in your hand, the sweat, would rust it. 'Don't touch that boy!' he'd say, and he made 'em back up: he had a big old walking cane." Family legend has it that the vehicle was given to Thompson by Henry Ford in recognition of his fiddling. While this may have been the case, there is no record in any of Thompson's contest documentation about his winning such a prize.

Sometime in the fall of 1923, Thompson, then seventy-five, decided to drive his truck down to Texas. In those days the trip took from a month to five weeks, but this was no problem to Thompson. As he himself said in a 1926 interview, "When I got tired, I'd jest drive it in the first open place I found by the road and ask if I could stay all night. 'Yep,' they'd say, and I'd drive it in, fix my bed, and git out my fiddle" (*Nashville Tennessean*, January 1, 1926). His main purpose was to go to Dallas for another fiddlers' contest. There he won a gold watch that was engraved on the back. But the trip had a more significant effect: his success at Dallas inspired him to seek a wider audience for his music. "When he got back, that contest was all he would talk about. He was keyed up to try to do something about his music. He felt like he had something, and he wanted the world to know about it," said Katherine Thompson.

The year 1923 saw the very first commercial "hillbilly" records by Fiddlin' John Carson, as well as the start of old-time music on radio stations like Atlanta's WSB. By the next year, the boom in old-time music was on in both media, radio and records, and Thompson watched it with increasing interest and anticipation. Katherine Thompson remembered:

> When the record market got so big and people got so interested in making records, and radio, and all, it really made him more anxious. He would just sit and daydream all the time after he had heard radio and records—why, he thought it would be wonderful to make records of his music, or to play it on the air. "I want to throw my music out all over the Amerikee," he used to say. (He wouldn't say "America," but "the Amerikee.") He really wanted to record and to go on the air. He wanted to get his music "caught." was the way he said it.

Recording fever finally got the best of Thompson, and in the summer or early fall of 1925 he decided to take matters into his own hands. He took Katherine along with him. She said:

The first time he made a record I was never so tickled, but I was never so mortified; it embarrassed me so. He wanted me to go with him and make a record up in this building on Church Street in downtown Nashville. Somebody had a little recording outfit up there, and they were going to make him a little record for, I don't know, a dollar or so. He wanted to have some records made real bad. He was supposed to pay for these, and that's what embarrassed me so. We got in there and made this record—I think it was "Flying Clouds" with me playin' the banjo back of him. And this man played it back to him, and it made Uncle Jimmy mad. He said, "Why, hell, thar, that don't sound like my fiddle. That don't sound a bit like me a-playin' my fiddle. There's just something wrong with your machine, or you don't understand catchin' it one!" I felt like going through the floor, and that man, he didn't know what to say. He tried to be nice, said Uncle Jimmy could take the record for half price. But Uncle Jimmy said, "Why, I ain't a-gonna give you no half dollar; I ain't a payin' you nothin' for that. You can just break that 'un right now!" Out he stormed; he put his fiddle in his case and wouldn't make no more records. And it was a little aluminum record, about the size of a saucer, and it didn't have much volume to it, and it did sound tinny. That started him, though; he was wantin' to get into the record or radio business bad after that, wantin' to get his music caught so it could be throwed out across the "Amerikee." So it wasn't long after that that Eva took him up to the broadcasting station.

There are several different versions of how Uncle Jimmy Thompson actually got to the WSM studios for the first time. According to relatives of Aunt Ella, a member of the Manners family first took Uncle Jimmy up to WSM so he could simply tour the station and see how it worked; while there he mentioned his fiddling, and was asked to play a little. Unknown to Thompson, the engineers turned on the transmitter and broadcast his fiddling. A similar version is given in the 1969 official Opry picture and history book, where it is alleged that Thompson came up to tour the station on a Thursday night. His guide happened to be the program manager (George Hay), and when Thompson mentioned his fiddling abilities, Hay asked him to return the next night (Friday) to broadcast. (However, the twenty-eighth of November, which Hay always gave as the date Thompson first played, was a Saturday.) But according to Eva Thompson Jones, the event occurred with less serendipity. Eva had been performing on WSM as a singer of light classical music, and a pianist. Eva told Don Cummings that Hay had not been satisfied with the direction of the station's shows and asked her for suggestions. She suggested her uncle and invited Hay to meet him for an informal audition at her home on Friday night, November 27. He did, was impressed, and invited Thompson to appear the next night (Cummings, *Birth of the Grand Ole Opry*). Katherine Thompson, for the record, agrees that it was Eva who really got Uncle Jimmy onto the show.

Whatever the case, he broadcast on Saturday, November 28 (the exact date is confirmed by the *Tennessean* radio column of a week later). His first tune was supposedly "Tennessee Waggoner," and it was carried across the country by the 1,000-watt transmitter. Hay recalled, in his history of the Opry, that "Uncle Jimmy told us he had a thousand tunes," and Hay then announced that he would answer requests. Telegrams poured into the station. After an hour, Hay asked Thompson if he wasn't tired, and the old fiddler snorted, "Why shucks, a man don't get warmed up in an hour. I won an eight-day fiddling contest down at Dallas, and here's my blue ribbon to prove it." Eva recalls that then building superintendent Percy Craig entered the studio with an armful of telegrams and announced that they had received a telegram from every state in the union.

Uncle Jimmy and Eva continued to play Saturdays throughout the month of December, and letters continued to come in praising his fiddling. One of the first letters was dated December 6 and came from listeners in the Missouri Ozarks, some 400 miles to the west. By the end of December, WSM had instituted, somewhat reluctantly, a regular program of fiddling on Saturday nights. Their press release in the *Tennessean*, December 27, 1925, announced that Uncle Dave Macon and Uncle Jimmy Thompson would answer requests. The story emphasizes Thompson more than Macon and provides several interesting new details about his life. It suggests that Thompson's repertoire included "375 different numbers," certainly a more realistic figure than the "thousand" that Hay claimed he knew.

The local newspapers at once became fascinated with Uncle Jimmy Thompson and throughout January and February 1926 constantly published stories about him and pictures of him. But it was the speed with which radio made Thompson famous that is so astounding; within a month of his first broadcast, he was known across the country. This became obvious when, during the first days of January, Uncle Jimmy received a challenge from fiddler Mellie Dunham of Maine.

Dunham had recently been crowned World's Champion Fiddler by Henry Ford and was attaining widespread popularity in the North due to Ford's promotion of old-time fiddling. After he had played at Ford's house, Dunham had been deluged with theatrical offers from the stage and vaudeville circuits. On January 2, a Boston newspaper ran a story in which Dunham challenged Uncle Jimmy Thompson and Southern fiddling in general. Dunham, the story read, was "tiring of the challenges and criticism heaped upon him by other fiddlers throughout the country," and "is anxious to meet 'Uncle Jimmy' Thompson, recently nominated by unanimous vote as the greatest barn dance fiddler in the South, for a championship contest." The article concludes:

> Considerable has been published about the "WSM" star in this section [i.e., of the Boston paper], and repeatedly Dunham has been called upon to comment. The Maine fiddler takes exception to the crowning of Thompson as America's champion barn dance fiddler following a contest which lasted eight days in Dallas.
>
> "He may have defeated 86 opponents in the Dallas contest," declared Dunham today, "but they were all Southerners, and they don't know as much about barn dance fiddling in that section as they do 'down in Maine.' I'm ready to meet any and all of them, but I'd rather like to meet Uncle Jimmy Thompson, who claims the title, first."

Accordingly, Dunham sent a telegram to Thompson, care of WSM. "Mellie Dunham held at Keith's for third week. Sends challenge to Jimmy Thompson of WSM fame. Eager to meet Southern rival."

Dunham's challenge raised a furor in Nashville, and a dispute quickly developed as to where the contest was to be held. George Hay volunteered to serve as a "medium" for the contest, and, with Thompson's blessing, sent a telegram to Dunham accepting the challenge. Hay suggested Dunham and Thompson have the contest on WSM Radio "any Saturday night in the near future that suits you." WSM would pay all expenses for the contest. "Let the radio public of America be judge. Our radio station reaches all points of the United States. What happened next is unclear. Hay recalls that Dunham's advisors, "realizing that he had nothing to win refused to allow him to accept. Whereupon Thompson remarked, 'He's affeared of me.'" But about the same time in Boston, Dunham's employers, a vaudeville circuit, denounced the telegram Dunham sent as "undoubtedly a fake." If the telegram was a publicity stunt, as now seems likely, Thompson was certainly not involved in it. (The story apparently originated in Boston, though WSM was certainly exploiting it for as much publicity as they could.) But Thompson was not even in town at the time, and came in only the next week "to find out what all the fuss was about." Though the contest itself never came off, one thing that came out of the whole affair was the delightful interview Thompson gave a local reporter:

"Let Mellie Dunham Come Here," Says "Uncle Jimmy," Eager for Contest

Champion Fiddler Chats About Contest, Leatherpants Dances and How He Learned to Play

"Uncle Jimmy" Thompson knows the difference between jig and leather-breeches dances; he knows enough old-time tunes to play all night without repeating a single selection; he recalls the eight days of playing in Dallas about 19 years ago when he won the nation's championship in his class against nearly 100 contestants.

And being champion, "Uncle Jimmy" knows that it is the challenger's place to let him say where he shall defend that title. That is why "Uncle Jimmy" will insist that Mellie Dunham of Maine, who challenged him Saturday night, must come to Nashville if he wants a chance at the Tennessee veteran fiddler's crown.

"Uncle Jimmy" came to Nashville Monday from his home in Martha, Tenn., to find out what all the fuss was about. He chatted enthusiastically about a fiddle he has had more than 30 years and refuses to sell; about the scores of quadrilles, schottisches, reels and waltzes he likes so well; and about his 73-year-old wife who "hits the floor" when he strikes a favorite tune.

EAGER TO MEET MELLIE HERE.

"If Mellie Dunham will come down here to this WSM station, I'll lay with him like a bulldog," the fiddler declared, emphasizing his statement with a sudden lifting of his chin that seemed to shake his thick, white beard. "Now wouldn't that be fine. I'll play him and let ev'ybody jedge."

Through all of "Uncle Jimmy's" talk of old-time contests—and he has never lost one, he asserts—he frequently referred to numerous simple facts connected with his 82 years of home life, all but 10 of which have been spent in Tennessee. He lived in Texas that long.

In his humble home, in Smith county, "Uncle Jimmy" lives alone with his wife. His three children are "married and gone away"—Willie Lee Thompson, 31, but called the baby, in Nashville; Jesse Morgan Thompson in the Rio Grande Valley of Texas, and Sallie King Callicut, his only daughter, near Seattle, Wash.

But his existence is not a lonely one. "Someone's always stoppin' in," the selfmade musician said, "and we have a big time."

LEARNS MUSIC BY SELF.

Asked about how he learned to play, he chuckled: "Huh! Never took a music lesson in my life. I'd jest as soon look a mule in the face as look at a sheet of music. I been playin' over 60 years and I learned it all myself."

He refused to name his "favorite piece."

After all, music is only an avocation for "Uncle Jimmy," and he takes pride in many other achievements. "I run a naked truck from Nashville four years ago, made a bed for it myself and drove the thing to Texas two years ago. When I got tired, I'd jest drive it in the first open place I found by the road and ask if I could stay all night. 'Yes,' they'd say, and I'd drive it in, fix my bed and git out the fiddle."

With one eye failing him, however, and with his 82 years of cares beginning to tell, "Uncle Jimmy" says he would not want to attempt another drive to Texas. Nor does he want to go to Maine, much as he would like to play in a contest with Mellie Dunham.

"I'll lay with him like a bulldog," he repeated, "if Mellie'll come down here."

Other contests did take place, though, and throughout 1926 Thompson was busy participating in fiddling contests across the South. This year saw the peak of the old-time fiddling craze that swept the nation, spurred on by the enthusiasm of Henry Ford. During the second week of January, the Ford dealers in Tennessee, Kentucky, and Indiana sponsored a series of local fiddling contests. The main purpose of these contests—in addition to fostering fiddling—seems to have been to draw people into the Ford showrooms to look at the new cars, and this was successful: several Tennessee contests averaged between 1,000 and 2,000 in attendance, and in the dead of winter. The winners of these local contests did not get much cash, but they were allowed to go on to the regional contest. For Tennesseans, this contest was held in Nashville, and from there six winners would go on to compete in the "Champion of Dixie" contest in Louisville. Winners there would go to meet Mr. Ford himself.

Thompson won the local contest (held at nearby Lebanon) with ease, and participated in the regional contest in Nashville. Because of the Mellie Dunham incident, tempers were running high; "On to Detroit!" became the battle cry of the contest. According to contemporary newspaper accounts, the twenty-five winners who played in Nashville on January 19–20, 1926, had collectively played to between 30,000 and 35,000 people in eliminations. All day, on the day of the contest, according to the newspapers, "groups came from various sections of the whole hill country of Tennessee came to the city . . . to boost their respective contestants." "Coming from some localities in groups of 200 or more, the clans of the hills of Middle Tennessee swarmed into the city. . . ." "The overflow crowd [Ryman auditorium, where the contest was held, seated then about 3,600] bore earmarks of rurality. The presence of family groups, father and mother and children, was noticeable throughout the audience. Their approval was frank and hearty, if inclined to boisterousness, and they certainly did enjoy the fiddling." A Reverend Roberts, who opened the contest with a short talk, declared that "the real significance of the meeting lay in the fact that this section, by this contest, was paying tributes to the homes of the pioneers, where such music abounded long ago." Undoubtedly some of the news reporters and participating civic leaders like Rev. Roberts were caught up in Henry Ford's romanticized notion of what American fiddling meant. Once the fiddling craze died down, many Nashville citizens were quick enough to repudiate this precious heritage as it manifested itself on the barn dance. But there is no denying the enthusiasm of Southerners for Ford's contests, as the Nashville event demonstrates. Ford and the South were alike in their love for fiddling, though probably for different reasons. Ford saw fiddling as a dying tradition to be resurrected; most Southerners saw it as a vibrant and living tradition to be developed.

Thompson's competition here was stiff by any standards. Among those he went up against were Uncle Bunt Stephens, the famous Lynchburg fiddler; Mazy Todd, lead fiddler with Uncle Dave Macon's Fruit Jar Drinkers; W. E. Poplin of Lewisburg, leader of the Poplin-Woods Tennessee String Band which later recorded for Victor and became an Opry fixture; and John McGee, from Franklin, the father of Opry pioneers Sam and Kirk McGee. Marshall Claiborne—a one-armed fiddler from Hartsville who held his fiddle between his knees and fiddled with his left hand, and was very popular in the middle Tennessee area—also played. The *Nashville Tennessean* referred to the fiddlers as "exponents of the art of Old Ned."

Thompson won by playing "Fisher's Hornpipe" and "The Mocking Bird." Claiborne took second, and Bunt Stephens third. All three journeyed the next weekend to Louisville for the tri-state championship. There their competition included "Blind Joe" Mangrum of Paducah, Kentucky, a fiddler who was later to play often on the Opry. But to the disappointment of Tennesseans, the first place was won by an Indiana fiddler, W. H. Elmore; Bunt Stephens won second, and Marshall Claiborne third. To everyone's surprise, Thompson did not place. A Thompson family story, which family members are unsure about accepting, holds that certain parties knew about Uncle Jimmy's love of moonshine and plied him with drink just before the contest. Supposedly, when his time came to play, he was barely able to make it onto the stage. Thompson some years later tried to visit Henry Ford in Detroit but was unable to get an appointment with him; perhaps he was wanting somehow to redeem himself. Bunt Stephens's performance in the contest, incidentally, was the start of a long and interesting career for him.

The Louisville debacle hardly slowed Uncle Jimmy Thompson's career though. He continued to headline the barn dance program throughout the first six months of 1926. He and Eva usually started the

program at 8:00 P.M. for an hour, though on occasion he was scheduled for as much as two hours. In April he was selected by Tennessee
Governor Austin Peay to represent Tennessee in a radio fiddling contest staged at station WOS, Jefferson City, Missouri, which had challenged fiddlers from all states bordering on Missouri. The governor
also selected fiddler Fulton Mitchell of Nashville to represent Tennessee, and "urged all Tennesseans to back their representatives" at the
contest. But since the contest was judged by the "amount of applause
in messages" received at the station, Missouri fiddlers obviously had
the edge.

Thompson temporarily left the barn dance in May 1926 when he
broke his fiddling arm, but by July 3 he was back on the air, with a good
deal of fanfare, and played throughout July. He played less regularly,
but steadily, throughout the rest of the year. On November 1, 1926, he
and Eva were in Atlanta, where they cut their first commercial records,
for Columbia. Four sides were recorded: "Mississippi Sawyer," "High
Born Lady," "Karo," and "Billy Wilson." Only the last two sides were
issued, however, on Columbia 15118-D. Oddly, there was no mention on
the label of Jimmy's WSM affiliation. Most of the tunes are traditional
fiddle standards. "High Born Lady" is probably an instrumental of "My
Gal's High Born Lady," favorite of Uncle Dave Macon. "Karo" is
Thompson's version of "Flop Eared Mule." "Billy Wilson"—not the clog
tune of this name still popular—is related to the Texas "Bull at the
Wagon" (recorded by the Lewis Brothers for Victor in 1929) and the
West Virginia "Red Bird" of Clark Kessinger. Sales from the Columbia
record seem to have been only average, and Thompson received little
royalty from them; like most old-time musicians, he probably recorded for a flat fee of $25 or $50 a side.

After 1926 Uncle Jimmy Thompson began appearing on the Opry
less and less. His time slots were also becoming shorter: as early as the
fall of 1926 he was playing for only a half-hour at a time, as opposed to
the two-hour stints of barely a year before. During all of 1928 he
appeared on the show only once. Since recordings he made in 1930
show him still to be an excellent fiddler, one might well question his
departure from the Opry.

There seems to be a number of reasons. One might simply be his
age: he was seventy-seven when he first played on WSM, and shortly
after that he had a stroke which left him blind in one eye. It certainly

became more difficult for him to get around, and the thirty-mile trip from Laguardo to Nashville was not an easy one in the twenties. But a more basic problem was that the Opry was becoming much more formal and structured, and Uncle Jimmy was more attuned to the leisurely nineteenth-century style of performing than to the hectic clock-watching twentieth-century mode. Laguardo resident Bert Norther recalls one significant night toward the end of Thompson's broadcasting career:

> I remember one night when Bill Bates, had the store here, we went down there one Saturday night to listen to Uncle Jimmy on his radio. Bill Bates called down there and told George Hay to get Jimmy to play "When You and I Were Young, Maggie." He cut loose on it and he never *did* quit. Finally they had to stop him, got him out of the way. He'd just had one drink too many.

The drinking was another problem. Thompson associated drinking, dancing, and having a good time. It was normal for him to take along a bottle when he played on the radio. Neighbor Sam Kirkpatrick recalls:

> I'll never forget the last night Uncle Jimmy played. He kinda liked his bottle pretty well, he was playing and before he finished his piece there was this stopping, and we didn't hear nothing for a minute, then George Hay come on and said Uncle Jimmy was sick tonight or something. Come to find out later he had just keeled over and passed out.

The drinking caused bad blood between Jimmy and WSM, and eventually led to a falling-out. Neighbor Jim Thompson says: "They would have to watch him—in fact, they told him they didn't want him to come down there drinking. His business down there just finally played out on that account."

It was a cruel irony: Thompson in the end becoming a victim of the medium that had originally brought him to fame. It must have been bitter.

* * *

In the last few years he continued to tour a little, farm a little, and play for his friends. Touring was more lucrative than playing the Opry anyway; Katherine Thompson recalls that WSM originally paid Uncle Jimmy $5 a show for fiddling, and he could make four times that amount by passing the hat at local fairs. He was still able to do some farming; even in his eighties he was strong enough to carry a bushel (150 pounds) of corn on his back to a mill several miles away.

In April 1930 he went to Knoxville to record again, this time for Brunswick-Vocalion. He did "Lynchburg" and a medley of "Flying Clouds" and "Leather Britches," and recorded some charming dialogue with recording supervisor Bill Brown.

> *Brown:* How old are you, Uncle Jimmy?
>
> *UJT:* Eighty-two—and I've got grown grandchildren, and great big greatgrandchildren; running cars and trucks yet, and a-playin' the fiddle yet. And I love to look at a pretty woman just as much as I ever did.
>
> *Brown:* Say, Uncle Jimmy, were the girls as pretty back in 1866 as they are now?
>
> *UJT:* They prettier—they healthier. Stout. Fat and plump.
>
> *Brown:* What kind of clothes did they wear?
>
> *UJT:* They just wore nice, good clothes—plenty width in the skirts, and they was long enough to come down to the shoes.
>
> *Brown:* That ["Flying Clouds"] is as peppy as a drink of good whiskey, isn't it?
>
> *UJT:* Yes, it's all right. All it lacks is a good set to dance after it.
>
> *Brown:* Uncle Jimmy, did you use to get good whiskey when you were a young man?
>
> *UJT:* Sure, get good whiskey, fine as could be. It was whiskey that jest made you love everybody. Make a fellow love his poor old grandmother.
>
> *Brown:* What'd you have to pay for it?
>
> *UJT:* Twenty-five cents a gallon. Right to the still and get it. Go to the stillhouse, didn't have very far to go. It made you love everybody instead of wanting to fight.
>
> *Brown:* Say, I've got a fellow here that plays guitar. Want you to listen to him, see what you think of him.
>
> [Guitar solo]
>
> *UJT:* Well, a guitar pretty, but they ain't near as pretty as a violin. They're the finest musical we've got in American. . . . I call fiddle, some call 'em violins, but fiddle just as good as violin, people know what they mean.

Less than ten months after he spoke those words, Thompson was dead. He passed away of pneumonia at his home in Laguardo, about 3:00 P.M. on Tuesday, February 17, 1931. Even his death is shrouded in legend; there are at least five different versions of how he died. Some stories hold that he passed out one night and froze to death; others say he caught pneumonia trying to repair his car in a snowstorm. The Thompson family says that he caught pneumonia one night when his house caught fire; dressed only in his long underwear, Thompson managed to put out the fire by drawing buckets of water from his well, but while doing so soaked his long johns. The underwear froze on him and he fell ill the next day. The day of his funeral was cold and icy, and Eva Thompson Jones was the only member of the Opry cast to attend.

*   *   *

The facts can reveal a picture of Uncle Jimmy Thompson's role in the history of country music, but what of Uncle Jimmy the man? Glimpses of his personality can be gained by talking with his old friends, neighbors and relatives. Here is a sampler of some of their favorite "Uncle Jimmy" stories.

> He wasn't a trick fiddler—he was serious about everything he played. He was always real entertaining, though. He'd always have some kind of little story to tell about something that was interesting to him. He could tell you just where he learned each fiddle tune, tell you where he first heard it played and who played it. And he used to tell about when his daddy or his uncle had this distillery, and they had a big flock of geese. Them geese would get up there at the mill dam where they had the grist mill—they had their still above that. And this water would come through there, where they poured the whiskey mash. Well, the old geese would get drunk, and—it just tickled you to hear him tell about how crazy them geese flopped around. (Katherine Thompson, daughter-in-law)

*   *   *

> We had a ferry down here at the river, and he used to go to the other side of Gallatin to get his bootleg. There was a gate across the road . . . there was no fence laws at the time, and we had to keep fences to keep the people's cattle from comin' down here in the

corn. One day my father and I went over there and fixed that gate up, next day or two Uncle Jimmy went over there at Gallatin, got him some whiskey, got drunk. Had one of those little Model T roadsters, and he hit that gate, and he tore that thing all into splinters. Didn't hurt the car much. Uncle Jimmy said, "The damn car wouldn't open the gate." Tore the gate all to pieces, we never did fix it up. That wound the gate up. (Sam Kirkpatrick, Laguardo neighbor)

* * *

He would get into a buckboard and drive the team at a fast run into town, and frighten anybody who was with him. (Eva Thompson Jones)

* * *

He took exercise every morning; he never failed. Would get up and take calisthenics. One time, it was 1918, the year of the war, my husband and I lived in Gatlinburg and he came to spend the night with us. Uncle Jimmy shared the room with cousin Jack Womack, the man we were living with as boarders. Uncle Jimmy, he got up the next morning. It was gettin' up time; I hadn't called them for breakfast. He got up and was goin' through all of that exercising and kicking—he'd always kick his feet. So after he went home, cousin Jack was a terrible religious old man, he said to me one morning, he blared his eyes real big when he'd talk, he said to me: "Let me tell you something. That poor old man is in bad shape. I seen him a-havin' the awfulest fight with the devil that you ever seen in your life. He was kickin' and a-snortin' and a-beatin' hisself in the breast—he was havin' the *awfulest* fight with the devil." (Katherine Thompson)

* * *

He would chew a whole package of gum at a time, but he would then put it in a Vaseline jar he kept in his vest pocket. Would carry it there. He said he'd biled that jar out, and would stick the gum in there when he finished chewing it. Always said, "You can't wear that gum out"—so he could chew it over and over again as much as he wanted to. (Jam Thompson, Laguardo neighbor)

* * *

The first time he got his engagement on the Opry, Eva made him
have his pants pressed. So she took his pants and had them cleaned
and pressed, and he came in there when he got ready to put them
pants on, hollered in there and said, "Hey, thar, who ironed them
damned wrinkles in these britches? I like my britches smooth and
round. Fit my knee-caps. Don't want no crease in 'em." (Bill
Thompson, grandson)

* * *

He was fond of Texas, always braggin' on Texas. Fellow that run
the store down there, Mr. Bill Bates, made up with this salesman
one time to knock Texas. So Uncle Jimmy come in, and this salesman started talking about how he was in Texas one time and there
was a fellow out there had a pair of oxen driving, and one of them
froze to death, and he was gonna go out and skin him and before
he got him skinned the other one died from overheat. And Uncle
Jimmy, he jumped up and said, "That's a damned lie!" And Uncle
Jimmy got mad at Bill, and he'd walk right by his store a half-mile
on up the road even if he wanted a nickel box of matches. (Sam
Kirkpatrick)

* * *

I once asked him how he liked to stay out at Eva's house when he
came into town [Nashville] and he said, "I wouldn't have it, I
wouldn't have it." I says, "Why?" And he says, "Well, there ain't
nowhere for to spit when I chew my tobacco." I says, "Couldn't
you get you a little bucket of ashes?" "Why," he says, "there ain't
a damned ash thar." (Katherine Thompson)

* * *

I remember we had a little colored community over here, not too
far from his house, and he liked to go over there and play for them
from time to time. And he'd get real hot if anyone said anything to
him about it. (Jug Stewart, Laguardo neighbor)

* * *

He knew all about the stars. He used to tell us about them, what their names were. He could tell where he was just by looking at the stars in the heavens. That's how he was able to never get lost when he was traveling around. (Mary Irwin, relative)

* * *

He called his fiddle "Old Betsy." He told the history of it lots of times, but I don't remember it now. He kept rattlesnake rattles in it, and in his case, a piece of red flannel. And he'd spread it over Old Betsy's breast every night—he'd "put her to bed," he'd call it. (Katherine Thompson)

* * *

Acknowledgments

Mrs. Katherine Thompson, Greenbrier, Tennessee; Fred & William Thompson, Greenbrier; Dwight Manners, Boston; Mary Irwin, Nashville; Jug Stewart, Laguardo; Mr. & Mrs. Jim Thompson, Laguardo; Sam Kirkpatrick, Laguardo; Bert Norther, Laguardo; Virginia Braun, Lebanon; the Manners Family, Laguardo. Special thanks to Bill Harrison, Madison, Alabama, who led the drive to erect a marker for Uncle Jimmy's unmarked grave and did some of the initial research in piecing together the story of Uncle Jimmy Thompson.

Fiddlin' Powers and His Family

T HOUGH EVERYBODY CALLED HIM SIMPLY FIDDLIN'
Powers, his full name was James Cowan Powers. He was born in
October 1877 in Russell County in southwest Virginia, where he
was to spend almost all of his life. Details about his early life are
sketchy, but a favorite family story describes his older brother "Uncle
Billy" Powers buying the first fiddle in the family, sometime around
1887. Uncle Billy was a great dancer, but not much of a fiddler, and he
soon lost interest in his new purchase. Young Cowan did not, though;
he waited for the times when Uncle Billy would leave home, and then
would sneak the fiddle out of its case and work on it. The young man
must have learned from other area fiddlers, or from other family members. Aside from the memory of the tune "Old Molly Hair" (which he
later recorded) being in the family tradition, we don't know how Powers acquired his distinctive style or repertoire that he was to become
famous for years later.

About 1900 or 1901 Powers married Mathilda Lambert, a local girl
who also came from a musical family. "Dad and Mother played music
long before we kids came along," recalled Ada Salyer, Powers's
youngest daughter. "They played music at community functions. Mother played the five-string banjo and Father the fiddle, but she could play
the fiddle as well, and the older children remember them exchanging
instruments, swapping instruments, while they were playing." It was
natural that when the couple's children started coming along, that they
would have musical talent, and that they would be encouraged to
expand the family stringband. (Charles was born in 1902; Orpha in

1904; Carrie in 1908; and Ada in 1911.) "In those early years Daddy would bring home an instrument for each child," said Ada. Charles got the banjo (he later doubled on guitar), Carrie got the guitar, Orpha the mandolin, and Ada, the baby, a ukelele.

The family soon relocated on a farm in Russell County, in the center of the area bounded by St. Paul, Dungannon, Nicklesville, and Castlewood. In addition to farming, Powers soon became known for his leather work. "He had his own special pattern for making leggings. He would order a whole cowhide at a time," said Ada, "and would make the legging to fit the person. He doubled stitched them, and waxed his thread, and hand tooled them. And there was other leather business too. At that time every young man in the county had to have an underarm holster, and he had to make a lot of those. Now that tells you something about the times back then." Powers also worked as a carpenter and helped build many of the houses in Clinchfield (then called Moss). "His main job was that he knew how to cut rafters, and one day the foreman asked him to teach the younger men there how to cut rafters. And Daddy had only had one day of school; he went to school one day and learned to write his name and never went back. But he had it up here."

All this was to undergo a severe change in 1916 when Tilda suddenly died. She was only thirty-five, but had contracted tuberculosis, and suddenly Powers was left with himself as sole head of a family of four children aged from three to fourteen. He continued to work as a carpenter for a time, but he often had to be gone for a week at a time, and this meant leaving the three girls alone in a remote farmhouse with instructions to never let anyone in the house. Perhaps because of this, perhaps because of the booming wartime economy, perhaps because of some other unknown reason, Powers decided to turn his family band into a professional entertainment troupe. He himself was widely known as a fiddler through his years of winning local contests. At thirty-nine he was no spring chicken, but he had learned about how to please an audience, and something about how to book "entertainments" in the coal towns and schoolhouses of the Southern mountains. "We started traveling with our music in 1918," Ada remembered.

> I remember that it was still World War I, and that daddy had to
> carry me to the train station. I was so young then I didn't have an

instrument yet; my part in the show was to dance. I can't remember when I didn't dance. It was war times, and money was plentiful. When I would dance, they would throw me down eight or ten dollars in silver under my feet. I heard someone once say, "Look—she doesn't even stop to pick up her money." But I never even thought about that; I just knew I was supposed to dance.

By war's end, the Powers Family was establishing enough of a reputation that Cowan decided it could be made into a full-time occupation, and for the next ten years did so. "The circuit that we traveled most was the five state area of Virginia, Tennessee, Kentucky, West Virginia, and North Carolina," said Ada.

We made our best money on those West Virginia and Kentucky mining towns. It was not unusual in there to take in over $200 a night—at 25¢ an adult and 15¢ a child. At first Daddy would go ahead a month or so before and book the shows for us, and then later he had several men who did that and did our advertising. At first we traveled by train, but then Daddy bought one of the first two Model T Fords in the community, and we went in that. I can hear those old curtains in the back flapping in the cold wind; it wasn't enclosed, and all we had in the back was those curtains. Then later he bought a big Essex coach, which had an enclosed top—the only car with a closed top in the community.
Daddy got the idea that Carrie needed some lessons in the guitar, so one day he brought Byrd Moore home with him. He said Byrd was a pretty good box player.

Indeed he was. He was to emerge as the leading guitarist in southwest Virginia, performing with everyone from Tom Ashley to Melvin Robinette, and recording dozens of times under his own name and with others. This was 1923, and even though Byrd had not yet recorded, he had an enviable reputation among local musicians. "He stayed with us about a month and taught Carrie guitar. We didn't know exactly where he was from. He was pretty much of a gypsy, moving around a lot, but he did have a half-brother in Wise."

A typical show would last about an hour, and while the entire group sang and performed on many numbers, each also developed specialties. Charlie would knock down on the banjo old tunes like "Shout Lula" or

"Coal Creek March" (which he later taught to Dock Boggs), and take up the guitar to sing songs like "The Little Old Log Cabin in the Lane" and "Rambling Reckless Hobo." Carrie would play variants of "Coney Isle" on the guitar, and Orpha would do "Don't Let Your Deal Go Down" on the mandolin. The sisters would sing some numbers by themselves, and on a select few pieces, such as "Rocky Road to Dinah's House" and "Turkey in the Straw," Powers himself would sing.

In the spring of 1924, an event occurred in Johnson City, Tennessee, about forty miles south of Dungannon, that was to have considerable effect on the career of the family. The United Commercial Travellers put on a fiddling contest and show at the Deluxe, then Johnson City's largest theater. The Powers Family got off the train to find they were the only stringband there, and they were promptly invited to play at the banquet Saturday night, alternating with the brass orchestra that had been booked to perform. Meanwhile, Powers signed up to enter the fiddling contest Friday night, where he went up against well-known local talents such as Dedrick Harris (from Asheville), Uncle Am Stuart (from Morristown), and Charles Bowman (from Johnson City). When the dust settled, young Bowman, who was months away from his recording career with the famous Hill Billies band, approached Cowan and said, "Mr. Powers, the way I see it, one of us will get first and the other one second." He was right; Powers took the $50 gold piece for first, and Bowman got the $25 second prize.

The star of the evening, though, was Fiddlin' John Carson, already a well-known recording star and master showman. He too was quite taken with the Powers family and impressed Cowan a lot for his showmanship and fiddling ability. As an example of the former, Ada remembered that Carson called her out on stage that evening.

> He had composed and had recorded this song, "You Will Never Miss Your Mother Until She is Gone." He called me out on stage—I was just a little girl, remember, about twelve—and he asked me how long my mother had been gone. I told him that she had died when I was three. He said, "Now I am going to play and sing for you an old song. I have the ballets printed out, and I am going to ask this little girl to pass them through the audience, and whatever you want to give for one, you drop it in the hat. It goes to her." That was a big theater, and I started out, but soon someone asked

my other two sisters to help out, and loaned them hats, and each took a hat in hand and a sheaf of ballets, and it seemed everybody there wanted one. When it was over, we had three hats full of money, and we went into the room off stage and dumped it all out on the table. My oldest sister went and called John Carson in there and said. "Now you take what you want out of that." He didn't want to, but she insisted, said it wouldn't be right, so he said, "OK, to make you happy," and reached over and took out two or three big bills. And next night coming home on my train—in those days they had a train butch that came through selling fruit, candy, papers—and going home we girls just about bought out the news butch. We had the money and we spent it.

John Carson also represented to Powers and the other musicians there the potential of the new mass media on their music. His recording career, which had begun by accident barely a year before, had won him instant fame and given him a huge new audience. The lesson was not lost on the local audience either. Bert Pouder, a Johnson City business, announced to Powers that he planned to get him a recording contract like Carson's. Powers and his crew went on back home, but within a few weeks Pouder wrote them saying that he indeed had lined up a recording appointment for them in New York City. (Pouder apparently was originally from New York, or knew his way around there quite well.) In August the family finalized plans to go. Charles had temporarily quit the band and left home, working at various odd jobs in the area. He was contacted and asked to come back to begin rehearsing with the band. He did, and shortly after that the group met Pouder in Johnson City and took a Pullman car to New York. Pouder was functioning by now as their manager, and they paid his expenses for the trip up there. He lodged them in the McAlbert Hotel on 34th Street, and picked them up in a cab on the morning of August 11 for their first audition.

Their first audition was at the Victor Record Company's offices, where they made an unnumbered and unissued test of a song called "Way Down in Georgia" on August 11, 1924. The Victor executives were impressed—they were becoming very much aware of the success their arch-rival Okeh was having with John Carson—and scheduled a full recording session for the group down at their studio in Camden, New

Jersey, across the river from Philadelphia. This was set up for August 18–19, 1924. Meanwhile, they also auditioned for Edison, and for the Keith-Albee vaudeville circuit. (The latter never bore fruit, but the former did—see below.) They also received an offer from Columbia Records to record as well, but Powers thought their offered royalty rate of one half cent per record was too low and held out for a full cent per side. Columbia held firm, and Powers went on with his Victor deal, which garnered them a flat fee of $100 per side. In between seeing the sights, the family also broadcasted for the first time, over station WJZ (owned then by the RCA corporation). They were surprised to learn that while they were on the air the station received numerous calls and telegrams from the little mountain towns where they had played, telegrams requesting favorite numbers fans recalled from their live shows.

Finally, the day for the sessions dawned, and the party made its way down to Philadelphia and crossed the river to the Victor factory in Camden. The Victor engineers had never seen a stringband before and were quite intrigued. The secretary who made out the session sheets was puzzled by the fact that the band performed entirely by ear, and typed "No Music" in the ledgers. They set up the strange aggregation in Room No. 2 of the studio and did a run-through on the first tune to be recorded, "Brown's Dream." It took several tunes to get the balance right—in fact, none of the first three tunes ("Brown's Dream," "Old Swinnie," and "Three Forks of the Kentucky River") was ever issued. Ada recalled some of the difficulties:

> They had a curtained booth back in there where the recording machines stayed; through this curtain protruded five metal horns. They placed us in a semi-circle and a horn came out toward each instrument, to each player. There was a red light in the hall, and they said to watch the light and when it comes on, start playing. Then we'll turn it off, but you keep noticing that light, and if there's anything wrong, we'll turn it on again for you to stop. They stopped us a time or two. Once there was wax that had somehow gotten in the groove and they had to remove that. We started again. They came out shaking their heads saying, "That little ukelele's just drowning out everything." I wore a thumb pick and a finger pick and my own style of playing I had. So he stood me

over behind my daddy and took the horn that I had been standing
in front of away. You know, that did awful things to a little red-
headed girl, but then he came out a second time still shaking his
head. Then he backed me up another six feet, and that's the way
we recorded.

The rest of that day they recorded three more songs: "The Little Old
Log Cabin in the Lane," "Old Joe Clark," and "Sour Wood Mountain,"
all of which were deemed suitable for release. Charles sang on "Sour
Wood Mountain" but for "Little Old Log Cabin" the Victor producer
insisted on bringing in a Victor studio musician to sing. This was none
other than Carson J. Robison, a few short years away from his successful recording career with Vernon Dalhart. This move angered the Powers Family because, as Ada put it, "he just didn't have that Appalachian
twang in his voice, and anyone could hear that he wasn't a real mountain singer."

The next day, August 19, 1924, the band got into high gear and cut
eleven songs: "Cumberland Gap" (unissued), "Buck Creek Girls" (unissued), "Billy in the Low Ground" (unissued), "Birdie" (unissued), "Patty
on the Turnpike," "Sallie Goodin" (unissued), "Callahan's Reel,"
"Rocky Road to Dinah's House" (unissued), "Sugar in the Gourd,"
"Cripple Creek," and "Ida Red." Carson Robison returned to sing the
vocal on the last cut. In two days, the band had recorded seventeen
selections, though only eight of them (four double-sided records)
would ever be issued.

The historical significance of this Victor session should not be min-
imized: it represented the first commercial recording of a full mountain stringband which had been playing together regularly outside of
the studio. It was also the first recording of a Southern musical family
group in history. Strictly speaking, the first full stringband to record
was John Carson's Virginia Reelers—two fiddles, banjo, and guitar—
who had recorded for Okeh in Atlanta in March 1924. However, evidence suggested that this was a "studio" band rather than a regular
working band, as Carson continued to do personal appearances by
himself or with his daughter. Eva Davis and Samantha Bumgarner
recorded for Columbia in April 1924, but only as a fiddle-banjo duo. In
July 1924 Henry Whitter took fiddler Henry Sutphin and banjoist John
Rector from Galax to New York to record two Okeh titles as the Vir-

ginia Breakdowners, but this too was a pick-up band, not a regular one. The Hill Billies made test records for Victor in the summer of 1924, but the company had trouble recording the full band, and they were rejected. Thus the Powers recordings can be seen as the first real documents of the Southern family stringband tradition, and the trouble the Victor engineers took to balance the sound was, in the end, historically justified.

Later that year when the Powers records were issued, Victor made them the centerpiece of their first catalogue brochure featuring traditional American music. It was a four-page handout called "Olde Time Fiddlin' Tunes," and it contained descriptions of Eck Robertson's fiddle records, as well as pseudo-folk music by the likes of Vernon Dalhart, Wendell Hall, and ex-Tennessee governor Alf Taylor's gospel quartet. Powers's eight recordings, more than any other, dominated the text, and the Victor company even reproduced a photo of the band. The writer of the brochure seemed aware of the historical first that the Powers sides represented: "These old tunes rarely get into the cities, but mountain folk have sung and danced to them for generations. . . . The tunes are mostly simple, and they are repeated over and over and over until they get into your blood and you will want to dance to them all night. Writers of books and plays of late years have gone into the mountains and studied the life of the people there, but this is almost the first of their music that has come into public notice." The writer seemed also aware of fiddling styles, since he noted that Powers's "Patty on the Turnpike" was "given more than average brilliancy by the fiddler's playing it in a high key."

The four Victor records that were issued were quite successful, so much so that when Victor began using the electrical recording process three years later, they asked Ernest Stoneman to remake the Powers sides with the new recording process. (It is unclear why they did not seek out Powers himself to do this.) In the records, Powers's liquid style does come across, though rather little of the fancy work that won him so many contests and influenced so many younger fiddlers. One of his pupils was Melvin Robinette, from Gate City, who later recorded for Gennett on his own. Robinette recalls that before he met Powers, he had been experimenting with various odd tunings, and that Powers showed him how to use standard tuning and to use his fingers to play in different keys. "He would double-note everything in a tune," Robinette recalled. "Not just an occasional note like we do. He would double-note even those fine [high] parts of numbers like 'Arkansas Traveler.'"

The next year, on October 2, 1925, the family made another trip to New York, this time to record for the Edison company. They did at least ten sides at the Edison studio between October 2 and 7, most of which were repeats of the Victor session: "Old Joe Clark," "Ida Red," "Sourwood Mountain," "Cripple Creek," "Sugar in the Gourd," "Rocky Road to Dinah's House," and "Little Old Log Cabin." The Edison sides allowed four minutes of music per side, and Edison did not saddle the band with an inappropriate dude singer: Charlie did most of the singing. And there were some new songs recorded here as well: "Cluck Old Hen," "Wild and Reckless Hobo," and "Pretty Fair Miss," though the latter was apparently not issued. Some of these records were issued as cylinders, others as flat discs.

Meanwhile, as recording stars, the Powers band began to expand their bookings. "String band artists of Old Virginny. Artists for the Victor Talking Machine Company," blazoned the posters. They appeared on WOPI in Bristol in the late 1920s and had a date to appear over KDKA in Pittsburgh, but an auto accident prevented them from getting there. They did one tour in 1926 with Byrd Moore, Tom Ashley, and G. B. Grayson, and another one through Kentucky in 1928 with Dock Boggs and the Scott Boatright family band. Carrie married John L. Porter, a harmonica player, in November 1925, and dropped out of the band for a time. As the other girls were quickly coming of courtship age, and as Powers himself began to think of marrying again, changes were in the cards.

Meanwhile, there was time for one final recording session. In July of 1927, Polk Brockman, the man who discovered Fiddlin' John Carson in Atlanta and persuaded Okeh to record him, arrived in Norton, Virginia, and held auditions for a new recording session Okeh was planning that fall in Winston-Salem. Cowan Powers called Carrie and her husband to rejoin the band and went over to audition. While he was there, he watched Brockman audition a skinny young yodeler from Asheville named Jimmie Rodgers. "Are you going to record that young man?" Cowan asked Brockman. "I want to, but he's on his way home to Mississippi, and I'm sure not going to bring him back from Mississippi," said Brockman.

He did, however, send the Powers family to the Zinzendorf Hotel in Winston-Salem, where, on September 27, 1927, they cut six final sides. These were to be the only electrical recordings the group ever did, and the Powers daughters naturally feel they were the best. All the group contributed to the singing, and John Porter ("Steamboat," as he was called on the records), added his harmonica to the doings. "Old Molly Hair" and "Did You Ever See a Devil, Uncle Joe" made up one coupling, and a two-part skit called "Old Virginia Reed, Parts 1 and 2," comprised the other. In the latter, each member of the family got to play a brief solo. Two sides, "Shady Grove," and "Johnnie Karo" (mislisted in the Okeh files as "Charlie Karo") were not issued.

The Okeh session, which could have been the start of a new recording career, instead became a swan song. The family was growing up and breaking apart. In 1928 the other two daughters, Ada and Orpha, had twin weddings and soon started their own families; Cowan himself remarried a younger woman named Janie Horn and started a second family. Charles had a brief marriage and then joined the army in 1928, starting a career that was to endure through the 1930s and which was to end tragically on the infamous Bataan death march in World War II.

Through the 1930s and 1940s Cowan Powers continued to be a familiar fixture at local fiddlers' contests and with a variety of bands on tri-state radio. Apparently he never sought to record again, though he enjoyed spending long hours with old friends like Charlie Bowman, swapping tunes and playing "remember when." By the early 1950s he was playing off and on with Carter and Ralph Stanley—"the boys," as he called them—and one evening while he was on stage with them in Saltville, Virginia, and he was finishing "Cluck Old Hen," he suffered a massive heart attack. They took him to a hospital in Abingdon, Virginia, where he died the next day.

In recent years, the Powers Family has been inducted into the Bristol Music Hall of Fame, and in the early 1970s the Powers girls resurrected their band for a time. Members of the family still occasionally perform today, carrying on a tradition of one of the genuine pioneer stringbands of the South.

Sources

Most of the material in this essay was drawn from personal interviews with Ada Powers Salyer, Dungannon, Virginia, August 13 and 14, 1983; tapes of these interviews are in the author's files. I have supplemented this with material from Mrs. Salyer's scrapbooks, as well as interviews with Cleo McNutt (Gate City, Virginia) and with Melvin Robinette (Tullahoma, Tennessee, 1977). Tony Russell made available details from the Powers Victor recording sessions.

Mr. Grayson's Train

SOMEDAY, WHEN A SERIOUS HISTORY OF SOUTHERN fiddle tunes is written, someone will have to give some thought to just what aspects of these tunes are distinctively "Southern." A great many of the older tunes are like Child ballads—they can be traced back to England, Scotland, or Ireland. But there is a considerable body of such tunes that correspond to what folksong collectors call Laws ballads—"native American" balladry partly modeled on older, imported forms, but partly forged from uniquely American aspects. There are numerous Southern fiddle tunes that, like Laws ballads, have distinctive "native American" aspects as well, features that are seldom if ever found in British tunes. There are, for instance, numerous rags and ragtime-like tunes that were influenced and inspired by the classic ragtime pieces of the 1890s; there are various blues, with their sliding notes and unorthodox bowing patterns. There are various kinds of imitative pieces, such as the old Texas versions of "Lost Indian," in which the fiddler added his vocalese to the fiddle sound; there are the lonesome waltzes with the drone harmonies derived from Cajun fiddling. And there are a series of tunes like "Train 45," "Going Down the Lee Highway," and "Orange Blossom Special," which have an open-ended C part to which measures can be added at the fiddler's discretion. This C part gives the fiddler a chance to improvise around the sketchy melody, gradually building tension in the manner of a jazz soloist, until he decides to "release" by returning to the A part. This last technique might be the most uniquely American of all these features, and the most dynamic of all fiddle tune types. It is a favorite of professional show-off fiddlers even today, and its basic technique has even been borrowed by rock guitarists. All of which is a necessary prelude to attempting to explain the popularity and influence of Appalachian fiddler G. B. Grayson.

In 1927, Grayson recorded two versions of a song he called "Train 45." It was a variant of an old mountain banjo tune usually called "Reuben" or "Reuben's Train," a "chording piece" that was often one of the first numbers a young banjo player learned. Grayson adapted it for the fiddle, worked out an arrangement which utilized part of the "open-ended" bridge, added a few floating stanzas, and came up with blueprint for a mountain and bluegrass standard. His Victor recording of it sold over 50,000 copies and then was reissued on the Bluebird label to sell a few thousand more; it remained in print until 1934. The next year it would be re-recorded by Wade Mainer (as "Riding on that Train 45") and would become a hit all over again. After World War II dozens of bluegrass bands would record it, including those of Bill Monroe, Flatt & Scruggs, and the Stanley Brothers, and it would become a standard at fiddling contests. Folksingers of the sixties used the tune to create a popular lyric they called "900 Miles."

Another classic early country song from the 1920s is one called "A Short Life of Trouble." Though the song was based on an old folk ballad, it might well have been written to describe the life and career of G. B. Grayson, one of the Appalachian region's most influential fiddlers and singers. Unlike other early country greats like the Carter Family or the Skillet Lickers, Grayson, along with his partner Henry Whitter, had an effective recording career that barely spanned two years. Whereas the Carters ran up a total of some 350 sides, Grayson & Whitter managed a grand output of only some forty sides—five of those were remakes. Yet these sides were some of the most important and influential in the music's history. Grayson & Whitter songs would be re-recorded and performed over and over again, all the way up to the present day. To paraphrase Winston Churchill, never have so many owed so much to so few. And though the pair will never make the Country Music Hall of Fame, their music still echoes at fiddle contests, bluegrass festivals, folk concerts, and even occasionally on the stage of the Opry.

Though both Grayson and Whitter have been gone for decades, friends and family remember enough about them to let us piece together their story. One source of confusion has been Grayson's exact name; official documents list it as Gilliam Banmon Grayson, and he was the son of Benjamin Carroll Grayson, a veteran of the thirteenth Tennessee Cavalry in the War Between the States. The family itself hailed from Scotland, and had settled in Ashe County, in a corner of extreme western North Carolina, not far from Mountain City, Tennessee. G. B. himself was born in 1871 and grew up listening to war stories of his father and uncle. One of the stories his uncle told involved the hunting down and capture of a local killer named Tom Dula. Dula had stabbed a girl named Laura Foster, and James Grayson, G. B.'s uncle, led the posse that captured him in Doe Valley, Tennessee. Dula was then returned to North Carolina and hanged. Soon a song arose about the event—whether or not G. B. had anything to do with it is uncertain—and in later years it became known as "Tom Dooley." And though it would become a national bestseller for the Kingston Trio in 1958, Grayson would be the first to record in 1930.

When G. B. Grayson was barely six weeks old, his vision was seriously damaged. His daughter said that G. B. had spent a day staring out a window at new fall of snow, with bright sunlight glittering off it. "He took cold in the eyes," she explains, and it did permanent damage to his vision. He was not totally blind—he could make out a figure of a person and could tell time by holding a watch close to his eyes. But as he grew up, this was enough to prevent him from farming, logging, store-keeping, or any of the other vocations available to mountain boys. Like most rural Southerners with such a handicap, he turned to music. Soon he had mastered guitar, harmonica, mandolin, organ, piano, but especially the fiddle. He developed a haunting, bluesy style with a unique tone. He also became a fine singer, holding the instrument down on his shoulder so he could sing and fiddle at the same time. He was soon busking around the mountains—playing on street corners, courthouse lawns, at train stations, pie suppers, dances, fiddling contests, medicine shows, and carnivals—anywhere he could make a little change. In the 1890s he had married, moved to nearby Johnson County, Tennessee, and started a family. Soon he was supporting a wife and six children by his fiddling and singing.

Grayson was in the center of the southern Appalachians, in the heart of classic folk ballads and fiddling, and he absorbed most of the music of the area. He played with some of the area's best-known musicians, including Clarence Tom Ashley and the banjoist Doc Walsh. But in the summer of 1927—at the same time that Ralph Peer was discovering the Carter Family and Jimmie Rodgers in nearby Bristol—Grayson met a man named Henry Whitter at a fiddler's convention in Mountain City. Whitter, a former millhand from Fries, Virginia, had actually traveled to New York four years earlier and made some of the first country records, including "Wreck on the Southern Old 97" and a harmonica piece called "Fox Chase." He was an adequate singer and average guitarist, but Whitter was a good promoter and knew how to talk his way into record contracts. He sensed in Grayson an immensely talented mountain fiddler and singer who knew nothing about the record business, and knew at once that they could help each other. Soon he had arranged tryouts at Gennett and Victor. The talent scouts there grinned with satisfaction; here, for sure, was *real* mountain music, not the stiff-necked mewing of studio singers like Vernon Dalhart or Mac & Bob.

Between October 1927, when the pair traveled to Richmond, Indiana, to record their first sides for the Gennett label, and September 1929, when they did their final session for the country's biggest label, Victor, Grayson & Whitter recorded an amazing number of songs that would become standards. Among the first were "Train 45," though we have no idea of just where or how Grayson worked up the piece, and "Handsome Molly," an old Irish ballad that would later be recorded by the Rolling Stones' Mick Jagger. At a 1927 Victor session they did two famous mountain murder ballads, "Omie Wise" and "Rose Conley," later featured by the likes of Doc Watson and Charlie Monroe. Then there was the war lament "He Is Coming to Us Dead." Later hits included "Nine Pound Hammer," learned from the Johnson City fiddler Charlie Bowman and later popularized by Merle Travis and Bill Monroe; and "Going Down the Lee Highway," a bluesy fiddle tune also known as "Lee Highway Blues" and a staple in bluegrass bands. In terms of sales, none quite matched the total of "Train 45." Their Victor version of "Barnyard Serenade" (a.k.a. "Old Hen Cackle") sold 9,000 copies, while the ballad "Red and Green Signal Lights" managed 6,000 copies. "Lee Highway," issued on July 17, 1931, only sold a little over 1,300 copies in its original incarnation.

Though the Depression was slowing down sales of Grayson & Whitter's records, the pair was still full of plans. They made a guest appearance on the Grand Ole Opry in 1930 and were well received, and

Victor was planning on making more records. But then tragedy struck. On August 16, 1930, Grayson set out for his brother's home and soon hitched a ride. He was apparently hanging onto the running board of the car when the car hit a log truck near Damascus, Virginia. Grayson was thrown out and killed. His death certificate noted that he was forty-three years old and that his occupation was a musician. Henry Whitter's widow recalled that he never really got over the death of his friend and partner, and that he eventually died of diabetes in 1941.

Today many veteran fiddlers and musicians in the central Appalachians still remember G. B. Grayson and play his songs. Doc Watson knows his music, as does Ralph Stanley. LP reissues of his old records have remained in print now for four decades, giving younger artists, whose grandfathers might barely have heard Grayson, a chance to drink from the well. His seminal 1927 recording of "Train 45" was the beginning of a line that hasn't run out yet.

Sources

Many of the details about G. B. Grayson I obtained through conversation and correspondence with his grandson, Jim Meadows, of Johnson City. Mr. Meadows also shared with me some of the family papers and some of Grayson's song sheets. I also benefited from reading Ray Parker's essay, "G. B. Grayson: A Short Life of Trouble," in *Old Time Music*, which also contains a complete discography. I have also been set straight in certain facts by Joe Wilson, a country gent now living in Washington, D.C. He provided me with a copy of Grayson's death certificate. He also authored the excellent liner notes to *The Recordings of Grayson and Whitter* (County LP 513).

Doc Roberts: Behind the Masks

IN THE 1920S AND 1930S FIDDLERS IN KENTUCKY WHO wanted to record their music found themselves at a disadvantage. The commercial record companies who eagerly set up temporary studios in states like Georgia, Texas, and Tennessee for some reason ignored Kentucky. During the golden age of old-time music, they only scheduled two field sessions in Kentucky—a 1928 Brunswick one in Ashland (which attracted primarily West Virginia acts) and a 1930 Victor one in Louisville (which did not attempt to attract local talent and was designed to record the Carter Family with Jimmie Rodgers). The Kentucky fiddlers who wanted to record generally had to go north to Indiana, where the Starr Piano Company had recording studios in Richmond, Indiana, or to Grafton, Wisconsin, where the Wisconsin Chair Company owned a record company called Paramount. The bigger of the two was the Starr Company, which issued their records through a company called Gennett. Even by the 1920s standards, Gennett records were poorly recorded, cheaply made, and were not well distributed. Compared to the major labels like Victor, Columbia, and Okeh, they didn't sell many copies, and the ones they did sell wore out quickly. Worst of all, the company issued the records on a variety of "stencil" labels like Supertone, Challenge, Champion, Silvertone, and Superior. For most of these secondary issues, the artists were only paid half the regular royalty. And to add insult to injury, Starr often issued the stencil labels under phony artist names, depriving the musicians of their fleeting chance at fame.

This was especially tragic in the case of Kentucky fiddlers, since the state had one of the strongest and most complex fiddling traditions in the South. It included fiddlers like Charlie Wilson, Leonard Rutherford, Ted Gossett, the black fiddler Jim Booker, Andy Palmer, Frank Miller, Draper Walter, Blind Bill Day ("Jilson Setters"), Cliff Gross, Les Smitha (of Jimmy Johnson's String Band), Crickett Garrett (with the Hack String Band), W. M. Stepp, John V. Walker, Tex Achison (of the Prairie Ramblers), and others. Most of these musicians were saddled with leaving their legacy in the unsteady hands of Gennett, and it was a precarious process. Some of the records, especially in the early 1930s, sold so few copies that virtually no copies of them are known to have survived; others exist only in single copies, heard only by a handful of students and collectors. In 1980, when Guthrie Meade and Rich Nevins compiled the best of these rare discs into a three-LP set called *Old Time Fiddle Band Music of Kentucky*, it was a revelation to both fiddlers and fans. Most of the records were so rare that it was as if they had been issued for the first time.

The Kentucky fiddler who best overcame this handicap was a young man from the central part of the state named Doc Roberts. He succeeded in recording more commercial sides than any other fiddler in the state—over eighty solos and as many more as an accompanist—and he probably made as much money from his records as any other fiddler. In terms of raw talent, repertoire, and style, he was probably the equal of Arthur Smith or Clayton McMichen. In terms of influence, he was not. Some of his records were, indeed, as rare as many of the other Gennetts, and some of his masterpieces, like "Rye Straw" (recorded in 1929) and "Deer Walk" (1930), sold only in the hundreds of copies. But even the ones that were popular didn't win Doc Roberts much fame or influence: few of them were issued under his own name. To the fiddlers and music fans of the 1920s, most of his music was known under names like Fiddling Jim Burke, Fiddling Frank Nelson, Uncle Jim Hawkins, the Old Smoky Twins, the Quadrillers, the Lone Star Fiddlers, the Kentucky Thorobreds, Carl Harris, Billy Jordan, and Fiddling Bob White. Only on the original Gennett issues—the rarest and poorest-selling of all the stencil issues—were Roberts's early records released under his own name. Only when he changed record companies in 1931, and began working for the American Record Company, was he able to insist on billing his work as the Doc Roberts Trio. The whole situation was symptomatic of problems Roberts had with his professional identity throughout his career, and his case illustrates just how hard it was for some Southern traditional musicians to assert themselves enough to make it as a professional.

In Doc Roberts's case, the problems started with his name. It all began on a Monday, April 26, 1897, in an old log house on top of a hill just off the Curtis Pike in Madison County, Kentucky. The Roberts family, fixtures in the county since before the Civil War, were about to get themselves a new baby. They called on the local doctor to help with the delivery. His name was Doctor Phillips, only everyone called him Doc Phillips, and after a successful birth, the grateful Roberts clan decided to name the new baby boy after him; the child was christened Dock Phil Roberts. A bit unusual for a proper name, to be sure, and throughout the boy's life he had to constantly correct people who thought "Dock" was a nickname and wanted to call him Phil. He also had to correct the way people spelled the name, valiantly insisting that it should be "Dock" with a K. In 1925 when the boy had become a man and had started making phonograph records, he spelled his name with a K on all his contracts and correspondence. The record companies paid no heed, apparently thinking that anyone who played the fiddle so well should be a doctor of some sort. After a few years, Dock Phil Roberts gave up and gave in and decided that if the world wanted to call him Doc and spell his name wrong it was easier to roll with the flow.

Rolling with the flow became Doc Roberts's style. It was one of the reasons he never commercialized his music the way Arthur Smith or Clayton McMichen or Bob Wills did. By 1935, when country music was just becoming a profession at which you could make money, when Arthur Smith was playing every week on the Opry and Clayton McMichen was touring with Larry Sunbrock's fiddling contests, Doc Roberts was in virtual retirement from music, serving as the county poorhouse keeper back in Madison County. Time and again he rejected chances to make the big push into full time, big cities, bright lights, radio barn dances. He seemed to prefer his farm, his family, and fiddling at local square dances.

Roberts himself admitted that he began playing the fiddle when he was seven, and that he picked up a lot of his tunes from other central Kentucky fiddlers around Madison County. "I wouldn't fool with the sorry ones," he remembered. "I would always pick the best we had." In fact, one of the better ones was Doc's oldest brother Liebert, who in later years actually beat Doc in a contest playing a tune called "Waynesborough." Liebert, in turn, had learned many tunes from a local African-American fiddler named Owen Walker. Born in 1857 and growing up during the Civil War, Walker was only one of a number of skilled black string musicians in the region. His band flourished about 1915, and he traveled as far away as Louisville playing for wealthy white patrons as well as black audiences. He never recorded, but passed onto the Roberts brothers some of his best tunes and some of the most distinctive and unusual tunes. These included numerous pieces that Roberts later recorded: "Old Buzzard," "Brickyard Joe," "Waynesborough," "Martha Campbell," and "All I Got's Done Gone." He also gave Roberts the idea that professional musicians had to dress in white suits with bow ties. Roberts later said that Walker "helped me every way in the world. . . . He was the fiddlingest colored man that was ever around Kentucky. He played like a white man, only he could beat a white man." Guthrie Meade, who interviewed Roberts and studied his repertoire extensively, estimated that as much as 70 percent of Roberts's repertoire originated with Walker—either passed on directly to Doc or indirectly through his brother Liebert.

When he was thirteen, young Doc spent one semester attending the school at nearby Berea, but by 1913 had dropped out to get married. He married Anna Francis Risk, and the couple soon started a family that would eventually number eleven children. To support this team, he began sharecropping tobacco and corn for his mother, who owned a large farm adjoining one of a neighbor named Dennis Taylor. Roberts's main concern was to support his family, but he found time to do some fiddling, and even to listen to the newfangled talking machine owned by his uncle John Murphy. By the mid-1920s he and his neighbor Taylor spent long evenings talking about how Victrola records were made, and how the musicians got money for them. He found that Taylor knew quite a bit about the record business, and how it was starting to get interested in the new field of old-time music. Taylor began managing a local band that included Roberts and a singer named Welby Toomey, and in October 1925 managed to get them a date to make some records up in Richmond, Indiana, for the Gennett Company. Appearing at the studio, located beside a busy railroad track in Richmond, they met a third musician, a guitarist named Edgar Boaz.

Boaz was from nearby Marion, Indiana, and though Roberts and Boaz had never played together before, both were skilled musicians, and it didn't take them long to figure out some duets. They did four fiddle tunes: "Martha Campbell," "All I've Got Is Done Gone," "My Baby Loves

Shortening Bread," and "Dixie." All were successful, both commercially and artistically. "All I Got Is Done Gone," the most popular of the lot, bears no relationship to the tune of the same name by Uncle Dave Macon. It was one of Owen Walker's tunes, "revised" by Roberts. "Martha Campbell," later to be recorded by fellow Kentucky fiddler Jilson Setters, "the singing fiddler of Lost Hope Hollow," was well known to Kentucky fiddlers at the time. "Dixie" was also revised, this one to include the fine part of "Soldier's Joy," while "My Baby Loves Shortening Bread" was not quite the familiar piece from the minstrel stage.

In spite of the impromptu nature of the session, and the fact that Gennett was still using the old-fashioned acoustic recording process, the records were successful and launched Doc Roberts on a career in records. In the following twelve months, Roberts and Boaz did two more Gennett sessions. They worked together so well, in fact, that Boaz soon moved down to Richmond, Kentucky, to work with Roberts. In 1926–1927 the pair began booking out of E. H. Munsey's furniture store, a local headquarters for musicians. Munsey would furnish the team with a car, gas, expenses, and advertising, and receive a percentage of the take in exchange. Roberts and Boaz soon became known at theaters and schoolhouses. "They would go out for a week at a time and come back with $75 to $100 each," recalls Roberts's son James. It was Roberts's first attempt to promote his music, and he did so only while he could keep up on the farm.

By now Dennis Taylor had visions of himself becoming a stringband music entrepreneur of sorts and was scouting around central Kentucky for other musicians. His general method was to take musicians to his farmhouse, board and rehearse them, drive them up to Richmond to record, and negotiate with the record company. In exchange, he would get part of the royalties. He had signed an "exclusive" management contract with Roberts which apparently prevented him from recording on his own, and by early 1927 Roberts was starting to realize that this was a bad deal and that he needed to get out of it. He started corresponding directly with F. D. Wiggins, head of the Gennett division, who was more than eager to work directly with one of their best-selling artists. At one point, when the recording machine at Richmond was down, he asked Roberts if he would be interested in driving to New York to record several hot songs. In January Roberts wrote asking if Gennett would object to his recording for other record companies under the name "Phill Roberts." They did not, as long as he did not use the name "Fiddlin' Doc Roberts," though they suspected his contract with Taylor might prevent it. (This was ironic, since Gennett was releasing most of Roberts's records on stencil labels under various pseudonyms.) One of Roberts's problems was that Boaz had gotten into some trouble and had to leave Kentucky, and he was having to find some other back-up musicians. He found them in Dick Parman of Corbin Kentucky, and in Ted Chesnut. The three eventually traveled to Chicago to record for Paramount, where they recorded a long session. Their vocal numbers were released under the name the Kentucky Thorobreds, and their fiddle numbers under the Quadrillers.

In the meantime, Roberts's struggle with Taylor continued. He notified Gennett that he did not want to make any more records for Taylor because "he has lost me money," and Roberts refused to go to a session that Taylor scheduled for May 1927. By August he had reached a compromise with Taylor, and he found himself helping out on one of the most unusual sessions in the annals of old-time music. Taylor had brought up a black stringband from Jessamine County, the Booker Family, lead by fifty-five-year-old fiddler Jim Booker. The family had been known for generations in the central Kentucky area, and shared much of the repertoire of Owen Walker. In May 1927 Taylor had brought Jim Booker up for an earlier session with a pick-up band that include white banjoist Marion Underwood and white singer Aulton Ray, with the titles being released as Taylor's Kentucky Boys. The result was some splendid music, and what was probably the first integrated recording session in the annals of country music. However, when it came time to make a band photo for the Gennett catalogue, Jim Booker was not invited and in his place Dennis Taylor posed, holding a fiddle he didn't know how to play; the image the catalogue presented was that of an all-white stringband.

By now things were so tense between Roberts and Taylor that Wiggins himself tried to step in and mediate, trying to talk Taylor into releasing Roberts from his contract. "He still wishes to retain your service," Wiggins reported to Roberts. In the meantime he had learned that Boaz had left and that Roberts was looking for a new partner: "We want you to bring a good singer as this is very necessary." Fiddle records were fine, but vocal records were what paid the bills. The squabbling continued with Taylor, and in August Wiggins finally lost patience and told both men that if they couldn't work out their differences, "it would be better to cut the whole thing out."

This apparently frightened both into settling up, and in September Roberts returned to the studios. This time Taylor brought up Jim Booker and his entire family stringband, which included Jim's younger brother, Joe, as well as a third brother, John. John and Joe, with a mandolin player named Robert Steele, recorded two sides under the name "Booker Orchestra," one of the very few instances of a black stringband making a commercial record. Taylor also had Roberts join them for three more sides, to be released as Taylor's Kentucky Boys. On these Roberts played twin fiddle with Jim Booker, and in doing so created the second integrated recording session in country music. Only one of the three cuts, "Sourwood Mountain," was ever issued, however, and it finally came out under the name "Hill's Virginia Mountaineers" on Supertone, a Sears label. Roberts was unhappy with the recordings, and was soon writing Wiggins asking that if they didn't come out well, could he re-record them? In October 1927 Wiggins replied saying that the other two numbers with the Bookers, "Turkey in the Straw" and "The Old Hen Cackled," were being "held up." "These are not nearly as good as your fiddle numbers." After he heard the test pressings, Roberts agreed, and wrote back asking that none of his tunes be released under the name Taylor's Kentucky Boys. It is unclear whether Roberts requested this because he didn't think they were all that good, or because he didn't want to be associated with Taylor's name. Wiggins agreed, though, and the only Taylor's Kentucky Boys sides released were those Roberts wasn't on. By the fall of 1927, Roberts had won a couple of important battles in his struggle to assert himself with the record companies, and to preserve his own identity as an artist.

At that same September session, Roberts recorded eight fiddle tunes with a young guitarist and singer he had discovered, a man who would be closely associated with him for the rest of his career: Asa Martin. Born in Clark County in 1900, Martin was the son of a piano teacher and an old-time trick fiddler who wanted their son to go to medical school. The money didn't hold out, though, and by 1920 Martin had taken to the vaudeville stage, and to making music for silent movies. When the talkies came in, Martin began to think his career was over; then he met Roberts at a fiddling contest and learned all about the record business. He turned out to be a fine back-up guitarist, as well as the kind of "good singer" Mr. Wiggins wanted. For some seven years he would record with Roberts, with his young son James, and with Ted Chesnut (one of the Kentucky Thorobreds). It was James and Asa Martin that provided the sweet harmony duet vocals on pieces like "There's a Little Box of Pine on the 7:29," and Martin who did the solo singing on hits like "When the Roses Bloom Again for the Bootlegger" and "The Virginia Moonshiner."

Surprisingly, though, Martin and Doc Roberts did not tour much together. Roberts seemed to be put off by Martin's attempts at promotion and showmanship, and felt that some of his advertising claims were exaggerated. The Gennett company, unlike modern companies, seemed lukewarm about their artists touring. In June 1928, for instance, when Roberts wrote to say he was touring, they responded: "We are glad to note you are making a tour, playing the theatres and high schools. Anything which you might do in this way of advertising the Electrobeam Gennett record will, of course, result to our mutual benefit." Thus, while Roberts continued to work with Asa Martin in the studio, he formed a "road band" to do what traveling he did—much in the manner of a modern Nashville singer. This band consisted of a cadre of Lexington area musicians that included his son James Roberts, guitarist Arthur Rose, and fiddler Oney Muse. Continuing to call themselves the Kentucky Thorobreds, this band worked on local radio WLAP in the early 1930s, and for about eight months, worked at Council Bluffs, Iowa, in 1932. For a time the band did three shows a week plus a Saturday night barn dance over WLAP. During these months, the bookings got so good that Roberts actually left the farm and lived for a time in Lexington.

Another brush with the big time came in 1928, when the popular singer Bradley Kincaid got Roberts to come up to his station, WLS, in Chicago for a tryout on "The National Barn Dance." Roberts went, stayed all of two weeks, and was offered a job on the show with Kincaid for $50 a week plus a percentage of tour income with Kincaid. It was a good offer and would have almost at once given Roberts a huge national audience for his fiddling—comparable to those enjoyed by Arthur Smith and Clayton McMichen. But Roberts refused, telling Kincaid that he couldn't sleep in the city with the elevated trains clanging all night, and that he just couldn't see bringing his large family to Chicago. It was also a hard place to get tobacco; Roberts was used to getting his plugs of Navy Star at the local general store, and when he got to Chicago he went into the first store he saw, assuming it was a general store as well. "I want a plug of Navy Star tobacco," he ordered. The startled clerk replied, "We don't sell anything but hardware here." Roberts shot back, "Then give me a plug of that."

Whoever made the ultimate decisions about what got recorded on Gennett must have had a good ear and a special fondness for fiddle tunes. In the end, the company produced as many or more good, pure, old-time fiddle tunes as any other commercial company. The correspondence in the Roberts files show that Doc would generally be in charge of working up the tunes he wanted to do, and this meant that a nice amount of the unusual central Kentucky fiddle tunes that graced his repertoire got preserved. These included such pieces as "Cumberland Blues" (1927), "Old Buzzard" (1927), "New Money" (1927), and "Hawk's Got a Chicken" (1930). Some of the more interesting pieces were original. "Drunken Man's Dream" (1930), with its long, bluesy lines, came from the fiddlers' occupational disease, drinking. "My father had a bad stomach ulcer all his life," recalled Roberts's son James. "He liked to drink John Barleycorn quite often, and this caused him to have nightmares. As a child, I'd hear him scream out at night, and mother would ask him about it the next morning, and he said he dreamed he was being butted by a goat. That might have been the drunk man's dream." Another popular original was the haunting "Jack's Creek Waltz" (1929), named after a creek in Madison County. Like so many older Kentucky fiddlers, Roberts plays the waltz almost as fast as a breakdown. "Rocky Mountain Goat," which Roberts recorded himself twice and which was also recorded by fellow Kentuckians Ted Gossett, Charlie Wilson, and Cliff Gross, was one Roberts learned from an eighty-year-old fiddler named Dude Freeman, from Beattieville on the Kentucky River. "Daddy claimed Dude was one of the best hornpipe players he ever heard in his life," says James. "Daddy ran into him at a fiddle contest when he was young." In addition to revising tunes by people like Owen Walker, Roberts would also occasionally rename an older tune to get it on record. Such was "Way Down South" (1934), Roberts's version of the nineteenth century sheet music song by Kerry Mills, "Whistling Rufus." James remembers: "A lot of the recording executives couldn't tell one fiddle tune from another, and the fiddlers soon figured this out. When some studio boss rejected a tune title because he already had out a version on that label, a lot of fiddlers just changed the name of the tune and went on and recorded what they liked."

There were occasions, however, when the company asked Roberts to do "cover" versions of tunes that were hits for other labels. In May 1928 F. D. Wiggins wrote Roberts explaining that the company had recently won a contract with the mail-order giant Sears to provide records for their catalogues, producing records on Sears's own labels, Silvertone and Supertone. Sears was not especially interested in artists, but in songs; thus Gennett did not hesitate to use false names on most Sears products. According to Wiggins, "We have just been requested by Sears Roebuck to make four special Old Time numbers for their next catalog to replace the same numbers which are not of our manufacture." Sears had some records in their catalogue that had been there for almost ten years, and had been recorded in the old acoustic process. The ones they wanted Roberts to re-record were a 1919 Federal side by Northern fiddler Joseph Samuels, "Old Zip Coon & Medley of Reels," and an old 1922 Silvertone record by Kentucky fiddler William B. Houchens, "Dance with the Girl with a Hole in Her Stocking" backed with a medley of "Leather Breeches" and three other tunes. Though Wiggins suspected Roberts already knew the tunes, he thoughtfully enclosed a set of the old records. Roberts dutifully learned them and re-recorded them five days later at Richmond.

Roberts also learned on his own from phonograph records as well. His uncle John Murphy had a huge collection of old-time records in the late 1920s, and both Roberts and his son James spent hours listening and learning from them. Roberts expressed a strong appreciation for the music of Tennessean Charlie Bowman, who recorded with the Hill Billies and then later on his own, and for fellow Kentuckian Leonard Rutherford, who worked with Dick Burnett and John Foster. He liked McMichen—especially in the Georgia Wildcats band—and on occasion did guest spots with them. His 1932 version of "I Don't Love Nobody," one of his more successful ones, came directly off the old Skillet Lickers recording, and "Charleston # 1" came from the 1929 Okeh hit by the Mississippi duo Narmour & Smith. "Wednesday Night Waltz" (1931) was doubtless done to give the American Recording Company a version of the popular hit by the Leake County Revelers and the Kessinger Brothers.

Roberts was one of the few old-time musicians who kept his royalty statements—indeed, he was one of the few who got royalties instead of a flat fee—so we have some idea of how his records were selling and how much he was making from them. If his records were to be his main legacy, his claim to immortality, they were fraught with irony. There was the fact that most of them were released under various false names, except for the last sequence, done for the American Recording Company. And the sales of his individual records were small compared to those of the Skillet Lickers or Burnett & Rutherford. Roberts's best seller for Gennett was a novelty coupling in which he played mandolin to Asa Martin's singing: "She Ain't Built That Way" backed with "There Is No Place Like Home for a Married Man." It sold over 20,000 copies. The unadulterated fiddle tunes were much less successful: "Run Smoke Run" sold slightly over 9,000, "The Devil in Georgia" around 8,000, and "Rocky Mountain Goat" about 8,000. A final irony is that many of the sides were released on the "original" Gennett label, and then on the Champion and Supertones under pseudonyms. Yet the average sale of a side on the Gennett label was only 335, where a Champion averaged 5,300 and a Supertone about 4,100.

In spite of all this, Roberts was able to get decent royalties during the late 1920s because he recorded so prolifically. A statement he got on April 1, 1930, which covered royalties for January, February, and March of that year, listed almost 100 sides that were still selling. For the stencil labels, which constituted most of the sales, Roberts was getting a little less than 1/2 cent a side. On this statement, sales ranged from over 5,500 (for a Dick Parman vocal called "We've Been Chums for Fifty Years") to ten (for the Supertone issue of the fiddle masterpiece "New Money"). His total for all the sales over this quarter was $478.13—not really all that bad in 1930. If his previous averages were in line with this, he might well have been making an annual record income of almost $2,000 a year. Certainly it was better than the deal he was able to strike with his next record company, the American Record Company.

A little less than a year after he got his $478 check from Gennett—a year, to be sure, in which the Depression struck with full force—he accepted a deal from Art Satherley to travel to New York and record twenty numbers for the flat rate of $300. Satherley mailed the group train tickets and even told them what train to take out of Winchester, Kentucky. "Mr. Calaway will meet you at the station here," Satherley wrote. "But in case you should miss him please go to the Breslin Hotel which is located at 29th St. and Broadway and they will take care of you there." If Roberts had any doubts that the times were changing, this ended them. He made his records for the new regime, and they were probably distributed better than any of the others. ARC had even more stencil labels that Gennett: the new records came out on Conqueror, the new Sears label, as well as several dime store labels like Romeo, Oriole, Banner, Perfect, and Melotone. The name "Doc Roberts Trio" was on all of them, but Roberts never learned just how popular they were; his flat fees of $15 a side didn't entitle him to royalty statements. Small wonder that he quit the business after a last session in 1934.

It would be a cliché to say that Doc Roberts was a fiddler's fiddler, but in many ways he was. He made a good run at the golden ring, but decided in the end that he just wasn't willing to make the compromises and concessions he would have to make to get it. He could copy the big hits of other fiddlers, yet when he did he couldn't resist "Robertsizing" them into his own unique style. He could travel around and do the radio station game that McMichen and the others were doing, but he finally admitted to himself that he really hated the travel and the ceaseless self-promotion. He could come up with clever original showpieces, but he really loved the old tunes that were common to the old central Kentucky fiddlers. Fans today see him as a superb technician, his style defined by long, flowing, melodic lines, by a tendency to utilize the first two strings as much as the latter two, by a wonderfully rich tone, and by a subtle sense of timing so characteristic of Kentucky bowmen. Historians will eventually see him as an important conduit to the lost world of African-American fiddling, a world which had one of its richest outposts in central Kentucky, in the work of men like Owen Walker and Jim Booker. Fiddlers have also respected Roberts's fondness for subtle improvisation in the middle of a performance, such as is heard in "The Devil in Georgia." (James Roberts recalled that his father would often play square dances, where a tune would run on for fifteen minutes at a time, and that he would often mix into a performance strains of several tunes, or even short quotes from other tunes.) Roberts also liked the blues, and, more so than either Smith or McMichen, used them in his music. As a result, many Roberts records have a distinctly modern cast to them, and resemble those by the better current contest fiddlers.

Though Roberts was effectively retired in 1935, when he was only thirty-eight, he couldn't completely leave the music business alone. He occasionally made guest appearances over radio stations WLW or WHAS, but confined most of his playing to local dances. "I played all over this country everywhere for them," he remembered. "All night long, many a night, until one o'clock, many of them." About 1960, when he was sixty-three, Roberts finally lost interest in playing and hung up the fiddle. Ironically, it was about this time that folklorists Archie Green and Norm Cohen rediscovered Roberts and began documenting his role in old-time music. He became the subject of a chapter in Green's influential book *Only a Miner* (about recorded coal mining songs) and his records were documented in a long series of articles in the *JEMF Quarterly*. All of this led to a renewed interest in Roberts's music; he was coaxed into appearing at several concerts at Berea College, and oversaw preparation of a reissue of some of his old records on a Davis Unlimited LP. By the time he died, on August 4, 1978, he had been visited by a parade of folk music fans, scholars, fiddle players, and enthusiasts. He must have felt at least a little vindicated for his struggle, for his stubborn integrity, for his high standards, and for the sad masks he had been forced to wear.

Sources

The bulk of this material is drawn from personal interviews with Doc Roberts at his home in July 1975, and from numerous interviews with his son James at his home in Lexington. James Roberts has also made available to me his father's files of correspondence and royalty statements, and allowed me to photocopy them. I have also relied on an unpublished interview of Roberts by Guthrie Meade in the Reuben Powell collection at the Traditional Culture archive at Berea College in Kentucky. Other sources include "Tapescript: An Interview with Doc Roberts," *JEMF Quarterly*, VII, pt. 3, no. 22 (1971), 99–103; "Roberts-Martin-Roberts Discography," *JEMFQ*, VII, pt. 3, no. 23 (1971), 103–104; pt. 4, no. 24 (1971), 158–162; VIII, pt. 1, no. 25 (1972), 15–17; pt. 2, no. 26 (1972), 73–76. Also see Ivan Tribe, "Fiddling Doc Roberts," *The Devil's Box*, vol. 10, no. 1 (March, 1976), 43–45, and Guthrie T. Meade, notes to *Old Time Fiddle Band Music from Kentucky* (Morning Star 45003–05, 3 vols. 1980). I have also benefited from conversations with Steve Davis, Bill Harrison, Loyal Jones, and Norm Cohen. Many of the original recordings mentioned here are reissued on the Morning Star LP, or on the County collection *Old Time Tunes* (County 412).

II

Masters of the Long Bow

Clayton McMichen:
The Reluctant Hillbilly

"EVERYBODY KNOWS McMICHEN." SO READ A HAND-
bill for a 1929 concert in Chattanooga featuring blue yodeler Jimmie Rodgers. Rodgers was then at the height of his fame, and his
supporting act was a suave fiddler from north Georgia named Clayton
McMichen. The fact that he could be so billed in 1929, only four years
after he had made his first recording, suggests how quickly McMichen
had become a legend. For the next twenty-five years, "Mac" was to
dominate Southern fiddling: he was to win the national fiddling championship crown no fewer than eighteen times; he was to broadcast on
nearly every major radio station; he was to work across the South in
shows staged by promoter Larry Sunbrock; and he was to record for
almost every major record label. He and Fiddlin' Arthur Smith are the
two people almost every old-time fiddler mentions when he talks
about "the good old days" or "the great old-time fiddlers" or "the
grandfathers of bluegrass fiddling." Bill Monroe recalled that "back in
the early days, Clayton was the best. I've played with Clayton, and after
Clayton left the Grand Ole Opry and went to Louisville, he come back
down here and talked with me about bluegrass music. If you check the
way I would play a fiddle number like 'Fire on the Mountain,' and
check the way Clayton plays it, you'll find it note for note the same
way."

Everybody agrees that McMichen has played a major role in the
development of fiddling styles, and, indeed, the very commercializa-
tion of country music itself. However, it becomes a little more com-
plicated when you try to pin down just what that role was. In one way,

McMichen's career can be seen as a chaotic jumble of contradictory impulses, wasted energies, and corrosive frustrations. For instance, at the same time he was playing on tour with Jimmie Rodgers in 1929, helping create songs like "Peach Picking Time in Georgia," he was more widely known as the key figure in the Skillet Lickers, the nation's most popular old-time stringband, but one whose sound and style was a generation older than the kind of semi-pop country music that Rodgers was trying to develop. In the 1930s he led an incredibly tight, hard-swinging stringband, but watched Bob Wills and his Texas bands reap all the glory for inventing western swing. In the 1940s he led a Dixieland jazz band, replete with trombones and trumpets, over Louisville radio. But he still entered all sorts of fiddling contests, where he stepped forth to play old-time tunes from his childhood in a classy solo style and more than a little brash self-promotion. Throughout it all, however, was an unwavering devotion to elevate fiddling to an art. McMichen spent a lifetime trying to fight against the "hillbilly" image of the old-time fiddler: the moonshine drinking, hound-dog holding, comic rube who hollered and danced and dressed up in funny hats. "I was serious about fiddling," he said in one of his few interviews. "When it came to fiddling . . . there's no foolishness in it, in other words."

Clayton McMichen was born January 26, 1900, in a village some forty miles northeast of Atlanta called Allatoona. His family, Scots-Irish who came into Paulding County around 1790, was rich in musical traditions. Some of them read shape notes and sang from old religious songbooks. His grandmother played the fretless banjo, and his mother "beat the straws," tapping the broomstraws on the bass strings of a fiddle. "They beat on the bass strings of the fiddle," he remembered, "and when you got to playing on the bass strings, turn the fiddle over so she beat on the E and A strings. But she had to beat it clear there. So when it ringed, she played where the E and A chord had been in there. You didn't need to have a banjo." Both McMichen's father and grandfather were well-known fiddlers in the area, and he learned a lot of his older tunes from them: "Billy in the Lowground," "Nancy Rollin," "Pretty Little Widow," "Rickett's Hornpipe," "Cincinnati Hornpipe."

"My dad was one of those sophisticated Irish violin players, and he's the one I learned all this fancy fiddling from." He knew how to read music from tune books, and played for a variety of venues in turn-of-the-century Georgia. "He'd put on his long tail coat and his high hat, you know, and get in front of the mirror and play for himself." He and another fiddler, joined by a pianist, would dress up and go play Viennese waltzes and "crinolines" at local society balls. Such music made an impression on young McMichen. Some of his first recordings would be made with a "sweet" band called McMichen's Melody Men that featured a clarinet, McMichen's fiddle, and a repertoire of dance waltzes like "Sweet Bunch of Daisies" and "Let Me Call You Sweetheart." McMichen was playing by the time he was eleven, and by the time the family moved to Atlanta in 1913 he was eagerly exploring all kinds of music. He recalled that he hung out with a band of gypsies for a time and learned some of their music. From 1914 to 1918, he hung out at Mays Badgett's fiddle repair shop, where some of "these long-haired fiddlers" from the Atlanta Metropolitan Opera "dropped in and gave me some lessons in technique." In his spare time, McMichen worked as an automobile mechanic, developing an expertise in applied technology that would stay with him throughout his life.

About the time McMichen arrived there, Atlanta was developing into a major center for fiddling contests. Annual contests down at the new Municipal Auditorium attracted thousands of spectators and dozens of fiddlers, mostly from north Georgia. The conventions were widely reported in the local newspapers, starting with the first modern one in 1913, and were even written up in national publications like *Musical America*. An association of fiddlers was soon formed, and a set of strict rules and judging criteria were established (straw beating and the ability to read music were special concerns). In spite of this, though, local favorites continued to be "showmen," like "Laughing" Gid Tanner and Fiddlin' John Carson, who liked to do comedy, cut up, sing with their playing, and do trick playing. McMichen, as well as some of his young friends, objected to this, and even tried to form their own fiddlers' association—without much luck. It wasn't until 1922 that McMichen's name appeared in a list of winners of the contest, when he placed second for his version of "Arkansas Traveler."

In about 1923 McMichen would meet a musician who would have a major effect on the direction of his fiddling, and on his musical career. This was Marcus Lowell (Lowe) Stokes, born in 1898 in Gilmer County, Georgia, but reared in the Rome area, some sixty miles northeast of Atlanta. Stokes was a tough, handsome boy, some two years older than

McMichen, and by the time he was seventeen, his father, an old-time mountain fiddler, had taught him enough that the boy was winning major contests. In November 1924 Stokes won the big Atlanta contest, beating out John Carson, A. A. Gray, and a host of other favorites. And though he was actually twenty-six by then, a Hearst newspaper account mistakenly referred to him as a fourteen-year-old. This caused a sensation of sorts and suddenly everybody was interested in the drama of a young teenager beating the best old-time fiddlers in Georgia at their own game. Follow-up pieces appeared in *The New York Times* and in *Literary Digest*. One of those impressed was the well-known poet Stephen Vincent Benet. In March 1925, he published a poem about the event, "The Mountain Whippoorwill, or How Hill Billy Jim Won the Great Fiddler's Prize." It has remained a favorite piece of Americana since, though it had little impact on Stokes's own career.

Compared to McMichen, Stokes had traveled widely and been exposed to all sorts of music. Early in his career he had played in a local band led by Bud Silvey, a popular fiddler who, in the manner of many north Georgia bowmen, would tune his fiddle up as high as he could get it. "You broke a lot of strings when you played with Bud," he later recalled. "A good bow would last a month." Stokes was thus interested when, around 1913, he met and heard another fiddler from the Rome area, Joe Lee. A native of Etowah County, Alabama, Lee had been born in 1884, and by the 1920s had what was considered the best stringband in the area. Though he himself never tried to record commercially, Lee emerged as a major teacher of many of the best north Georgia fiddlers, including Bill Shores. What impressed them all about Lee was his ability to play a "long bow" style. As Richard Nevins explained, "Lee's style of pulling a long smooth bow and his tendency to keep his strings run down to standard or lower pitch gave his music a mellower and less rhythmically oriented sound." Stokes adapted his own playing to this new style and was soon making graceful, gliding bow strokes that let him craft sparkling cascades of notes and innovative ornamentation.

The fateful meeting between Stokes and McMichen occurred in 1923, the same year John Carson made his first phonograph record and introduced Georgia fiddling to the world. They met at a show at Tipton, Georgia, and hit it off. The two roomed together for a year in Atlanta, often playing fiddle contests and dances, each backing the other on guitar. Stokes recalls that when he first met McMichen he was still playing the short bow—"jiggy bow" style, the older mountain style that featured short, rapid bow strokes. Once Stokes introduced him to the kind of bowing he had learned from Joe Lee, McMichen was at once impressed and saw the advantages of it. During their year together, Stokes taught McMichen as much as he could of the new style. Years later McMichen would explain that the new style was not only musically important, but it could be used as a style of showmanship. "It's a lot of bow action, that stuff I was doing, that flipping the bow up there. Take a full length stroke every time, and, boy, they think you're really going then. . . . Play sixty-four strokes all the way through it, and you're really fiddling then."

McMichen made some inconsequential records in 1925, but the next year he found his real forum as he began recording with the Skillet Lickers. At first, this was a studio band, the brainchild of Columbia Records' A&R man Frank Walker. Its name came from an old pick-up band that had been a novelty act at the Atlanta Fiddlers' Convention, the Lick Skillet Orchestra. (Though there was an old community near Atlanta called "Lickskillet," most authorities think the term was just a derogatory stereotype, like "Possum Trot.") Walker formed the band by bringing together Gid Tanner, a tall, red-headed chicken farmer, singer, banjoist, and fiddler from Dacula; Riley Puckett, a blind guitarist and singer who had recorded with Tanner for Columbia a couple of years earlier; and Fate Norris, a banjo-playing comedian who also performed on a homemade one-man band contraption.

For the lead, Walker decided to use three fiddlers: Tanner, McMichen, and McMichen's brother-in-law, Bert Layne. It was a configuration unheard of in regular fiddle bands at the time, and just whose idea it was remains unclear. There had been a handful of earlier recordings featuring twin fiddles: Eck Robertson's very first session featured duets with Henry Gilliland; the West Virginia band, the Tweedy Brothers, had done a series of records in 1924 and 1925, many of which were sold on Sears' labels; and in 1925 the Hill Billies featured the twin fiddles of Charlie Bowman and Fred Roe on several records. The first commercial Cajun recordings, many of which featured twin fiddles, were still two years in the future. In both the Tweedy Brothers and the Hill Billies bands, the fiddles usually simply "doubled" each other—i.e., they played in unison. "In my dad's time," remembered Lowe Stokes, "they played two fiddles in a band, but they sounded like one." In the earliest Skillet Lickers sides, though, Tanner and McMichen usually played a unison (or near-unison) high part while Bert Layne added a low baritone harmony. In classics like "Bully of the Town," the effect is a wonderful, dense, bluesy texture that had bands across the South trying to imitate it.

At first the band was billed as "Gid Tanner and the Skillet Lickers," since Tanner was the best known of the individual band members, at least in north Georgia. Almost at once, McMichen and Puckett protested, and later labels read, "Gid Tanner and the Skillet Lickers with Clayton McMichen and Riley Puckett." Their first recording session was held on April 17, 1926, at a temporary studio Columbia had set up at 15 Pryor Street, in downtown Atlanta, just a block east of Peachtree Street. (It was actually on the second floor of a building used by Columbia for a regional office and was full of boxes and freight.) The session yielded six sides: "Hand Me Down My Walking Cane," "Watermelon on the Vine," "Bully of the Town," "Pass Around the Bottle and We'll All Take a Drink," "Alabama Jubilee," and "Turkey in the Straw." A month later in May, the first Skillet Lickers side was released: Columbia 15074, "Bully of the Town" backed with "Pass Around the Bottle." The sales were everything Walker could have hoped for; Columbia 15074 became one of the highest selling entries in the Columbia old-time series, eventually running up sales of over 207,000 copies. It was one of the best-selling, if not the absolute best-selling, fiddle band record of its age. Rivaling it in sales, though, was the second Skillet Lickers release, in September 1926: a coupling of "Watermelon on the Vine" backed with "Hand Me Down My Walking Cane." It rang up sales of over 180,000—at a time when a typical Columbia release was lucky to sell 30,000 copies.

None of these tunes were, strictly speaking, traditional fiddle tunes. "Bully" had originated in a St. Louis bordello called the Castle Club in the 1880s and was later cleaned up and popularized on the national vaudeville circuit by a singer named May Irwin. By the 1920s it was well known to Southern fiddlers and banjoists, and by the time the Skillet Lickers recorded it, it had already been waxed by Fiddlin' John Carson in 1925. Later in the decade, fiddlers like Sid Harkreader, Harry Tweedy, Earl Johnson, and Lowe Stokes cut versions. "Watermelon on the Vine" was an old minstrel song, as was "Hand Me Down My Walking Cane." In fact, all of these first four "career sides" for the Skillet Lickers featured vocals by Riley Puckett, which supports an allegation that

McMichen made in interviews that although many of the later Skillet Lickers' sides were exciting fiddle tunes, it was the ones with Puckett's vocals that sold.

By the fall of 1926, it was clear to Frank Walker and his bosses at Columbia that his plan had worked, and the Skillet Lickers' image was well on its way to being in place. Soon the image included not only the multi-fiddle ensemble and Puckett's lead vocals, but Gid Tanner's falsetto shouting and harmony, and McMichen's corn-pone introductions. "Folks, here we are again, the Skillet Lickers, red hot and raring to go," he announces at the start of "Liberty." "And maw, don't you let 'em dance on your new carpet. You make 'em roll it up." In April 1927 Walker and his assistant, an Atlanta native named Bill Brown, got the idea to have the band do a skit—what the company ad writers would later describe as a "rustic comedy sketch." This was a pastiche called "A Fiddler's Convention in Georgia," a send-up of the old Atlanta contests featuring solos by the group and ersatz introductions. It sold so well that the next session they did a second skit, this one done by Walker and based on stories he had heard the boys telling during the recording sessions. It was "A Corn Licker Still in Georgia," in which the boys portray fiddling moonshiners who "play a little tune" as they run off the mash and entertain customers. McMichen plays the leader who has to keep his boys in line, especially when they want to sample the wares too soon. "I know you," he says. "If you started drinking liquor, there won't be no music." The skit became their third best-selling record, topping out at 160,000 copies. Amazed, the Columbia bosses insisted on a series of follow-ups; eventually there were fourteen parts to the skit. Additionally, the band was prevailed upon to do a series of other "rustic" skits, such as "The Kickapoo Medicine Show," "A Night in a Blind Tiger" (a bootleg joint), "Hog Killing Day," and "Possum Hunt on Stump House Mountain." The series helped bolster the image of the Skillet Lickers as a band of uncouth backwoods Georgia hillbillies, when in fact they were probably the most innovative, influential, and original stringband masters of the day. As their reputation grew, it did so without the benefit of the one medium that so many other old-time stars had: radio. The Skillet Lickers made their name through their records and through personal appearances—though their records were so full of comments and dialogue that their fans might well have seen them as a substitute for radio.

Amidst the comedy, the falsetto shouting, the booming group

vocals, and the strained skits is some very fine fiddling. After the third
Skillet Lickers session, Bert Layne dropped out, so on the fourth session (October 1927) McMichen tried to continue with just himself and
Tanner on fiddles. Though Tanner was a good old-time mountain fiddler, his style was quite different from McMichen's (who had little
respect for it), and Walker at once noticed the difference. We really
need that third fiddle, Walker told them after their first day's work.
McMichen quickly spoke up and said that he had a young friend who
could help them out. His name was Lowe Stokes, and he lived up in
Rome. Walker liked the idea and held up the session while McMichen
jumped in his car and took off on a sixty-mile drive to Rome. He finally found Lowe and asked him if he would like to join the Skillet Lickers. Soon they were both burning rubber on the road back to Atlanta,
and the Rome newspaper was running a story about how a local boy
had made good.

By October 1928, when the band made their famous recording of
"Liberty," Stokes had taken his place as the band's lead fiddler, with
McMichen playing a close harmony to the individual notes of the
melody. (Often Stokes used a mute on his bridge to better balance
McMichen's sound; he also said that this idea of playing close harmo-
ny came from his listening to jazz fiddler Joe Venuti, who was then in
his heyday.) Tanner was by now reduced to filling in here and there,
and in later records abandoned fiddle entirely for banjo or Jew's harp.
During the last three years of their existence, 1928 to 1931, the Skillet
Lickers produced their share of hardcore fiddle records, with less of
Puckett's singing or Gid's horseplay. Those spotlighting the Stokes-
McMichen lead included "Cotton-Eyed Joe" (1928), "Slow Buck" (1928),
"Pretty Little Widow" (1928), "Mississippi Sawyer" (1929), and "Rock
That Cradle, Lucy" (1929). By 1930, Bert Layne had rejoined the group,
giving the last records an exciting three-fiddle (McMichen, Stokes,
Layne) sound that would not be duplicated again until Bill Monroe's
experiments with it in the mid-1950s. These include "Ride Old Buck to
Water" (1930), "Whistlin' Rufus" (1931), and "Don't You Cry My Honey"
(1930).

In spite of the fact that Stokes played lead on most of the records,
it was McMichen the general public heard of. His name appeared on all
the record labels, and it was his voice that introduced the members on
the discs and moderated the skits. Stokes was generally kept in the

background, a sort of "silent partner," and his role as the unsung hero in the band remained unappreciated until researcher Rich Nevins discovered him living in retirement in Oklahoma during the early 1970s. Stokes's own career had been seriously disrupted in 1931 when he lost his right hand in a shooting incident.

As the Skillet Lickers were making their final records, the Depression was wrecking sales. Some of the last releases sold fewer than a thousand copies—which was still more than a typical 1931 release would sell—and some of the best of their three-part fiddling was heard by relatively few people in its original release. But in the 1960s and 1970s, as younger fiddlers and various old-time "revival" bands discovered the Skillet Lickers, many of these rare sides were re-released on LPs, and many of these actually sold better than the originals. Bands like the Highwoods String Band were especially attracted to the multi-fiddle sound and intricate harmonies, and McMichen himself mad a comeback of sorts during the folk revival, even appearing at the Newport Folk Festival.

Though the original Skillet Lickers didn't make many radio appearances—they had no regular program nor were they ever a part of an organized variety show like the Grand Ole Opry—they did do extensive touring. Stokes recalled: "We'd put on a big show, and they'd play our records out on the street that day and announce where we'd be for the show." Columbia's A&R assistant, Bill Brown, would handle many of the bookings. The show would cost 25 to 30 cents admission, and the band would generally get 70 to 80 percent of the take. Three hundred to four hundred people at a show was usually a minimum. Fiddler Bill Helms, who substituted on these tours when one of the regular fiddlers was unavailable, recalled that the tours went into some of the more remote areas of the mountains. "Hardly anybody up there rode, lessen it was in a wagon. They'd be coming to hear us, down out of these mountains, on mules and horses, wagons. Used lanterns in those days, didn't have any electric light at all. Old kerosene lanterns: you could see 'em like little bugs at night coming way back cross the mountains there, coming down there totin' those lanterns along, have it in the wagon with them, so they could see which way they were going. I'd never seen nothing like that before." The band played Georgia, North Carolina, South Carolina, Alabama, Kentucky, and Tennessee. In 1927 they did a major concert and fiddling contest on the stage of the Ryman

Auditorium in Nashville, long before it became the home of the Grand Ole Opry.

McMichen, meanwhile, continued to record extensively on his own. He recorded ten or so sides with his "sweet" band, McMichen's Melody Men, and its offshoot, the McMichen-Layne String Orchestra; a series of duets with Riley Puckett, including a fine version of "Cindy" (1927), an influential "Old Molly Hare" (1928), "Rye Straw" (1929), and "Paddy Won't You Drink Some Good Old Cider" (1928); an unusual solo record, "St. Louis Blues" and "Fiddling Medley" (1927); a number of sides released under Lowe Stokes's name; as a vocalist under the name "Bob Nichols"; a couple of Victor sessions with Jimmie Rodgers; and dozens of back up jobs with just about anybody who came into the Columbia studio and needed help. From 1926 through 1931, Atlanta became the center for country music recording activity, and Columbia would have two marathon sessions—one in the spring and one in the fall—in which they would record the lion's share of their old-time product. McMichen, along with Stokes and Puckett, were so versatile and experienced that Columbia finally put them under contract. McMichen got $3,000 a year, with an obligation to make ten of his own records per year (twenty sides), as well as play back-up when needed. His fiddle was heard on everything from the vaudeville singing of Oscar Ford to the gospel music of Smith's Sacred Singers. As such, he and his colleagues became some of country music's first studio session men.

Overall, the success of the Skillet Lickers made music history and convinced record companies that fiddle music would sell. Yet except for McMichen, few other members of the band really considered themselves full-time professional musicians. In one of the skits, each of the members introduces himself, and states his occupation. Gid Tanner, for instance, says he is a chicken farmer. But when it comes to McMichen, when someone asks what he does, he says, "I don't have no vocation, I just play the fiddle." Even this early, McMichen had determined to make his living from his music. This meant that he had to do more recording, be more versatile, become more aware of things like copyrights, and try his hand at songwriting, as he did with his "Peach Picking Time in Georgia," which he got to Jimmie Rodgers and which subsequently made him a lot of royalties. He also tried some singing—he had a rather pleasant, well-mannered voice in the vein of Carson Robison—and recorded numerous sweet, sentimental duets with the likes of Puckett and Hugh Cross. The first of these, "My Carolina Home" (1926), became a huge best seller, ringing up sales of over 260,000 copies, more than the biggest Skillet Lickers seller. Later efforts like "Don't You Remember the Time" and "Let the Rest of the World Go By" sold well above average as well. Ironically, these records reinforced what McMichen was starting to see as a straitjacket for his music. He was seeing the music changing around him and was especially intrigued by the experiments Jimmie Rodgers was making with his arrangements and accompaniments. Western swing was starting to develop, and musicians like Joe Venuti were expanding the possibilities for the violin. McMichen was feeling more and more confined with Puckett and the Skillet Lickers; "the band stunk," he would later write, and he came to feel that he had to give up a good thing and strike out on his own.

Thus it was at the final Columbia Skillet Lickers session in 1931 that McMichen showed up with a new band, the Georgia Wildcats. He recorded a last round of tunes with Puckett and Tanner, and then unleashed his new sound. Slim Bryant, his new guitarist, played dead-string "sock" chords and did single-string take-off solos while McMichen played a classy, swinging violin. Instead of "Whistling Rufus," the new band played fare like "Yum Yum Blues" and "When the Bloom Is on the Sage." The new records were nice, but by 1931 no one could afford them any more than Skillet Lickers sides, and only a few hundred got out to the record stores.

And with them, McMichen continued his long, lonely battle to take country music uptown, to open the music up to experimentation, to technical expertise, and to professional musicianship. The trouble was, the music didn't want to go uptown just yet. Throughout the 1930s McMichen would struggle to integrate the sounds of pop music, of jazz, swing, even crooning, into his own music. He would maintain his Georgia Wildcats for the next ten years; they would perform, broadcast, and record throughout the South and Midwest. The band would include some of the best young musicians of the times: Slim Bryant, the innovative guitarist who, some say, helped teach Les Paul; Carl Cotner, who would later move to Hollywood and become Gene Autry's musical director; and Merle Travis, who made his first records for McMichen before he too went to the coast and wrote such favorites as "Sixteen Tons."

The Wildcats made a string of records for Decca that were as eclectic as they were stunning: swooping twin fiddle ensembles, take-off solos by fiddle, guitar, and even tenor banjo; harmony scat-jazz singing à la the early Mills Brothers; and smooth Crosby-like vocals by Kenny Newton. The band's repertoire was as diverse as anything heard during that age. It ranged from a romping "Farewell Blues," in an arrangement lifted almost note for note from a jazz recording by Benny Goodman and Joe Venuti, to modified mountain standards like "Free a Little Bird." It included revamps of "Please Don't Sell My Pappy No More Rum" to haunting originals like "Georgiana Moon." Yet the new records didn't sell a fraction of what the old breakdowns had sold. "Georgiana Moon" was especially disappointing to McMichen. In later years he recalled: "It was one of the most beautiful tunes I ever wrote in my life. We thought we were gonna get rich on it. Heh. We didn't sell enough to pay for the first pressing. I got about 75 or 80 cents for writing it." Today, "Georgiana Moon" has become a standard at festivals throughout the country, and is often thought of as a public domain song.

Many of the musical ideas McMichen had were echoed in the music of Bob Wills, Bill Boyd, and Milton Brown as they popularized western swing in the 1930s. McMichen seemed especially to resent Wills's success. When asked about Wills in later years, he responded, "Deal me out. I know him well, but 'No comment.'" But this was only part of his larger frustration. In 1935 he wrote and recorded a song in which he sang:

> Can't get nothing from old-time fiddlin'
> I'm gonna learn to swing.
> I ain't gonna waste my time a-whittlin'
> It doesn't mean a thing.
> Gonna sell my farm and move to town
> Buy me a horn and toot around
> Hi-de-ho is what I'll play
> With a razz-ma-tazz in a swinging way
> Get me a job with a big jazz band
> I'm gonna learn to swing.

He did learn to swing, but found that many of his fans still insisted on his old-time fiddling. Later in life, McMichen once again met up with his old producer Frank Walker (who himself became the producer of Hank Williams). "It's awful easy, McMichen, to play too good," he told him. "We couldn't make money because we didn't have that hillbilly whine, like Bill Monroe." On another occasion, McMichen said: "A lady wrote me a nasty letter asking why do you play those silly old tunes? On the air I replied to her: I notice in my thirty-five years of show business that there's 500 pairs of overalls sold to every one tuxedo suit. That's why I stick to swamp opera." McMichen was indeed finding his commercial niche, but he remained bitter about it. Later in life he became impatient with younger people who persisted in honoring him only as the fiddler in the Skillet Lickers and ignoring his other thirty years of musical accomplishments.

Even when he had to play the role of the old-time fiddler, though, McMichen did it with characteristic élan. In 1932 at one of the National Fiddling Championships held in Cincinnati, McMichen defeated over 100 competitors from across the country by playing what was described as a "Brahms-Gershwin version of 'Arkansas Traveler.'" As early as 1927 he recorded for Columbia an amazing solo fiddler version of "St. Louis Blues" with all kinds of curious "gypsy" variations. When he did play traditional contest favorites, he would do tunes like "Fisher's Hornpipe," a tough enough tune in any key, and take it through five different keys (F, B-flat, G, D, and back to F). His 1939 Decca recording of "Fisher's" goes through three keys in about sixty-five seconds. By his own account, his favorite tune was "Bile 'Em Cabbage Down," which he claimed and copyrighted. "I won the national championship sixteen times playing that thing," he recalled. He generally played it in a cross-key tuning, throwing in some shuffle rhythm around the second or third chorus. Often he would improvise on the melody, like a jazz soloist or modern bluegrass musician. Some later fiddlers have even absorbed part of his improvisation as a normal part of the tune. He justified his playing the best of the old breakdowns by saying, "Hoedowns are Irish classics, not hillbilly."

While he was adept at competing in authentic fiddling contests, he also helped create a new venue that might be described as a "commercialized fiddling contest." Even in the Skillet Licker days, McMichen would combine with the concert a fiddling contest in which members of the band would take on any local talent. Starting in 1933, he joined forces with promoter Larry Sunbrock to refine this idea even more. In many of these, Sunbrock would set up a sort of "showdown" between two well-known fiddlers. Like modern staged wrestling matches, the contests would evolve as a "grudge match" between the "good guy" and the "bad guy." It was an odd sort of morality play, in which fiddlers served as heroes and villains, replacing the classic western movie heroes. In some cases, McMichen actually wore a white hat, and his opponent was a colorful showman who billed himself as Natchee the Indian. (His real name was apparently Clifford Storer.) Sunbrock took one particular showdown contest on tour from Cincinnati to Louisville, Nashville, Atlanta, and elsewhere; in St. Louis, he claimed that the show played to 24,000 people on one single day.

Veteran fiddler and promoter Dolph Hewitt was involved in some of these contests, and in 1994 he recounted a vivid description of one to fellow fiddler Byron Berline. He and McMichen found themselves competing in preliminaries in the afternoon. Hewitt said, "Before I came out they introduced Natchee the Indian. He had a white Indian costume clear to his feet—bells on his feet. He come flying out of them wings with that fiddle playing 'Wild Horse.' Went in like a horse and all the kids just went up in the air. Place was full of kids in the afternoon. . . . He beat me and Clayton both. Clayton was mad about it too. . . . He said, 'What are you going to do about that goddamned Indian, Dolph?' I said, 'I don't know what you're going to do about him, but I'm going to fiddle his ass off!'"

That evening, when there were fewer kids and more adults, Natchee was assigned to play last. "Clayton went out and he played. He walked out there [on stage] and he said, 'Ladies and gentlemen. . . .' He's about six-foot-two tall, you know, had a hand like a ham of meat. 'Ladies and gentlemen, I want to tell you who I am. I'm Clayton McMichen. I've won this contest twenty-one times before. This will be twenty-two. I'll win it tonight. I've seen these guys fiddle this afternoon and they're not in my class.' Oh boy! If you ever seen a guy sell hisself, he had it down to a T." McMichen did indeed beat Natchee, with his bells and dragging headdress, but he was outplayed by Hewitt.

McMichen's actual association with Sunbrock only lasted about a year; he was replaced by another showman fiddler, Curly Fox. He didn't give up the commercialized fiddling contests entirely, though. In the 1940s he occasionally did them with such worthy opponents as Roy Acuff (when both were on the Opry at the same time).

From 1945 to 1955, McMichen turned his stringband into a Dixieland jazz band and broadcasted daily over station WAVE in Louisville. For years he was featured on a noontime show done from Howell's furniture store. The band was another curious mixture of forties swing and fiddle band fare. One member, Bernie Smith, recalled: "All of the Dixieland tunes were especially arranged; during the war, we even had an arranger out at Fort Knox who had made arrangements before going into service for big bands like Les Brown and Tommy Dorsey. We really had a swinging band. Our band sounded so great that people came all the way from New Orleans to hear and see us." A typical show would start out with the theme, "Sweet Bunch of Daisies." (This was another tune Clayton had made into a fiddle standard. Though he didn't write it, it had a special meaning to him. Not only was his wife named Daisy, but the tune had been his first big hit—selling almost 100,000 copies—under his own name back in 1927.) Then "Pappy," which was what McMichen was then nicknamed, would play a fiddle tune. Next would come a vocal, done either by Pappy or Bernie Smith, followed by a Dixieland number featuring the whole band. Louisville loved it; one survey indicated that as many as eight out of ten people were hearing the band's noon show. For a time in the early 1950s, the group even had a local TV show.

It was during this time that McMichen also met up with George Barnes, one of the unsung pioneers in using the electric guitar to play "country swing." Barnes recalled that McMichen taught him how to play old fiddle tunes on the guitar, and he went on to specialize in picking breakdowns. When he joined the famed WLS band, the Prairie Ramblers, in the late 1940s, he spread the tunes across the country via the Ramblers' broadcasts.

In 1945 an entrepreneur and promoter named Joe Davis bought the rights to some of the old master recordings McMichen had made in 1932 (the year after he started the Wildcats) for the old Crown record company. He wrote McMichen to discuss reissuing them. McMichen eagerly replied, asking for a chance to record some new sides with his new Dixieland band. Davis wasn't interested, however, and by the war's end McMichen was dismayed to see ghosts from the past coming out as "new" records: titles like "Hog Trough Reel," "Arkansas Traveler," and the like. Finally McMichen decided enough was enough. In 1955, the first year Elvis Presley hit it big, he decided to retire from the music business and open a tavern. Maybe his Skillet Lickers' past would finally leave him alone.

He was wrong. As the folk revival began to pick up steam in the early 1960s, it made heroes out of people like the Kingston Trio and Joan Baez, but it also stimulated interest in genuine traditional and old-time performers. People began to "rediscover" veteran blues singers, fiddlers, and singers from the 1920s and to coax them out of retirement. The 1920s especially were romanticized as a sort of golden age of stringband music, and all kinds of people began to track down McMichen to ask him about his days with the Skillet Lickers. Generally McMichen tried to be civil enough to them, but he gradually began to tire of people who were ignorant or unsympathetic with the later, equally significant, aspects of his career, and who persisted in glorifying the five frustrating years he had spent in Atlanta. Even in his twilight years McMichen had to watch as the historians did to him the same thing that generations of fans had done: pigeonhole him as a funky, colorful, old-time fiddler.

McMichen made a brief comeback of sorts. As early as 1961, Birch Monroe, Bill's brother, had invited him up to the festival at Bean Blossom. Here he played for an audience that respected his whole career, and that was responsive to him as something more than just an ex-Skillet Licker. But in 1964 he was asked to appear at a Northern festival, the Newport Folk Festival, and for the first time encountered a young, urban, folk music audience. He was not impressed. "You're only interested in me because I'm old," he reportedly snapped to one such group. He played "Bile 'Em Cabbage Down" for them.

In 1964 McMichen was seriously injured in a car accident, and this probably prevented him from taking full advantage of the chances for a comeback during the revival. But by May 1965 he had recovered enough to do an important concert at the University of Illinois in Urbana. This concert was promoted by the Campus Folksong Club, an important organization which saw several of its associates go on to become major figures in folk music scholarship. By 1965 the club had over 400 members, and under the direction of Archie Green and others, it had gained a remarkable appreciation for genuine traditional music in its most authentic form. The club looked forward to seeing McMichen, one of the greats of the golden age of old-time music, and he eagerly turned out. When McMichen arrived, his guitarist brought out a big electric guitar and promptly plugged it in. Some of the audience was dismayed, and others did not know quite how to react. McMichen played well, but the concert was less than a success. Archie Green recalled later that "it was ill-timed." The young audience was simply not ready for the kind of eclecticism McMichen represented.

In 1966 McMichen did two more concerts at Bean Blossom, this time backed by Shorty Shehan, his wife Juanita, and a young Neil Rosenberg. Tapes of the concert reveal that McMichen's fiddling was still surprisingly strong. Indeed, he was still playing well enough to win the first prize at the Kentucky State Championship contest in 1968. But the emphysema he suffered from was getting worse and worse. He finally lost the fight on January 3, 1970, in Battletown, Kentucky.

Clayton McMichen was a victim of one of country music's earliest and most enduring stereotypes: the wise-cracking hillbilly fiddler. Unlike Bob Wills or Roy Acuff, he was never really able to transcend this (at least to the public eye), and most of his repeated attempts to do so were not commercially successful. Like jazz bandleader Fletcher Henderson, who had to watch Benny Goodman take over his ideas and get credit for inventing swing, McMichen had a career marked by bad timing and frustration. Ironically, he never at any time in his career really and fully embraced pure old-time fiddle music; he was always wanting to innovate, to experiment within the tradition, to challenge the rigid structure of the music. Perhaps he failed because his timing was bad: the early record industry was too stratified, feeling that they had to sell only pure stringband music to Southern whites, only blues to blacks, and only jazz to Northern youngsters. McMichen simply didn't accept this. Perhaps he failed because he tried to make his move during the Depression, a bad time for any sort of experiment.

But this isn't to say he failed by other, higher standards. Certainly he made millions aware of the potential for fiddle music, and influenced huge numbers of young fiddlers. He is owed more than just a tip of the hat, or a sentence of praise in a footnote.

Sources

The most important sources for details about McMichen's career include a lengthy interview of the fiddler done by Fred Hoeptner and Bob Pinson in 1959 and published in *Old Time Music* # 1 (Summer 1971), 8-10; # 2 (Autumn 1971), 13-15; # 3 (Winter 1971–72, 14–15 et.

al.); and # 4 (Spring 1972, 19-20 et. al.). I have also made use of the huge McMichen scrapbook in the Country Music Foundation archives, as well as a file of personal correspondence made available by Margaret Riddle. In addition, I made use of a second interview of McMichen, done in March 1964 by Robert Shelton, notes from which are in the CMF files. Quotations from Lowe Stokes are taken from an unpublished interview done by Rich Nevins in 1972, as well as the liner notes to *The Skillet Lickers—Volume 2* (County 526), also prepared by Nevins, and from Joe LaRose, "An Interview with Lowe Stokes," *Old Time Music* # 39 (Winter 1982/ Spring 1984), 6–12. The quote from Dolph Hewitt comes from an interview with Byron Berline published in *The Devil's Box*, vol. 29, no. 4 (Winter 1995), 20–33. This chapter is a considerably expanded version of Charles Wolfe's "Clayton McMichen: Reluctant Hillbilly," *Bluegrass Unlimited*, May 1979, with additions from Charles Wolfe's "McMichen in Kentucky: The Sunset Years," in *The Devil's Box*, vol. 11, no. 2 (June 1977). The Columbia sales figures are from the author's files and are courtesy of Tiny McCarthy and David Freeman. I have also benefited greatly from discussions and correspondence with Bill Harrison, Judith McCulloh, Archie Green, Ivan Tribe, and others.

Kessinger

IN THE SUMMERS OF THE LATE 1960S, THE GREAT SOUTHERN
fiddle contests found themselves awash in new fans. From Massa-
chusetts, New York, California, and Chicago came thousands of
young enthusiasts, caught up in the throes of the folk music revival,
hitchhiking and driving their way into the humid Southern summers
that must have seemed aeons away from the summer of love in San
Francisco. In Galax, Virginia, they poured into a small mountain town
where the Elks Club had held a fiddling contest for thirty years. With
their blue jeans, bare feet, long hair, and funny cigarettes, they reveled
in the stringband music, skinny dipping in the creek that ran beside the
fairground, shocking the local residents. The story was the same at the
other sprawling festivals: Union Grove, Pulaski, Richwood, Pomery,
even up in Weiser, Idaho.

All of the festivals had their favorites, performers who were suddenly elevated from local dances to the world of records, radio, and
national popularity. It was an age of rediscovery, and the young fans
searched out and coaxed into playing everyone from Eck Robertson to
Arthur Smith to Clayton McMichen. But one of the few veterans who
could really hold his own at the contests, who needed no patronizing
nor special consideration, was a lively, stocky fiddler who always wore
a small-brimmed hat. He loved to play, and was a master showman: he
would shake his hips, crouch like a batter, dance a little, and occasionally let out a spontaneous whoop. He didn't like the well-mannered
Texas styled fiddling that was in vogue at Southwestern contests, nor
the delicate figure skating of Posey Rorer and his imitators; he ripped

into a tune like a hungry man faced with a plate of fried chicken. He played "Ragtime Annie" with a feverish tempo and launched into "Sally Ann Johnson" in a way that dared anybody to keep up.

People who had heard his old records from the 1920s swore that, unlike the other resurrected fiddlers of those summers, he was actually playing better than he had then. He didn't have to be coaxed out of retirement; he roared out of it. By 1971, many of his fans had no qualms about using superlatives. "He is the greatest old-time fiddler around today," announced the Rounder Collective (Rounder Records founders Ken Irwin, Bill Nowlin, and Marion Leighton) after hearing him. Many agreed, and few in those Vietnam protest days didn't know his name: Clark Kessinger.

His was pure fiddling, with no real concessions to popular taste. In the seventy-plus sides he recorded for the old Brunswick company between 1928 and 1930, and the five LPs he made during his comeback in the 1960s, he had no novelty numbers, no funny vocals, no cute trick playing, no harmony singing. Except for a few square dance calls on his first records, it was all pure Kessinger; if you didn't like fiddling, it wasn't your music. Where Doc Roberts sprinkled his repertoire with vocal duets, where Arthur Smith became as well known for his vocals as his instrumentals, and where McMichen cut show-off pieces and hired smooth singers to sell his pop pieces, Kessinger stuck with what he always did best: fiddling.

He came by it honestly. He grew up in rugged Lincoln County, West Virginia, south of Charleston, across the Kanawha River. "I was born in Kanawha County, Charleston, right out of Charleston, South Hills, and I was raised there," he recalled in 1971. "I stayed up around Boone as much as I did around Kanawha. Boone County. We lived around Lincoln County when I was a boy. When I was about ten years old we moved there. We lived out there about three or four years. Farmed on a hillside farm. We moved back to Charleston then. South Hills that is. I was born twenty-seventh of July of July 1896. I was the youngest boy." Clark's father spent most of his time working as a molder in a local foundry, making wheels.

In later years Kessinger was a little cagey about just where he learned his fiddling. He admitted that "my great-grandfather fiddled. Also my great uncle on my mother's side, in Lincoln County. That was way back." He admired local fiddlers like George Dillons and the brothers Dave and Bob Glens. "One played slow music and the other played hillbilly." But probably his most important mentor was the legendary Ed Haley, the blind fiddler who never recorded commercially but whom many today consider perhaps the finest of all West Virginia–Kentucky fiddlers. "He was from over around Logan, close to the Kentucky line. He was a great fiddler, he was a smooth fiddler." Young Clark certainly inherited some of Haley's tunes, and most likely some of his unusual bowing technique. For much of his life Haley stayed around the Ashland area, and in later years openly admired Kessinger's playing—though he occasionally complained to friends that Kessinger always seemed to shy away from playing in front of him.

Clark had started playing music when he was only five and was playing for country dances by the time he was ten. Though his first instrument was the banjo, he later switched to violin ("I never saw a guitar"). "I just started playing, not to learn it. Just come natural to me." His first attempts at making money with music came when he was seven, in local saloons. "My dad used to take me there. My dad didn't drink; he used to take me there just to make money. I'd get ten or fifteen dollars a night, more than he made in a week, back in them times. The people who came in . . . throwing money at me. I used to dance, why I'd get out there and dance a little bit. That was quite a thing. . . . I'd play and dance, carry on just a little bit." Ironically, young Clark didn't even own his own fiddle through all this; he would borrow his brother-in-law's, or "someone would just hand me one." On one of these visits, he remembers learning one of the first tunes he played, "Marching Through Georgia."

When America entered World War I, Kessinger was twenty-one, and he found himself serving a stint in the Navy. Whether or not this stay had any effect on his fiddling is not clear, but by the time he got back to West Virginia he was starting to get a serious reputation for his fiddling. French Mitchell, a well-known fiddler from the area, recalled that by the early 1920s, he was known throughout the Kanawha Valley as a fierce competitor in local fiddling contests. At one such event, at Point Pleasant, Mitchell recalled that many of the contestants who had signed up suddenly dropped out when they learned that Kessinger was playing. (Such tales are probably quite true, but they were also told about other mountain fiddlers, such as Melvin Robinette of Virginia.) By this time he had started performing a lot with the son of his brother Charles, Luches Kessinger (1906–1944). Nine years younger than Clark, Luches (Luke) lived in Charleston and South Charleston. Unlike a lot of the older West Virginia fiddlers, Clark Kessinger did not like to play solo; he enjoyed a guitar accompaniment and especially liked Luches's playing. "He played it clear, clear as he could be. That's what I liked about him. He was right there with the notes . . . every note that I hit, why he'd hit 'em. He didn't slack down on you, he didn't speed up or nothing. Well, we were used to one another. We used to have a time playing around in different places. Play for nothing. Never get no money out of it." The pair also got their own radio show on the new station in Charleston, WOBU, when it opened in October 1927. The station was not all that powerful at first, but Kanawha County, full of factory towns and coal camps, could boast of around 10,000 radios, more than any other county in the state. The people in the area who had somehow missed Kessinger at fiddling contests and dances now had their chance to hear and admire him.

Next came the single most important event in the career of Clark and Luches: in February 1928 a major league recording company set up shop in Ashland, Kentucky, about forty miles from Charleston. The company was Brunswick-Balke-Collender, which released records on the Brunswick and Vocalion labels, and had recently inaugurated their "Songs from Dixie" series that featured releases by Uncle Dave Macon, Buell Kazee, and Al Hopkins & His Buckle Busters (the Hill Billies). Most of their old-time records before now had been recorded in New York, but following the lead of companies like Victor and Columbia, they had decided to set up temporary studios "in the field" and record in various Southern cities. No one had ever tried this in the Kentucky-West Virginia area, and Ashland seemed like a good bet. In charge of the activity was James O'Keefe, accompanied by Richard Voynow, a former piano player on some of jazz man Bix Beiderbecke's sessions.

For several months prior to the Ashland session, O'Keefe had networked through the region lining up talent. It would include an important cross-section of key musicians: singer Bascom Lamar Lunsford, Roy Harvey & the North Carolina Ramblers (Charlie Poole's old band), gospel singers Welling & McGhee, Jack Ready's Walker Mountain String Band, Warren Caplinger's Cumberland Mountain Entertainers, and the original Tennessee Ramblers (not to be confused with the later radio band). A temporary studio was set up at Carter's Phonograph and

Music Shop at 217 Sixteenth Street in Ashland. Later Kessinger recalled, "They sold the records right there at the furniture store. They sold them there after they got them made." Clark and Luches had been recommended to O'Keefe by a local violin teacher, Richmond Huston, who was an admirer of Clark's. "He wanted us to make some records. He said he could get us on. And sure enough, he did, he got us on." The Kessingers were asked to report at 9:30 A.M. on February 11, at the very start of the session. Like most companies, Brunswick didn't offer royalties for first time artists, but their lump sum payment was generous: $100 per "double-sided" record (two selections). The Kessingers would wind up recording fourteen sides, or seven records for a total of $700—pretty good money in 1928.

O'Keefe's roster was short on fiddlers, and he was interested to hear the Clark Kessinger everyone in the area was talking about. He also had a specific problem he hoped the Kessingers could solve. Arch-rival Columbia had just issued a hot new seller which was threatening to become the biggest hit of 1928: an instrumental by a Mississippi fiddle band called the Leake County Revelers and entitled "Wednesday Night Waltz." The piece had been recorded in April 1927 and released in November, backed by another waltz, "Goodnight Waltz." O'Keefe was right in his guess that the Columbia record would be a big seller: it did wind up being the biggest Columbia old-time seller of 1928, eventually totally almost 200,000 copies. Columbia kept it in print for decades, and it became one of the most influential of all country instrumentals. The waltz had originated with the fiddler for the Leake County Revelers, Will Gilmer, who admitted that he had picked up the tune "out in Texas somewhere." In the middle of the recording, though, the band would suddenly break into a faster tune called "Saturday Night Breakdown." It was a career record for the Revelers and helped them get later radio work, record contracts, and even a job playing for Huey Long's election campaign.

Other companies desperately tried to grab a piece of the action and frantically tried to find cover versions. Even Doc Roberts was pressured to try one for the American Recording Company, and Victor had Carson Robison do a vocal version. (It is sometimes thought that the idea of record companies doing a "cover" version of a hit by another company is something that dates from the 1940s; in fact it was quite popular in all fields of music by the late 1920s.) O'Keefe had sent a copy of the Columbia hit to Clark Kessinger and asked him to work up a version—of both sides. It was no problem for Kessinger, who loved waltzes anyway, and he and Luches added it to the session. It became Brunswick 220, the first Kessinger recording. (It was O'Keefe, incidentally, who decided to name the pair the "Kessinger Brothers" because "it just sounded better.") It took off about as fast as the Columbia original, and soon Brunswick had its own best-seller on its hands. In fact, it became the Kessinger Brothers' most popular record. "We'd have made a fortune if they'd paid us royalties," Kessinger said. There was no fortune, but its success did guarantee the Kessingers a recording career, and a chance to preserve some of the South's best fiddling. Without "Wednesday Night Waltz," the Kessingers might have been like most of the other artists at Ashland—artists who got one session and were not heard from again.

O'Keefe almost made another mistake. Many of the early fiddle records released by the companies were designed for a practical purpose: square dancing. To that end, they were festooned with dance calls, sometimes with the caller right up in the mike, often frustrating listeners who were trying to appreciate the fiddling. On about half the Kessinger sides from this first session, a caller named Ernest Legg was brought in. Fortunately, Legg was a local man who had had experience doing square dances with the Kessingers, and his calls did not distract all that much from the music. Indeed, they even added to the effect. Unlike the Northern or New England callers, who barked their calls in ugly, harsh shouts, Legg almost sang his calls, using a laid-back mountain tenor and long, cascading, internally rhymed phrases that actually echoed Kessinger's bowing patterns. Of the first twelve Brunswick sides, all but two featured calls on at least one of the sides. Soon the Brunswick bosses figured out that Kessinger's fiddling was attractive on its own terms and did not need to be marketed as a means to an end. After this first session, there were no more recordings using a caller.

The Kessingers' second record (Brunswick 235) was also a best-seller: it was a fine reading of "Turkey in the Straw" backed with the first commercial record of a tune that would become a standard, "Hell Among the Yearlings." (Some tune collections, including those of Ira Ford, have a number by this name, but it is not Kessinger's.) It was a tune that Kessinger himself continued to feature throughout his career and that became very popular on the fiddle contest circuit. Kessinger's arrangement featured a much-copied technique where he brushes the string with his forefinger, creating a subdued pizzicato effect. Other releases from the first session included more common tunes, such as "Arkansas Traveler" and "Forky Deer" (Brunswick 247), "Chicken in the Barnyard" and "Devil's Dream" (Brunswick 256), and "Girl I Left Behind Me" (Brunswick 267). Even these familiar standards were played with a drive and intensity that earlier versions lacked. Two of the odder tunes were "Garfield March" and "Kanawha March" (Brunswick 238); the former dated from the assassination of President James Garfield in 1881, and was originally a piece of sheet music called "Garfield's Funeral March." Kessinger had learned it from local fiddler Abe Glenn in 1903, when he was seven, and Garfield's death was only a generation away. His mellow "Sixteen Days in Georgia" (Brunswick 267) was a version of the familiar "Fourteen Days in Georgia."

Though the records would carry his name and his music across the country, Kessinger didn't know that at the time. He was working hard at a day job as a caretaker for a wealthy Charleston resident, Harrison B. Smith. Smith knew Kessinger as a good painter and all-purpose handyman, but did not know he was a fiddler. One of best legends about Kessinger described how he found out about it. Researcher Nancy Dols tells one variant: "One day the cook was playing one of Clark's records in the kitchen when Mr. Smith came in and asked, 'Who's that wonderful fiddler?' He was amazed to find out it was Clark, and immediately hired him to teach his son to play." Billy C. Hurt, from near Rocky Mount, Virginia, tells another variant: "Clark worked when he was a young feller—jobs were sort of scarce one time, and he sorta worked as a gardener for this big distinguished man there in Charleston. And he played the fiddle and this guy loved the fiddle so good, well, he loved the violin really, that he loved to have Szigeti and some of them big violinists come in and hold concerts 'round Charleston. And he didn't know Clark was an old country fiddler. So he heard Clark up there in his garden one day in his courtyard out there, playing the fiddle and his maid was a-dancing. Well, he come out there and got to listening at them and he just thought that was the greatest thing that ever was. He asked Clark how in the world did you ever learn to play like that?"

In later years, admirers of Clark Kessinger like Guthrie Meade, noting his bow control, tone, and precision, had assumed that he had had some formal training. Even today it is not clear how much he had. Kessinger himself insisted he was a "natural" musician, a self-taught country fiddler. But these comments came during the height of the folk revival, when "natural" and "self-taught" were tickets to the folk festival and old-time fiddling circuit. We know, for instance, that a formal violin teacher named Richmond Huston (who got the Kessingers their record contract) must have had some close connection with Kessinger. And by his own admission Kessinger knew and studied the records of such popular classical violinists as Fritz Kreisler, Joseph Szigeti, and Jascha Heifetz. All three toured widely in the 1920s, and all three had a wide variety of popular recordings on the market. Szigeti was Hungarian born, a child prodigy, a friend of Bartok, noted for his playing of Bach's unaccompanied pieces. By 1925 he had made his American debut, playing in a style which required holding the bow in an archaic way, with the elbow close to the body. Kreisler was a Viennese virtuoso, born in 1875, a popular figure in the United States since 1888. He was known for his liquid tone, his expressiveness, and what critics have called "the elegance of his bowing." He was also fond of using an intense vibrato. Though he recorded many of the standard extended works before coming to America, his many Victor recordings often featured short, light classical pieces, many of his own composition.

Kessinger not only knew the records of these masters, but he heard them in person and actually performed before Szigeti. When Kreisler and Szigeti gave concerts in Charleston, the son of Kessinger's employer was able to get him into the concerts. On one such occasion Kessinger met Szigeti. Billy C. Hurt tells the story:

> After the concert was over, he [Smith, Kessinger's employer] wanted Clark to meet Szigeti. So he went up and got word to Clark that Szigeti was going to be there and he wanted him to meet him, so we went up to the house and met Szigeti, one of the greater violinists, and Szigeti wanted him to play a tune and Clark played the "Mockingbird." And Clark said old Szigeti like to pulled his hair out, and he said how in the world do you do that, don't know no music? Clark said I just do it by ear, I don't know one note from the other. He said Szigeti got his genuine Strad out, and he said Szigeti started playing that violinist stuff. He said Szigeti didn't know it, but he [Clark] was watching every move he made. He was

getting all this stuff off of him. He was watching them hands and
them double-triple stops he's putting on the violin. And that's
where Clark got a lot of this violin touch that he had.

Kessinger himself later admitted his debt to Szigeti and Kreisler: "[I]
caught the touch they had. . . . Some of their kind of bowing, who I
could kind of add it in with hillbilly. Made it a lot better."

Throughout the rest of 1928, the Kessinger Brothers' records continued to sell better than any other fiddle records in the Brunswick catalogue. Some were issued on Sears labels under the name "Birmingham
Entertainers," and later some of the sides would even be issued on
French Canadian labels under the name "Les Deux Paroissiens." Convinced they had a major act on their hands, Brunswick invited Clark
and Luches to come to New York in early 1929 to make a new round of
discs. This session, spread out over several days, produced some twen-
ty-three sides, none with any square dance calls. It too produced its
share of classics. One was "Tug Boat," in its first commercial recording.
This record would make its way to, among other places, Texas, where
the influential Texas fiddler Benny Thomasson would learn it and
insert it into the Texas fiddle contest repertoire, where it remains to
this day. Another was "Salt River" (later redone), an old Irish tune
which would eventually make its way to bluegrass star Bill Monroe,
who would record it as "Salt Creek."

There was "Dill Pickle Rag," Charles Johnson's 1906 Kansas City
piece originally called simply "Dill Pickles," a popular rag with many
old-time musicians, played by Kessinger in all three of its original
strains. "Old Jake Gillie," another Midwestern tune called "Jake's Best
Reel," got its first recording here, and became one of the more popular Kessinger recordings. "Chinky Pin" (some Brunswick clerk's man-
gling of the word "chinquapin," a type of mountain chestnut) was a
tune that was already a mountain favorite on both fiddle and banjo,
under titles such as "I Am My Mama's Darling Child," "Pig Town Fling,"
and "Love Somebody." It was probably an old Irish bagpipe tune,
though Kessinger was the first to record it under "Chinky Pin." "Done
Gone" was Kessinger's tribute to Eck Robertson and was learned
directly off of Robertson's 1922 recording. He told Guthrie Meade that
he considered Eck to be "one of the best fiddlers he has heard." Generally, the Brunswick bosses shied away from Kessinger's more esoteric

pieces, yet chose to release the more familiar tunes like "Sally Good-in," "Sourwood Mountain," "Mississippi Sawyer," "Richmond Polka," and "Soldier's Joy."

Other sessions followed in June 1929 (twenty-four sides) and September 1930 (seventeen sides) before the Depression, and the sale of the Brunswick company, put a premature end to them. Many of these later ones were waltzes, such as "Black Hawk Waltz, "Over the Waves Waltz," "Midnight Serenade Waltz," "Wildflower Waltz," "Mary Jane Waltz," and "Lauderbach Waltz." "I like the waltzes best," Kessinger said in his 1972 interview for Rounder Records. "I'd rather play a waltz. They're harder to play. Well, in a way they're harder, in a way they're not. They are harder to play for the time. They're harder to get time to a waltz than it is to a hoedown. When you play a hoedown for an old square dance, you just play it so long as you keep the time, your beat, that's all you got to have, your rhythm. That's all it takes."

Even though these later recordings sold only a fraction of the earlier ones, due mainly to the Depression, many of them are considered true Kessinger masterpieces, and in spite of the low sales, key fiddlers somehow found them and kept the tunes alive. The one Kessinger called "Rat Cheese Under the Hill" was first thought to be a misnomer for the familiar "Natchez Under the Hill" ("Turkey in the Straw"), but in fact was a completely different melody. It was later recorded (by Ted Sharp) under the name "Pike's Peak," and in the 1930s by Bob Wills band as "Prosperity Special." "Sopping the Gravy" got into the Texas fiddle contest repertoire, probably again through Benny Thomasson, and in the 1980s was rejuvenated by virtuoso Mark O'Connor, who named one of his albums after it.

In addition to the traditional fiddle tunes, Kessinger drew upon a number of sources to fill out his sessions, with fascinating results. One was the body of quirky, unusual West Virginia–Kentucky fiddle tunes he had grown up hearing in the Kanawha Valley. These included items like "Poca River Blues," "Birdie," "Three Forks of Sandy," "Portsmouth," "Brownstown Girl," as well as the aforementioned "Old Jake Gillie." A second source was old pop songs, which Kessinger rearranged into fiddle tunes: Kerry Mills's "Whistling Rufus," "Steamboat Bill," "Little Betty Brown" (popularized as a vocal by the Hill Billies), Billy Reeves's 1869 hit "Shoo Fly," and "Little Brown Jug." In doing this, of course, he was following a practice that older bowmen had done for generations. A related source was Kessinger's unusual fondness for marches and polkas; not only did he do the popular "Garfield March," but he did "Under the Double Eagle," "Polka Four," and others. A final source was original pieces, or constructs, where Kessinger pieced together parts of different tunes: "Everybody to the Puncheon," "Kanawha County Rag," and "West Virginia Special."

Kessinger occasionally complained that the three-minute length of the 78 rpm records actually caused him to repeat a tune more times than he thought necessary. But often when he did this he managed to infuse the different choruses with subtle variations. A typical Kessinger arrangement often featured a series of short, rhythmic bow strokes where he actually lifted the bow from the strings, followed by a long, breathtaking, cascading run (as in "Tugboat"). Unlike those of modern Texas fiddlers, his variations stayed close to the original tune outline; as Nancy Dols notes, "the smooth, clean exterior of his playing sometimes almost hides the intricate things he does with the melody, rhythm, and bowing." He was fond of devices such as the "brushing pizzicato" effect heard on "Hell Among the Yearlings" and "Going up Brush Fork," and of using entire lines of double stops to enhance a melody. Like many of the older mountain fiddlers, he was fond of adding an extra beat to a phrase, creating an irregular meter, making it hard for a competing fiddler at a contest to duplicate his style.

On September 20, 1930, about a year after the stock market crashed, the last of the Brunswick recordings were completed, and Clark Kessinger effectively dropped out of the national music scene for the next three and a half decades. He married in 1929, and began a family that would eventually number six children, none of whom showed any special interest in playing an instrument. "I was a painter by trade," he explained. "I painted for years and years. I painted for one man for about eighteen years. One contractor. Mostly inside painting, decorating. I don't like the outside work. I never was no highclimber." His hand was so steady with the brush that he did not even have to use tape to protect the windows. During World War II he briefly left this trade to work as a guard at a local plant.

Not that he ever gave up fiddling. He and Luches played for a time in the 1930s over Charleston radio WOBU's "Old Farm Hour" and engaged in several of the highly promoted "fiddling showdowns" against Natchee the Indian. He appeared on stage shows with the Delmore Brothers, the McGee Brothers, Arthur Smith, Clayton McMichen, and others. They often played at City Hall for the mayor of Charleston. "One of the mayors was a good friend of mine," he remembered. "He was the Mayor Copenhavery. I used to play for him. I'd always played for him when he'd have any doings a going on. He liked the old-timey music. He was crazy about hillbillies." Clark and Luches also continued to play at dances and clubs, and in the late 1930s they actually appeared at the National Folk Festival in Washington, D.C. The end to this chapter came in May 1944 when Luches died.

Still, Kessinger kept his skills sharp by playing with different accompanists, whomever he could pick up, at various dancehalls and clubs. Rock & roll, with its electric guitars and Elvis imitators, came on the scene in the 1950s, but in the obscure corners of the Appalachians, Bill Monroe still held sway on the radio, and many of the rural dance halls still preferred fiddle bands. In 1963 Kessinger was working at a club called Westfalls, down on Route 60 just east of Hurricane, West Virginia. It was a center for local square dances, big enough to have three sets on the floor at one time. Kessinger had been playing there for some time, and word had gotten out. One of the people who perked up at the news was Guthrie Meade, then working for the Library of Congress and a devotee of Kessinger's old records. At the National Folk Festival that year at Covington, Kentucky, Meade passed on the information to a young man named Ken Davidson.

Davidson was a young Charleston resident who was deeply interested in traditional music of the area, and was responsible for discovering some of the area's best performers. He had discovered the remarkable fiddler French Carpenter, as well as instrumentalist and singer Jenes Cotrell. He not only encouraged his finds to get out and perform more, but he took them to fiddling contests and festivals, including ones as far away as the Newport Folk Festival. He also recorded them and formed a company called Folk Promotions to release his field recordings. Acting on Meade's tip, in the spring of 1964 he drove to Westfalls Inn and introduced himself to Clark Kessinger. He was amazed at how well Kessinger was still playing and urged him to go up and compete in a fiddle contest at Pulaski, Virginia. He agreed and took first place. A second win at Richwood, West Virginia, soon followed. By August he tried the granddaddy of all Virginia contests, Galax, and lit out down Highway 19. There he formed an impromptu stringband with two younger musicians, guitarist Gene Meade (from Draper, North Carolina) and banjo player Wayne Hauser (from Winston-Salem, North Carolina). Though Kessinger had never recorded with a full stringband, it fit his fiddling like a glove, and after a few rehearsals the group took first place in the stringband category, beating out sixty other groups. Later that year Davidson recorded the band in Charleston, and released the results on Volume Four of his *Folk Promotions* album series. Guthrie Meade wrote a booklet of notes and included a complete discography of the old Kessinger Brothers 78s. By the end of the year, fiddle fans knew that Clark Kessinger was back; fiddle novices knew there was a new gunslinger in town and that the level of play at Southern contests had just gone up.

Kessinger was sixty-six when Ken Davidson met him for the first time, and his comeback was to last about seven years. He quickly became the most colorful and intense fiddler on the contest circuit, winning dozens of prizes, including the World's Champion prize at the forty-seventh Union Grove affair in April 1971. He continued to record, including three more LPs for Davidson's label (which had by now changed its name to Kanawha). Some of the albums were later reissued on Folkways Records, and then on County. They were popular, and some of them probably reached a larger audience than did the original 78s. Gene Meade became Kessinger's regular guitar player, playing in a fluid flat-top style, both at contests and on records. Even today, many fiddle fans can still remember where they were when they first heard Kessinger play at one contest or another.

By 1971 Ken Davidson's company was effectively out of business, and he encouraged a newly formed company to take over his chronicling of Kessinger's music. The new company was owned by Ken Irwin, Bill Nowlin, and Marion Leighton—a trio of young Bostonians who were all veterans of the festival circuit and who had named their company Rounder. They drove to Union Grove and met Kessinger. After the finals, they drove over to the Vance Motor Inn in nearby Statesville and began recording the new LP. They got twelve good cuts, eleven fiddle tunes, and a guitar solo by Gene, and left with the tapes, planning to return in a few weeks for a follow-up session. A week before the scheduled session, though, Kessinger had a stroke and collapsed on stage at a convention in Virginia. He recovered, but his right hand was severely affected and he had trouble playing. Hoping against hope that therapy would improve Kessinger's condition, the Rounders waited for several months. Only when it seemed Kessinger would not play well enough to continue, they released the album as Rounder 004—a little short on titles, but containing some of the lovely, obscure waltzes Kessinger loved to play. One of them might have served as a theme song: "When I Grow Too Old to Dream." Kessinger died June 4, 1975.

Sources

The first serious writing about Clark Kessinger was a set of liner notes by Guthrie (Gus) Meade, "Clark Kessinger, Fiddler," that came with the original Folk Promotions album (828), Folkways album (FA 2336), and County reissue (733). Most of the quotations from Kessinger came from an interview done by the Rounder Collective and packaged with the LP *Clark Kessinger*, Rounder 004 (1972). A good overview of Kessinger's career and music is yet another set of liner notes, these by Nancy Dols, for *The Kessinger Brothers—1928–1930*, County 536 (1975). I have also drawn on conversations with Bob Kessinger (Clark's nephew), John Hartford, Steve Davis, Bill Harrison, and Ivan Tribe. The quotations from Billy C. Hurt are taken from David Reiner and Peter Anick, *Old-Time Fiddling Across America* (Pacific, Missouri: Mel Bay, 1989), p. 74.

Fiddlers' Dream:
The Legend of Arthur Smith

RIVE WEST FROM NASHVILLE TOWARD THAT CORNER of Tennessee formed by the Cumberland and Tennessee Rivers, and you get into Arthur Smith country. Down here you don't have to explain to people *which* Arthur Smith—banjo maker Arthur E. Smith, or "Guitar Boogie" Arthur Smith?—for down here there's only one Arthur Smith, *the* Arthur Smith, the one they called "the king of the fiddlers." Here his music and his memory still live; his songs are played at square dances in Waverly and at fiddling contests in Clarksville, Dickson, or Ruskin. Even the countryside reminds you of Arthur Smith's music and Arthur's tunes: you go through Cheatham County ("Chittlin' Cookin' Time in Cheatham County," "Cheatham County Breakdown") and then through Dickson County ("Dickson County Blues"), and you pass over Indian Creek ("Indian Creek") and drop down to the hamlet of Sugar Tree ("Sugar Tree Stomp"), or go up to the town across the river, Paris ("Paris Waltz").

If any one figure looms like a giant over Southern fiddling, that figure is Arthur Smith. Every year at contests in living room jam sessions, and even in Nashville studios, those old enough to remember Smith swap stories about him. Those too young to remember him find themselves unable to escape from his music, from clumsy bluegrass arrangements of "Walking in My Sleep" to awkward, tentative renditions of "More Pretty Girls than One." Almost all the old-timers in the Tennessee area speak of Arthur Smith as the ultimate source for much of present-day fiddling style: Southeast contest fiddling style starts here, with Smith. Whatever you call his style—long bow, rolling notes, finger-noting—it had a tremendous impact on Southern fiddling. Along with a few select others—Clayton McMichen, Clark Kessinger, Doc Roberts, Ed Haley—Smith elevated fiddling from simply a folk music to a folk art. Smith was by no means content to passively accept the fiddling tradition he found in middle Tennessee, and quietly, meekly preserve it for future generations. He added his own unique stamp to everything he touched, even the most traditional of tunes; and he wrote dozens of good, albeit difficult, breakdowns and rags and blues. At a time when fiddle bands were dying out, and fiddling was considered old hat, Smith made people sit up and listen—not dance—to hard-core, flat-out, no frills, plain good fiddling. He gave the fiddler a status he has hardly enjoyed since, in the world of professional country music.

Yet in spite of this, there has not been all that much good information available on Smith. Too much of what has been printed is little more than legend, folklore, and just plain gossip. Smith has become, for many, a shadowy figure, and his music more of a memory than a living force.

FORMATIVE YEARS

Arthur Leroy Smith was born on April 10, 1898, at the rural hamlet of Bold Springs, in southeast Humphries County, Tennessee, about halfway between the modern towns of Waverly and McEwen. There William Calvin Smith, Arthur's father, had a family farm, and it was there Smith received his grade school education. (He apparently never got much beyond the fifth grade—by no means an uncommon thing in those days.) One of the factors that cut short his education was the untimely death of his father in 1903 or 1904. As a young boy Smith spent most of his time working on his mother's farm on Blue Creek.

There is some confusion as to exactly how Smith began his fiddling. His father had the reputation in the area as a fiddler, but because he died when Smith was so young, he probably did not pass on too much to his son except, perhaps, a love and respect for music. The Smith family recalled that, even before he was able to hold the fiddle properly under his chin, the young Smith tried to play by holding the instrument upright on the floor. "Our grandmother said that when Daddy was just six or seven he would wake her up at night playing on the fiddle," recalled Lavonne Brown, Smith's oldest child.

Apparently Smith continued to fiddle as he grew up and began to play local dances with other area musicians. One of the guitarists with whom he worked was an attractive young girl named Nettie; she and Smith had been childhood sweethearts, and soon they decided to get married. They were married on September 27, 1914, just after the outbreak of World War I. Smith was just over sixteen, and his bride was two weeks shy of fifteen. They continued to live in a little house on his mother's farm, and to play for an occasional dance. By 1916 their first child, Lavonne, was born followed by a second in 1917.

Nettie recalled buying Arthur the first fiddle he ever owned about this time; she sold chickens to buy it for him. She apparently bought it from a neighbor at nearby McEwen, Grady Stringer. At least, Stringer remembered selling Smith a fiddle at about this time. At this point, stories became confusing. Stringer (who still lives near McEwen) was one of the early musicians who played with Smith during his formative years, and the person most frequently mentioned as an early fiddling influence on Smith. According to Stringer, "I sold Arthur one of my two fiddles for $6.50. It was a Sears Roebuck model called a Virginius. Arthur later said that he had been offered as much as $500 for it." Stringer was quite sure that Smith didn't begin to play seriously until he got that fiddle: "He had hardly played at all until he got that fiddle, but once he determined to learn it, and work at it, he learned fast. After he got to playing seriously and got to learning, Arthur could play anything." Smith must have played some on the fiddle before he met Grady Stringer and bought his Sears fiddle—otherwise he wouldn't have had such a great desire to own a fiddle—but it well might be that this sale marks the point at which Smith decided to become serious. As far as Stringer could recall, this sale must have taken place about 1917, for he remembered that Smith already had two small children.

Smith later admitted to Kirk McGee and others that Grady Stringer was one of his influences in developing his style, and it is important to look for a moment at Stringer's own career. Stringer never aspired to any sort of professional career, and for most of his life he fiddled for square dances and contests. He was born in Humphries County in 1897, just a year earlier than Smith; Stringer was thus hardly in the position to be much of a mentor to Smith, since they were almost the same age. However, Stringer had a brother named Jim Stringer who was older and who acted as a teacher for him. Stringer in turn passed on a lot of this to Smith. Another old fiddler from the area who influenced both Stringers and Arthur Smith was Walter Warden. Warden is widely recognized in the region today, and some of his tunes are still played by musicians like Omer Forster. One of the tunes Arthur Smith picked up from Stringer was "Forked Deer"; another was a tune the Stringer brothers called "Band Piece." They had learned it from another fiddler in west Tennessee, who had learned it from an old gramophone record by a brass band. The Stringers "added a little to it" and passed it on to Smith, who added a little more. When he recorded "Band Piece" years later, Smith dubbed the tune "Indian Creek," in honor of the road where the Stringers lived.

Talking to interviewers in later years, Stringer was fairly modest about just how much he taught Arthur Smith. "He learned some from me, I guess, but then I learned a lot from him too. He got ahead of me real fast. I think he did get some of his style from me. I picked up most of my own style from my brother Jim and from this Walter Warden. I just stuck it up and went at it. I used my fingers mostly. Some fiddlers put too many notes in the open with a bow to suit me. I've heard fiddlers play that played in A that played open note. A music teacher once told me that those open notes didn't count."

Smith continued to play in the area. In addition to the Stringers and his wife, he also played with a cousin named Homer Smith, and McEwen fiddler Floyd Ethredge, who was apparently no special influence on Smith but who went on to have a professional career in fiddling, playing for a time with the Crook Brothers on the Grand Ole Opry. (Incidentally, in the 1970s Ethredge still lived in McEwen and occasionally fiddled at local dances.) But the big change in Smith's life came in 1921, when he moved to Dickson in middle Tennessee and went to work for the NC & St.L railroad. His first job on the railroad was as a logger, cutting crossties, but he soon moved up to the job of linesman, where his work consisted of putting insulators on poles. At that time, the NC & St.L was one of the two main railroads crossing Tennessee. The L & N line ran north and south through Nashville, while the NC & St.L arced across the state from Memphis to Nashville and then down to Chattanooga and on into Georgia. The NC & St.L ran right through Humphries and Dickson counties, Smith's home ground. The line was known informally as "the Dixie Line" by everyone in the mid-South. Smith's work took him all up and down the Dixie Line (as he put it in "Walking in My Sleep"), and for a time he lived in railroad cars on the line. He took his fiddle along, and learned from and played with many of those whom he met. One such person was singer Jack Jackson—the first country singer to record in Nashvillewho met Smith in about 1922 or 1923 in Mt. Juliet, Tennessee. "Arthur had a floating railroad crew that would go from place to place, and he happened to locate in Mt. Juliet where I went to school and he stayed there for several months. When I found out that he was a fiddler—he lived in railroad cars fixed up for living quarters—I'd stay till he got in and pick with him until he got ready to go to bed, then I'd walk home."

Meanwhile in Nashville, the National Life and Accident Company decided to start a radio station. Since September 1925 a small local station called WDAD (or "Dad's," in deference to the fact that it was owned by Dad's Radio Supply House) had been broadcasting some old-time fiddling and stringband music by Dr. Humphrey Bate and his band. When WSM opened in October 1925, the management first tried to construct a "dignified" image by broadcasting all sorts of formal music. Later that year, though, two things happened to change this. George D. Hay, the "Solemn Old Judge," was hired as station manager, and Henry Ford decided to start promoting fiddling contests to "preserve the authentic American values." A fiddling craze swept the nation, and Ford dealers across the South sponsored fiddling contests. Hay noticed this fad, and decided to try some old-time music on WSM. On an informal basis, he let Dr. Bate, Uncle Dave Macon, and Sid Harkreader broadcast over WSM. Then, in November, he let a seventy-eight-year-old, white-bearded fiddler named Uncle Jimmy Thompson play for an hour. The response was overwhelming, and by December WSM had announced that it would broadcast a regular "barn dance" every Saturday night. (For further details, see chapter 3.)

It is quite likely that Arthur Smith was one of the musicians who appeared informally on the early Opry during its first year, but he does not appear in any of the newspaper listings. Smith's first documented appearance on the Grand Ole Opry (as the "barn dance" was renamed in 1927) was on December 23, 1927, where he is announced as "Arthur Smith, fiddler, of Dickson, Tennessee." He played thirty minutes from 9:30 to 10:00, and played solo; both his friends and his family recall that in his first few Opry appearances, Smith played with no one, nor did he sing. For thirty minutes he played old-time solo fiddle, in the manner of so many rural Tennessee fiddlers. He came on right after the spot by Uncle Dave Macon and Sam McGee. Another solo fiddler holding down a spot by himself on the Opry at that time was Whit Gayden, a west Tennessee fiddler who specialized in doing imitations on his fiddle. (I have been unable to determine whether Smith knew or played with Gayden, who later recorded for Victor.)

After several weeks of playing the Opry by himself, Smith joined forces with his cousin Homer Smith. Arthur and Homer appeared on the show for the first time on February 3, 1928. Arthur played fiddle, and Homer played guitar and sang. (Arthur at this time did not consider himself a singer.) Though Homer Smith played an important part in Arthur's career, I have been unable to find out much about him. He was Arthur's first cousin, was from Humphries County, and also worked on the railroad; he died around 1975. Arthur and Homer were popular, though, and quickly nailed down a regular spot on the Opry. This was usually at 10 o'clock, just after the regular segment by Paul Warmack & His Gully Jumpers, and just before Bert Hutcherson's thirty-minute solo spot. (Hutcherson was from all accounts a splendid solo guitarist in his prime, and for years was good enough to do an entire thirty-minute spot by himself. Sam McGee learned a lot of songs from him, and so did Arthur; one of them was "House of David Blues," which both Arthur and Sam later recorded.) Arthur and Homer were often referred to as the "Smith Brothers," though they were not. In 1928 Arthur and Homer appeared on the Opry twenty-eight times, more than any other act except DeFord Bailey. Throughout 1929 and 1930 the two continued to play regularly on the Opry, and by 1930 they were playing in the 10:07 slot that immediately preceded the most popular program of the time, "Amos n' Andy."

But regardless of Arthur Smith's popularity on the Opry, the pay in those days was hardly enough to support a growing family: it was only $5 per show. Like most of the other early performers on the programs, Smith could see his music-making only as a part-time hobby. He continued to work for the NC & St.L railroad and to play for the Opry only on weekends, as a part-time hobby. In 1928 he was promoted to the railroad's maintenance department, and he and his family moved to Bruceton, in Carroll County, a few miles east of Huntingdon. This placed him over 100 miles from Nashville, at a time when he was playing the Opry almost every other week. Of course, he was able to travel into Nashville on a free railroad pass, and in many weeks he found himself closer in because of his traveling with his maintenance crew. For a time he and Homer worked around Chattanooga, and they apparently played several times over WDOD.

This distance from Nashville, though, might have had one very significant effect on his career. By 1928 record companies had been busy for two years documenting the music of fiddlers who, in many cases, were less popular than Smith. Since 1925 the record industry had sent teams of scouts and engineers into the South to locate and record fiddlers like Smith. For the fiddlers there was little money to be made from such records, to be sure, but the exposure could certainly encourage a fledgling career. Why wasn't Smith recorded during this first wave of field recordings? There are no clear answers. Alton Delmore has written that Smith didn't think he was good enough to record, but Smith's friends and family dispute that. Even this early Smith took a just pride in his fiddling abilities. In 1928 the Victor Company set up in Nashville and recorded many of the pioneer radio artists on the Opry. Even though Arthur and Homer were one of the most popular acts on the Opry, they were not recorded. Why? One guess is that the recording sessions took place during the week, when Smith was possibly miles away working on the railroad. Many of the groups recorded were Nashville natives, who were close in and convenient for the recording session; Smith, living over 100 miles away, could usually get into Nashville only on weekends.

The railroad job, though, was still important to Smith. In fact, it had been a fellow Dixie Line employee, Harry Stone, who had gotten Smith his first job on the Opry. Stone was an early WSM announcer, and later became its General Manager. (Smith had other ties to WSM as well; the famous dance band leader Beasley Smith, whose band was a mainstay of the early WSM schedule, was another cousin of Arthur's.) Smith's house at Bruceton, where he continued to live until 1932, became a stopping-off place for other fiddlers traveling through the country, or on the Dixie Line from Memphis to Nashville. One of those whom Lavonne remembered visiting her father was Clark Kessinger, the West Virginia fiddler who made over seventy records in the 1920s. (See the preceding chapter of this book for more on Kessinger.) Smith and Kessinger had a great deal of respect for each other and kept up their friendship in later years. In fact, friends and family recall that Kessinger was one of the few fiddlers that Smith openly praised in those early years. (He knew of McMichen but was apparently not familiar with the work of Doc Roberts.) Though the styles of Kessinger and Smith are quite different (aside from both being "smooth, long-bow fiddlers"), it is possible that Smith did learn from Kessinger.

By 1930 Smith was featuring "Blackberry Blossom," one of his most famous pieces, and getting a great deal of mail at WSM. But then, for reasons which are not at all clear, he and Homer split up. Their last documented appearance on the Opry was in February 1932. They had not appeared on the Opry at all in 1931, and I have been unable to find out just where Smith was during this time. By the time Smith showed up again on the Opry, it was with a new band, one which was to become one of the show's most famous: the Dixieliners.

THE DIXIELINERS

On May 7, 1932, the Nashville Tennessean's radio schedule for the Opry carried for the first time a band listed as "Arthur Smith and his Dix-ieliners." This was a sort of super stringband that Smith had formed with Sam and Kirk McGee, and it quickly won a wide following both as a radio band and as a touring band. Both Sam and Kirk had had exten-sive experience before they joined forces with Smith. Sam already had the reputation as one of the area's best guitarists. His virtuoso flat-top picking style was already influencing guitarists across the country. Sam had been recording since 1926, both by himself and with Uncle Dave Macon, and he had toured widely with Macon in the late 1920s. Kirk had also recorded with Macon and his fellow Opry performer Blythe Poteet, and had had experience that ranged from medicine shows to singing conventions. In fact by 1930, Kirk had his own radio spot over Nashville station WBAW, and at one point was on the air opposite Homer and Arthur Smith on WSM. Both Sam and Kirk had played with Uncle Dave Macon, and were very loyal to him, but by 1932 Uncle Dave was using his son Dorris more and more in his act. Besides, Sam had had a falling out with Macon. Both McGees were interested in explor-ing new ways to further their careers.

Sam and Kirk had both known of Smith's fiddling, of course, and were interested in joining forces. Both McGees have said that they sought Smith out with the proposition to join, and in fact for some

*Eck Robertson (left) with fellow fiddlers
Lewis Franklin and A. P. Howard,
filmed by Fox Movietone News
in April 1922. (CMF)*

Eck Robertson, ca. 1922
Victor publicity shot. (CMF)

Uncle Jimmy Thompson, 1926.
(University of Louisville
Photographic Archives)

Record catalogue from the
Victor company, 1920s. (CMF)

Cover of Henry Ford's Dearborn
Independent. (Charles Wolfe)

Fiddlin' Powers and family.
(Charles Wolfe)

Curly Fox and Clayton
McMichen, 1930s.
(Charles Wolfe)

Clayton McMichen, 1930s. (CMF)

Doc Roberts and Edgar Boaz
at a recording session for the
Gennett company, in 1926.
(Southern Folklife Collection)

Fiddlin' Arthur Smith with
Sam and Kirk McGee, 1930s.
(CMF)

Clark Kessinger performing.
(CMF)

Bob Wills in
Columbia Records
ad, 1940s. (CMF)

The Cumberland Ridge Runners with Slim Miller on fiddle, 1931.
(Charles Wolfe)

Tommy Jackson (left, on fiddle)
at a Louvin Brothers recording
session, 1950s. (CMF)

Tommy Jackson. (CMF)

months would drive over to pick up Smith on Friday night, spend the weekend playing the Opry and doing live shows, and return him to the railroad Monday morning in time for him to go to work. It wasn't until the mid-1930s that Smith felt secure enough in his music vocation to quit his railroad job completely. However, as the Dixieliners got more and more tour bookings in the 1930s, he would often take off a week at a time from his work and somehow get away with it.

The McGees and Smith soon found they had a lot in common. They found that they knew many of the same musicians, and that they shared a common repertoire of middle Tennessee traditional and popular tunes. More importantly, all three were demanding and exacting musicians, superb technicians in the prime of their careers. Arthur was thirty-four, Sam was thirty-six, and Kirk was thirty-three. None of them had to make any serious adjustments when they began playing together. Kirk recalled: "As far as Arthur was concerned, he just added a banjo player and a guitar player. His fiddling didn't change; he had played that style all the time. Arthur didn't sing at first, though, not for a long time. Finally he got to singing, and then we couldn't stop him." Often, though, Kirk and Sam did the singing and picking, Sam did the comedy, and Arthur did the fiddling.

Shortly after the Dixieliners were formed, Smith decided the band needed a piano player. A number of the stringbands on the Opry at that time were using pianos: Dr. Humphrey Bate, Ed Poplin, Theron Hale, and for a time even the Gully Jumpers. Smith's oldest child, Lavonne, had been playing piano—Smith had bought a piano for his house when they moved to Bruceton—and now he asked Lavonne to play with the Dixieliners. Lavonne, who was still in high school at the time, began to play tours with the group in late 1932, and then played with the group on the Opry.

Lavonne recalled vividly her first time on the Opry: "He asked me to come and play with him on the Opry, and they said I could, and I got on the payroll the second Saturday night that I played. You had to sign your paper, or you didn't get your five dollars. . . . At least that's what I got. Judge Hay would always introduce us as Fiddlin' Arthur Smith, the Dixieliners, Sam and Kirk McGee, and Miss Lavonne! The first time I was ever on the Opry he had that steamboat whistle he would blow, and he was standing right over there behind me when he blew it, and I just pounded that piano. It scared me, it really did. And my daddy gave me the awfulest look you ever seen. It was a goof and Daddy didn't like goofs."

Smith was still working regularly on the Dixie Line, of course, though by 1932 he had moved his family back to Dickson. Still, there were many weekends when he would find himself quite a ways from either Nashville or Dickson on a Friday afternoon, and often would have to take the train in to meet the rest of his band in Nashville. In fact, there were many occasions when Smith would be coming in on the train from one direction, Lavonne would be taking the train in from Dickson, and Sam and Kirk would be driving in from Franklin. Somehow, they would find time to rehearse new numbers for the show. Their ten-minute segments proved popular with the Opry and its sponsors, and soon the band had a regular sponsor: an early type of all-purpose glue called Kester Metal Mender. Kirk recalled, "It was a thing you mended kitchen utensils with. Anything you had broken, like a tea kettle, you'd melt that stuff and pour it in the crack. It was a type of sawdust." The Kester company was a regular sponsor for the Dixieliners' part of the Opry for the entire six years the band was together.

The Dixieliners soon found that the fame they acquired over WSM's powerful 50,000-watt broadcasts made it possible for them to make money doing personal appearances and tours. In doing this, they were breaking the trail for the way that countless Opry acts would use their Opry experience: not for money, but for publicity.

At first, the Dixieliners would try to do the booking for personals themselves. "A lot of times," recalled Kirk, "people would write in wanting to book us. We'd go, but we'd get into the town, and there wouldn't be any advertising, nobody would know we were there, and there were times we played to less than 100 people." This kind of problem caused them to eventually hire an agent, one R. D. Wolfe (no relation to the author!), who handled bookings, took care of advertising, and in exchange got 20 percent of the take. But all the members of the group felt it was money well spent. The agent produced handbills and posters, and got them into the towns where the band was going to play. For a time the group advertised on "trailers," which followed the featured movie at local theaters where they were booked to appear. On these trailers, still photos of Smith and the McGees would be shown while fiddle music played in the background. (Ironically, this fiddle music was taken from records by Clark Kessinger, since the Dixieliners had not yet recorded on their own.) These trailers were purchased for $9 each and sent to local theaters where they would run for about a week prior to the Dixieliners' show date. At one time the group had as many as a dozen different trailers.

Another method of advertising was to show up at local radio stations and offer to do a free ten-minute show. Small-town radio stations were cropping up all over the South in the 1930s, and most of them had informal, unstructured program schedules. They were glad to make room, even on short notice, for a band from the Grand Ole Opry, and had no objection to the group plugging its latest personal appearance in the area. Sam McGee remembered that on one or two occasions the local radio station would be shut down for the afternoon, and the station manager would open up and go on the air just for the Dixieliners.

WSM was also taking steps during this time to help its artists attain the status of full-time professional artists. In 1933 the station organized the Artist Service Bureau, and began its own campaign to stimulate bookings by WSM artists. One early flyer the station sent out featured both old-time and mainstream acts (such as Lasses White and Beasley Smith), but the old-time acts were described on the front and the "pop" acts on the back. Even then, it seems, WSM knew where its real appeal lay. On this flyer the Dixieliners were described as "Arthur Smith, Sam & Kirk McGee from Tennessee, a sweet fiddle and two rural comedians." The Dixieliners were also pictured in a 1933 press book compiled for theater owners and booking agents; here they were listed as a "hillbilly" act, and their performance rates were listed as follows:

1 time per week $25.00
3 times per week $75.00
6 times per week $150.00

It is interesting to note that, while these prices are compatible with other Opry stringbands, the rates are only about a third that of the rates for the then popular vocal group, the Vagabonds. And it is also important to remember that these were 1933 dollars, a time, recalled Kirk, "when a dollar was as big as a wagon wheel." The WSM bureau got the Dixieliners even more jobs, but it took for its trouble an additional 15 percent of the revenue (on top of the manager's 20 percent). A lot of times local schoolhouses, where the shows were often held, demanded an additional 15 to 30 percent of the gate. (Many schools in the Depression actually needed this kind of income to keep afloat.) And, to top it off, when the group played mining towns, especially a company town, many of the audience paid their admission in company script, and the musicians often found that when they tried to exchange this script for cash at the company store, it was devalued by 20 percent. The Opry demanded each act that toured be in Nashville for the Saturday night show for a large number of nights each year. It was small wonder that Smith wanted to hang onto his railroad job during these early years.

Many of the trips the Dixieliners made were into small communities in and around middle Tennessee, but occasionally they made longer ones. Often they were part of a Grand Ole Opry package tour, and Kirk recalled being on traveling shows with Uncle Dave Macon, the Vagabonds, Blythe Poteet, and DeFord Bailey. Later Smith toured with the Delmore Brothers as well, and on a few occasions with both the Delmores and the McGees. Tours ranged as far as the eastern seaboard, though most of them were confined to the upper South: the Carolinas, Virginia, West Virginia, and eastern Kentucky. Kirk recalled: "One of the first times they booked us out of the state, they sent us up to Clintwood, Virginia. A little mining town. Those people went wild over Arthur's fiddling. They got a petition up and got us moved up an hour on the Opry, so a lot of miners could listen to us between shifts. Got a petition with 1,500 names on it. They got it done." On one occasion, Smith and Lavonne, accompanied by the Mulligan Brothers (a banjo-guitar act), went to Detroit, where they performed over WJR, played a few auditoriums, a sports arena, and, without Lavonne, a few bars.

What was a typical Dixieliners stage show like? Kirk remembered that when just three or four of them played, they all stayed on stage for the entire time. Numbers at the beginning and the end would feature everyone playing together, but the middle of the show would feature each person doing a series of specialty numbers: Arthur would do a few, Sam and Kirk a few, and, if Lavonne was along, she would play a couple of piano solos such as "St. Louis Blues" or "Darktown Strutter's Ball." Arthur and Kirk handled the emcee work, and Sam put on a red Toby wig to do comedy. Kirk feels that the 1957 album Smith and the McGees recorded for Folkways was a fair approximation of the kind of variety and tunes heard on these early shows. A typical show would run an hour and a half if it was the only show they did. "If we did an afternoon show in the town," recalled Kirk, "we'd make the night show a little shorter."

Smith played and toured with the McGees exclusively from 1932 through 1943. After that he began to play some with the Delmores, though he still did most of his touring and broadcasting with the McGees. They broke up for good in 1938, after playing together for six years and after making their mark on the music of the South.

RECORDING WITH THE DELMORES

In 1933 two young men from Alabama, Alton and Rabon Delmore, had joined the Opry. Alton played standard guitar, Rabon played tenor guitar, and they had a distinctive soft close-harmony singing style that was to influence generations of country musicians. Even before they had come to the Opry, Alton recalled, they had listened to the Dixieliners, and had been greatly impressed. In late 1934 the Delmores, like most younger Opry performers, were trying to build up their tour bookings, and among the people they began to tour with was Arthur Smith.

Blythe Poteet, who toured with the Delmores and Smith, recalled that the three men would often sit around in hotels jamming after hours, and that "the Delmores got the idea of using Smith on some of their records. If he would help them out on some, he had a few tunes he had written, and they would help him record." Smith, for his part, was impressed at meeting a musician like Alton, who could read and write music, and who could help with Smith's increasing attempts at songwriting.

Smith had never recorded any with Sam and Kirk, possibly because the prime of their relationship occurred during the worst part of the Depression, when nobody was getting recorded.* Also, neither Smith nor the McGees had any special connections to record companies.

* Some evidence suggests that the McGees-Smith band might well have been recorded informally. On August 26, 1934, the WSM station announced: "For the purpose of checking and comparing various programs on the air, WSM has added to its equipment the latest type of recording outfit. The recording machine will be used for auditions to be sent to prospective sponsors and for 'catching' shows on the air for the use of the pro-

When the McGees recorded with Macon for Gennett in 1934, it was the result of some audition discs Kirk had sent them out of the blue. The Delmores, on the other hand, had already recorded an extensive session for Victor in 1933. Their new vocal sound was quite appealing to the record company executives of the 1930s. All this tends to support what Alton Delmore wrote in his autobiography, *Truth Is Stranger than Publicity*:

> It was 1934 and we had a record session coming up down in New Orleans. I wrote to the company and got Arthur Smith a try-out. I knew he would make good. He paid his own way down there and his expenses, as was agreed when we first inquired. He had a free pass on the railroad trains because he worked . . . as a lineman. But when he got down to New Orleans, and Mr. Oberstein [the A&R man for Victor in charge of the field sessions] heard him play, the RCA Company paid all his expenses both ways. He made eight breakdowns, all very well played.

This session took place in January 1935. The makeshift studio was in an old building that faced an alley, and all day long the recording sessions were interrupted as heavy trucks in the alley caused the delicate recording equipment to vibrate. After the Delmores recorded their tunes, Smith recorded his, with Alton and Rabon backing him on guitars. Smith got through in a hurry, recording eight sides in two hours, and doing almost all of his numbers right on the first take. Alton recalled, "He played a lot louder than we did, and with our two guitars we could compete with the trucks pretty good."

The first record Smith made was "Lost Train Blues," a piece he probably learned from the Crook Brothers, who often featured it on the Opry. He also recorded two other "Smith classics" at this time, "Blackberry Blossom" and "Red Apple Rag." He did one of the first country versions of "Goofus," an old pop tune by bandleader Wayne King that later became a western swing favorite. He recorded "Fiddler's Dream," an original based vaguely on the chord changes of "Flop-Eared

gram and production departments. Harry Stone, manager of WSM, believes the recording device will be of great help not only to the station but to the artists who can, in a measure, hear themselves as others hear them." To date, though, I have found none of these air-checks.

Mule," and a nice version of "Mocking Bird," a tune popularized on the Opry by Theron Hale. Alton Delmore recalled all the tunes as breakdowns, but Smith also did two lovely waltzes, "Smith Waltz" and "Spring Street Waltz," the latter a "contest" waltz full of difficult double stops and trills. "Mocking Bird" and "Red Apple Rag" were even released on Bluebird's Spanish series as being by "Arturo Munez." The English-language records were released under the sole name, Arthur Smith; nothing was said on the label about the Dixieliners.

About a year later Smith did his second session for Victor, and on these he began singing. According to Alton Delmore, to sing was not exactly a matter of choice. When Alton wrote Oberstein about a time and place for the next session, Oberstein wrote back that he liked Smith's playing very much, "but he didn't do any singing, and his records didn't sell well enough to bring him back again." Alton then suggested that Smith work up some vocal material. Smith agreed, and Alton wrote this proposal back to Oberstein: "Mr. Oberstein liked the idea fine. He said that he didn't want to let Arthur go in the first place. . . . Mr. Oberstein had a boss too, and he had to take some orders, same as we did. So I gave the good news to Arthur and we agreed to get together on some songs suitable for records. He had some songs about finished and I helped him finish them . . . and together we got a good batch of material for the session. In this first session with us all singing, there were several good sellers and one hit record: 'There's More Pretty Girls Than One.'"

Starting with this session, Smith formed a pattern which was to characterize most of his later records. A session usually contained some singing, a few original numbers, a few older pop numbers, and some traditional numbers that Smith had reworked and rearranged. Between 1935 and 1938 he did a total of five sessions with the Delmores, usually releasing the sides as by "The Arthur Smith Trio," not the Dixieliners. Smith also backed up the Delmores on many of their records, and things eventually got to the point where it was hard to tell whether a record was a Delmore record or a Smith record. There are several cases (such as the famous recording of "House of David Blues") where the Bluebird release of a record would be by Arthur Smith, while the parallel Montgomery Ward release of the same record would read as by the Delmore Brothers. All told, Smith did some fifty-two sides with the Delmores under his own name, many of them well-known fiddle and vocal classics: "Pig in the Pen," "Walking in My Sleep," "Love Letters in the Sand," "Chittlin' Cookin' Time in Cheatham County," "Kilby Jail," "Florida Blues," "Nellie's Blue Eyes," and the most famous of all, "Beautiful Brown Eyes."

Smith also during this time participated in a number of the "commercialized" fiddling contests I have discussed elsewhere. These were stage shows which would feature a "showdown" between two or three leading fiddlers of the time. One of the biggest promoters of these contests was Larry Sunbrock, and he often hired Smith to go against fiddlers like Curly Fox, Clayton McMichen, Clark Kessinger, and Natchee the Indian, the fiddler from Oklahoma. Kirk McGee remembered one such contest where Clayton McMichen hired Smith and the McGees to come to Cincinnati for a show which included a fiddling contest, the winner to be determined by audience applause. Smith really won the contest, judging from applause, but McMichen finally stepped forward to claim the prize. Smith couldn't object, since it was McMichen who had hired him. Smith didn't enter too many "legitimate" contests after he turned professional, though.

During this time Smith had been spending more and more of his time away from his railroad job. He would save up his vacation time to do touring, and when he used up that he would simply take off time without pay from the railroad. Gradually, though, with income from personals and from records, Smith was making enough to enable him to quit the railroad and make music as a full-time vocation.

He was also finding some other work on WSM, and in 1937 was playing in addition to the Opry, with a pop-oriented country group called Jack Shook & His Missouri Mountaineers. Shook had come to WSM in 1934 and won fame as a fine guitarist and an average vocalist. In the mid-1930s he teamed up with two singers from the Opry's Big Yank show, Nap Bastian and Dee Simmons, to form a pop-country singing group that resembled, in the words of Blythe Poteet, "a poor man's Sons of the Pioneers." Later, accordion player Bobby Castleman joined the group, and then Smith joined as fiddler. The Mountaineers were a sophisticated group, and Shook soon had to teach Smith how to play from a musical arrangement. It was valuable experience and helped Smith out in later years.

Both the Delmores and Smith had the reputations around WSM as hard drinkers. This led to some wild scenes on the road. Kirk McGee recalled one scene in particular.

I remember once in Marion, North Carolina. Sam and I were on the first floor, and Alton and Rabon and Arthur were in a room on the second floor, and they were pretty drunk. People was callin' the manager, wanting to quiet 'em down. I went up there, said "Why don't you all go to bed?" And Arthur says, "We're gonna catch it when it comes around again." Well, they fell across this bed, iron railings and all, and bent 'em to the floor. I went back up there. And Alton, he talked real soft, he says, "Now Kirk, we're all together and we're gonna have to pay for this bed. You in your part?" And I said, "No, I never got in that bed." They had to pay for the bed.

Other aspects of the drinking were not so funny, and in 1938 this was one of the factors that caused the Delmores to leave the Opry. (It was not, however, the *only* factor.) It also got Smith into trouble with the Opry management. In February 1938, David Stone organized a special Opry tour group to go into a west Tennessee town. According to Alton Delmore, "A group of sponsors down in west Tennessee wrote in and said their sheriff could beat our best Grand Ole Opry fiddler, and wanted to put on a contest to prove it." When the night of the big show came, all the Opry acts showed up except Smith: the "best fiddler" that the sheriff had challenged. "The sheriff was there, with his bow all rosined up and his fiddle in tune, and he was raring to go. He was a politician, and this thing would help him out, win or lose. But our fiddler didn't show." Stone was furious, and when he finally found Smith he announced that he was going to suspend him for four weeks, and bring in a new band each week to play in his place. Alton says that Smith told him later what had happened that night: "his friends, who were bringing him down, stopped and got them some moonshine. They got too much of it and decided not to go to the contest, and they knew he was at their mercy. So they just laughed at him when he begged them to take him on to the town. He was given the horse laugh, and he learned a lesson not to trust a lot of people after that. He told David [Stone] the same story but David would not accept it."

The suspension was unfair to Smith and must have made him bitter toward the Opry. But it led to other important consequences: one of the four new bands that Stone brought in to replace Smith was a group from Knoxville headed by a young tow-headed singer named Roy Acuff.

THE TRANSITION YEARS, 1938–1945

One of the members of the Vagabonds, the popular vocal group that had toured with both Smith and the Delmores, was Herald Goodman. When the Vagabonds split up in 1938, Goodman decided to form his own band, and put together a group called the Tennessee Valley Boys. It was a young, exciting band which played a fine mixture of traditional Southeastern music and western swing: one of the numerous bands at the time that might be classified as "Southeastern swing" bands. The lead fiddler was a very young Howdy Forrester, and his brother Joe played bass; Billy Byrd played guitar; and an Ohio native named Virgil Atkins played banjo.

As Howdy Forrester recalled, Goodman was a clever showman who "knew he needed a well-known performer from the Opry to draw people. Smith was about the hottest act on the Opry then, so Goodman hired him. We toured all over east Kentucky, West Virginia, Virginia, and North Carolina." By 1939 Goodman had decided to quit the Opry and strike out on his own, and Smith agreed to go with him. In September 1938 the group did a session in Rock Hill, South Carolina, for RCA Victor-Bluebird. Goodman's group did several sides (including the exciting "Banjo Rag") and then Smith recorded ten sides with Goodman's band backing him. This included a fine version of "In the Pines," with Forrester twin fiddling with Smith, and the first recording of the popular "I've Had a Big Time Today." After this session, the group took off for east Texas.

Forrester recalled that Smith was a skillful and fascinating teacher, and he learned a lot from him. Also in the fall of 1939, Georgia Slim Rutland joined Goodman's crew, giving them three fiddlers—three of the most famous fiddlers in Southeastern music. What this band must have sounded like, God only knows. What ideas or techniques Smith and Rutland might have exchanged we shall never know. But the band did broadcast regularly over KVOO in Tulsa, Bob Wills's old stomping ground. By 1940 Smith had moved down to Shreveport to join the Shelton Brothers at KWKH. That station was just beginning to emerge as a powerful country music station and was actively building its roster of country stars. The Shelton Brothers were riding the crest of a long string of successful records for Decca, and were used to working with fiddlers of the caliber of Curly Fox. Other noted old-time artists on the station at that time included the Rice Brothers, fiddler Ernie Hodges, and old-time fiddler Charlie Bowman. The music of KWKH must have approximated that of the Opry in the early 1930s and should have been more congenial to Smith. It wasn't, though, and he didn't stay with the Sheltons very long. He played for a time with pick-up bands around New Orleans, and by the latter half of 1940 had relocated in northern Alabama.

He stayed with eldest daughter Lavonne in Decatur, Alabama, and organized a local band to play over station WMFO (now WMFL) in Decatur in the fall of 1940. This band included Arthur "Firecracker" Burns on guitar and Arthur "Happy" Parker on mandolin. "The whole band was named Arthur," joked Lavonne. Smith continued to compose songs during this time, and worked on "Crazy Blues" and "Yodeling Blues" that fall.

Smith had a scheduled session for Victor in October 1940, though, and did not have a band lined up to back him. His Decatur band did not really have the experience and seasoning, he felt, for recording demands. As the session approached, he returned to Nashville and found that young Bill Monroe, who had just recently joined the Opry with his new band, the Blue Grass Boys, also had a session for Victor scheduled in Atlanta at the same time his was. Thus on October 7, 1940, he rode with Bill and his band down to Atlanta. Bass player Bill Wesbrooks did the driving. "We took Bill's straight-eight Country Club Hudson," Wesbrooks recalled, "and drove down to Atlanta that morning, recorded sixteen sides in four hours, and drove back to Nashville that night. Arthur was kind of down on his luck at the time, and he didn't have anybody to back him on his records. He asked Bill if Clyde Moody and Tommy Magness and I could back him, and Bill said yes. We hadn't played with Arthur at all; we just followed him as best we could, and he did eight records right after Bill did his session." Wesbrooks got $120 for the two sessions, and laughs over the fact that Smith asked him to give him his (Wesbrooks's) share of union scale for playing on Smith's record. Wesbrooks refused.

That was a fruitful day in Atlanta. It was held in the Kimball Hotel at Five Points. "They had rented two big rooms down there, with a sliding door in between them," recalled Wesbrooks. The sessions were supervised by Frank Walker and Dan Hornsby, who had worked together in the pioneering Columbia 15000 series that documented so much of the old-time music of the 1920s. Monroe recorded his famous version of "Mule Skinner Blues" at the early session; in the later session, Smith and Tommy Magness did some incredible twin fiddling on "K.C. Stomp," one of Smith's originals. Later, Clyde Moody did some fine back-up work on "Crazy Blues" and Bill Wesbrooks's bass propelled Smith in one of his finest fiddle breakdowns, "Bill Cheatham." The session marked the start of one era, the end of another; it was the first recording done by Bill Monroe on his own, and it was the last of the famous Bluebird sessions for Smith. And, to top it all off, a year before the session Hitler had invaded Poland, and set off a chain of events that were to mark every aspect of American life.

In 1941 Smith continued to play in northern Alabama, first in and around Decatur, and then in Birmingham. There he joined Zeke Phillips & His 49ers, playing over Birmingham station WSGN. In 1942 the Bailes Brothers—Walter and Johnnie—played for a few weeks on WSGN and met Smith. Both were impressed with him. The Bailes Brothers had been regularly appearing over WSAZ in Huntington, West Virginia, on an Opry-like program called the "Tri-State Jamboree." When the Baileses returned to West Virginia, they prevailed on Flem Evans, their manager and promoter, to hire Smith for the show. Evans agreed, and by 1942 Smith was in West Virginia. For a time he was in Bluefield, but spent most of his time playing dates out of Huntington.

Walter Bailes recalled that Smith usually traveled with his brother, himself, and Little Evy, all regulars on the "Jamboree." "With us, he played pretty much the same stuff he had done with the Delmore Brothers. We had parts of the show where we featured his solos, and then there were some numbers where Arthur and I sang duets. One of his favorite numbers back then was 'Look What Those Blue Eyes Did to Me.' Another was an arrangement we worked out, sort of a novelty thing, of 'Orange Blossom Special.'" This latter number had been recorded only three years before by the Rouse Brothers—Ervin Rouse had composed it—but had not yet attained the wide popularity it now enjoys. Walter Bailes thinks Smith's frequent performance of the tune did a great deal to make it a fiddle standard; indeed, Smith played it as his showpiece throughout the 1940s. Bailes also notes that while with them, Smith played another fiddle tune destined to become a standard, Leslie Keith's "Black Mountain Rag." He did this in addition to playing his established favorites like "Pig in the Pen" and "More Pretty Girls."

Bailes was especially impressed with Smith's singing: "They say that Acuff was the Opry's first big solo singer, but I think if Arthur had stayed, he might have given *any* of them competition."

Smith was by this time putting more and more emphasis on his singing and songwriting. In 1943 he published two important songbooks, *Songs from the Hills of Tennessee* (which he published in Huntington to sell over the air and at personals) and *Arthur Smith's Original Folk Song Folio No. 1*, a more elaborate songbook with music transcribed by Alton Delmore and published by the American Music Company in Oregon. Both of these songbooks contain, obviously, only songs and none of the instrumental tunes with which Smith is normally associated. *Songs from the Hills of Tennessee* ("as composed and sung by Arthur Smith, formerly of WSM Grand Ole Opry") contains a number of songs which Smith apparently sang on the air and at personals, but which he never recorded. Included is "Low and Lonely," a tune normally associated with Roy Acuff, and others such as "Fort Worth Jail," "Honey I'm in Love with You," and "Baby Girl." Most of the "newer" songs are distinctly sentimental songs or "aching heart" songs. The American Music folio contains twenty songs, nearly all recorded by Smith, and many of them more solidly based in tradition. A close look at these two songbooks shows Smith's career in transition, though, from the tradition oriented music of the Dixieliners and the Delmores toward the new more popular country music of the 1940s.

Toward the end of 1943, the Bailes Brothers left WSAZ to join the Grand Ole Opry. For a time, Smith stayed on in the area and spent the first half of 1945 playing with the York Brothers in Bluefield, West Virginia, and in the latter half of the year he returned to Detroit and played at the Jefferson Inn with his son Earnest. After the war was over, he returned to Alabama, and early 1946 found him playing with the excellent cowboy singer Rex Griffith over station WSGN in Birmingham. At this time "western" music was sweeping the country, and the cowboy image was dominating country music. Smith found that he could play this sort of music very well and sensed that it was the wave of the future.

The West Coast Days

Sometime in 1946 Smith drifted south to rejoin for a short time his old boss Herald Goodman. Goodman was now known as "Cousin

Herald," and he had a regular program called "Saddle Mountain Round-Up" on station KRLD in Dallas. While he was there, Joe Frank, a well-known promoter and then manager of Gene Autry, put Smith in touch with cowboy singer and actor Jimmy Wakely. Wakely had started out as one of Autry's back-up singers and now was starting his own successful career as a single. Wakely was impressed with Smith's fiddling and invited him to come to California with him. Smith accepted.

Smith stayed with Jimmy Wakely for most of 1946, and all of 1947 and 1948. Jimmy has described in a letter to me (see facsimile) some of his own special memories of Smith. It is important to realize that during this time, Wakely was perhaps the most popular cowboy singer in the country, and he was getting wide exposure in clubs, on records, and in films. He had a number of big hits including "One Has My Name, the Other Has My Heart" and "Slippin' Around." He was doing several films a year—popular music-filled singing cowboy films for Monogram. During the time Smith was with Wakely, he probably reached more of an audience than ever before in his career. Smith had always had a great deal of regional (Southern) appeal; now, however, he was acquiring a certain national appeal. Jimmy Wakely's account of rich New Yorkers dancing between the tables at plush Las Vegas clubs when they heard Smith certainly dramatizes this fact.

He also became a movie star. Smith appeared in a number of motion pictures with Wakely, primarily as a musician. (On a few occasions Smith was filmed playing the piano.) Though he came from Tennessee hill country, Smith was no cowboy. Lavonne recalled on one memorable occasion the director got Smith aboard a horse, but when he gave the order for the camera to roll, the horse started moving, Smith did not, and one Tennessee fiddler bit the dust. Some of the more notable films in which Smith appeared include *Oklahoma Blues, Saddle Serenade, Song of the Range, Lonesome Trail,* and *Sunrise Serenade.* None of these were destined to become film classics—they were low-budget two-reelers produced for the Saturday afternoon Bijou circuit—but they were good, solid examples of the singing cowboy genre.

Smith was continuing to develop his considerable songwriting talent during these days. As usual, most of Smith's songs were in more of the popular country vein than in the old-time vein; many were senti-

Jimmy Wakely

4720 FORMAN AVENUE
NORTH HOLLYWOOD, CALIFORNIA 91602

Oct 30, 1977

Mr. Charles Wolfe   Re! Arthur Smith

Dear Charles:

Arthur Smith joined me on a tour in 1945. I left the coast
for an opening date at Pampa, Texas. Arthur came up from
Dallas Texas to join me. He stayed at our ranch after that
for roughly three years... toured with me.

Arthur never played on my records... He did work in several
western pictures with me at Monogram. His style was not
the sound I was using on records... but he could fit in real
good in pictures.

To a degree, Arthur was limited... but only to the degree
that he was so great as a fiddle player with a definate
style that he didn't have to play anything else.

He played the Last Frontier hotel with me in Las Vegas and
when he started playing, those people would often get up and
dance between tables... They would holler and yell... He really
made them let go. I am talking about the days when the very
rich came to Las Vegas to live 6 weeks and get their divorce...
Many from New York where they had never heard a country fiddle
player.

I first met Arthur at Tulsa when he was working with the
(Harold Goodman) Saddle Mountaun Roundup. He stood on the
stage at a filled auditoreum and played solo (no band) his
arrangement of ORANGE BLOSSOM SPECIAL and stopped the show.
This was in 1939 when I was working at WKY Oklahoma City.

I had been his fan since I listened to him on the Opry on
those Saturday nights in 1929... Its true, his story is
short... but it is good as he was a great fiddle player,
a n exciting artist... a good friend.

Sincerely Wakely

JIMMY WAKELY

mental love songs. A number of these later songs he co-authored with Jimmy Wakely, including numbers like "I'm Always Blue for You." At one point Wakely had quite a hit with one of Smith's songs called "Dry the Tears from Your Blue, Blue Eyes," and once Smith backed up Wakely as he made a special guest appearance on the Opry.

Smith also continued his recording career while he was on the West Coast. Though he never recorded on any of Wakely's hit records for Capitol, he did record under his own name for at least three different labels. In the fall of 1946 he did six sides for Black & White, one of the new independent labels that sprang up on the coast after the war. Most of the artists the label recorded were jazz musicians, though they made an effort to develop some country acts. (One of the other country artists they recorded at this time was Bennie Hess.) Smith did some stints touring to promote these records (he made one appearance at Buckley's in Nashville, autographing new Black & White releases), but they were less than successful, probably because of the limited distribution system of the company.

In October 1947 Smith went back into the studio, this time at Capitol, one of the biggest and most prestigious labels of the time. Wakely recorded for Capitol and this may have been a factor in getting Smith on the label. His first Capitol release, his first record in seven years, was "Crazy Blues" backed with his own arrangement of "Orange Blossom Special." The record was released December 15, 1947, and the record got national notices in the music press. *Billboard* reported, on December 6, 1947, that "Arthur Smith, who was featured for years on the Grand Ole Opry as hot fiddle and is now a member of Jimmy Wakely's troupe, is cutting for Capitol. . . ." "Crazy Blues" was a souped-up version of Smith's 1940 Bluebird recording and featured an exciting "take-off" fiddle solo by Smith—one of the few he recorded. There's also an interesting electric guitar solo by some unknown guitarist. (Smith's back-up band on all these West Coast recordings was a modern, electric country band, but none of the members have yet been identified.) It was a sign of the changing times that when Capitol released the record on its "Americana" series, the label read "The Original Arthur Smith, and his Dixieliners." The phrase "Original" was deemed necessary because of the recent popularity of North Carolina musician Arthur "Guitar Boogie" Smith.

Smith later told Kirk McGee that his drinking eventually caused him to leave Wakely and start wandering again. By 1949 he was back in

Dallas, playing again with Goodman, and on the famous "Big D Jamboree," which had been organized in 1947. One of the people he played with was Billy Walker, a future Ozark Jubilee and Grand Ole Opry star. In 1950 he was back in the Nashville area, playing with his old friend Blythe Poteet in the Tennessee gubernatorial campaign of Pat Sutton.

The low point of his career came in 1951. For the first time in over twenty-five years Smith didn't really play much music. He spent most of the time working in and around Nashville as a carpenter with his brother Raymond. He had earlier been injured in an accident—someone had hit him in the back with a rock—and he wasn't fully recovered from that misfortune. Then, to make matters worse, one of his songs, "Beautiful Brown Eyes," became a big popular hit when it was recorded by a number of singers, including Roy Acuff. Alton Delmore had worked out the lead sheet for the song with Smith, and Smith and the Delmores had recorded it under his name back in 1937; the song had been included in Smith's copyrighted song folio of 1943. Yet now Smith's claim was being challenged by two New York writers who were claiming the song was public domain. Smith was quick to defend his rights to the song. A letter that survives from April 2, 1951, gives insight into this, as well as into Smith's blunt, direct manner of dealing with controversy. He wrote to Mr. Sylvester L. Cross, president of American Music, Inc. (who had published Smith's 1943 songbook):

> If your letter of March 24, 1951 is based on true facts, there would be no reason for you to give me $1,000.00 for nothing, because, if the song is in "public domain" and if I have no right thereto, then I would have no right to sell something of which I have no part therein.
>
> However, I am advising you now that I am the composer of this song known as "Beautiful Brown Eyes" and that I have a contract with you which I executed some years ago. I am definitely not interested in selling my rights to this song or selling my contract on same.
>
> I am hereby notifying you that I want full and complete settlement with you, as per my contract on the song "Beautiful Brown Eyes."
>
> Please keep me advised on the success of "Beautiful Brown Eyes" in all details.

The members of the Smith family believe that this particular dispute was settled with a quitclaim in which Arthur had to settle on a lump sum instead of royalties. (Alton Delmore, who had also filed a claim on the song, had to settle his claim for $1,500.) Just what kind of settlement Smith finally arrived at is unclear, though the family thought they they continued to get some royalties on the song.

The event, however, was another unsettling experience for Smith, and one which climaxed one of his worst years.

THE FINAL YEARS

By the mid-1950s Arthur Smith saw a musical world that had changed drastically from the one he was accustomed to. Even the "modern" heart songs Smith had been writing seemed old-fashioned in the face of the new rockabilly and rhythm & blues sounds coming from Memphis. It was one of the bleakest periods in modern times for lovers of fiddle music, or for old-time music. It looked like the kind of music Smith knew and loved was inexorably doomed to extinction.

Still, there was some work to be found for a good all-around fiddler, which is what Smith had become by now. In 1956 Jimmy Wakely called him back to California for a series of radio shows. While there, Smith renewed his friendship with other West Coast musicians like Merle Travis.

When he returned to Nashville, he found that his former Dixieliners, Sam and Kirk McGee, had made contact with a young man named Mike Seeger. Seeger had heard the McGees perform the year before at a show at New River Ranch in Maryland, and had been very impressed with the authentic old-time music they had played. Seeger and number of other young musicians from the North and East had been exploring the roots of stringband music and were busy hunting up old musicians from the "golden age" of old-time music, the 1920s. Seeger was now in Nashville wanting to record the McGee Brothers for an album on Folkways Records. The McGees, somewhat bemused by their new status as "folk" musicians, were willing enough to record; they had continued to play on the Opry during all the years Smith was bouncing around the country, but the Opry had recently threatened to drop them if they didn't agree to tour more. Kirk suggested to Seeger that Smith be included in the session, and soon the Dixieliners were reunited for the first time in almost twenty years.

Seeger brought a portable tape recorder into Kirk's home in Brentwood in November 1957, and the three began to tape tunes. "It was sort of hectic," Seeger recalled later. "They'd get to playing something, and then stop and remember something else, and play some of that. You had to get one minute of one thing here, two minutes of usable stuff there." Sam, Kirk, and Arthur were stirring up a lot of memories. Arthur recorded a number of fiddle tunes he had played with the McGees but had never before recorded, like "Cumberland Gap," "Sixteen on Sunday," "Dusty Miller," and others. The men were rusty on some of the old tunes. All three had been playing more modern music in their day-to-day music careers. The session finally ended, and all three promised to get together soon to do some more songs to round out the album. This second session never really came about though. Seeger held onto the tapes for almost six years hoping to get the second session, but one thing or another kept the three from getting together. Finally, out of a sense of desperation, Folkways released the album in 1964, seven years after the tunes were recorded.

Smith, meanwhile, had found another outlet for his energies: bluegrass music. Lester Flatt and Earl Scruggs were revolutionizing the face of bluegrass with their incredible instrumental and vocal stylings, and Smith indirectly had a significant role in their success. By 1957 Flatt & Scruggs were making more personal appearances than any other Opry act. One of the mainstays of the Flatt & Scruggs band was fiddler Paul Warren, who had joined the band after spending fifteen years with Johnnie & Jack, another fine Opry group. Warren was a great admirer of Smith's fiddling and made no bones about the fact that he emulated Smith's style. He spent many nights jamming with Smith and recording him on his home tape recorder. Through his personal appearances with Flatt & Scruggs, he carried Smith's style and many of his tunes to a new generation of young bluegrass musicians. He also played on a number of the Smith tunes recorded by Flatt & Scruggs, such as "Pig in the Pen." Smith also jammed a lot with Earl Scruggs. On at least one occasion Earl recorded a fantastic home tape of himself and Smith playing through Smith's incredible repertoire of traditional fiddle tunes. This tape, which has been circulated underground for years, was supposedly the source from which bluegrass star banjoist Bill Keith learned his version of "Blackberry Blossom," which became a bluegrass standard after Keith and fiddler Billy Baker (another young Smith devotee) recorded it in 1965. To fans of the incredible fiddle-banjo duets that Paul Warren and Earl Scruggs used to play on the radio, the tape represents even more of an interesting source document.

None of this, however, materially affected Smith's career, and by 1959 he had returned again to Detroit, where he stayed with his son Earnest. He continued to work at his songwriting, with more than a little success. In 1959 a promising young singer named Marijohn Wilkin recorded a Smith tune, "Why Did You Go Away?" for Columbia Records. Then in 1963, Don Pierce of Starday Records in Nashville contacted Smith. Pierce, who had been having a lot of success with his move toward acoustic bluegrass music, had decided to record a series of albums by Opry old-timers, like Lew Childre, Robert Lunn, the McGees, and the Crook Brothers. Pierce wanted Smith to do an LP in this series. Smith agreed, and, accompanied by his son Earnest on guitar, cut an LP called *Rare Old Time Fiddle Tunes*. It contained fourteen fiddle tunes—no vocals—and included a number of Smith favorites that had never been recorded before: "North Carolina Breakdown," "Louise," "Dixieliners' Ramble," and "Cumberland Waltz."

About this same time, Smith began to hear from Mike Seeger again. Though it had had little effect in Nashville, the folk revival was in full swing among young people in the North and West, and in the urban centers of the nation. Much of this movement did little but enrich acts like the Kingston Trio and the Weavers. However, one of the by-products was a serious, but short-lived interest in the genuine traditional musicians who were the sources for much of the folk music. Pop Stoneman, Tom Ashley, Maybelle Carter, and dozens of other leading lights from the 1920s were being "rediscovered" and invited to play at colleges and concerts, before audiences that had little in common with the Southeastern tradition they represented. Sam, Kirk, and Arthur soon joined this circuit. The Newport Folk Foundation sponsored special concerts by the trio in New York, Boston, and Philadelphia. After Kirk and Arthur convinced Sam (who was reluctant) to make the trip into the North, the three found a warm and receptive audience for their old-time music. The climax, perhaps, came with the rousing ovation they received at the July 1965 Newport Folk Festival.

Partly as a result of this new-found popularity, Folkways recorded a second LP by the trio in 1968. Like the first, this LP featured a variety of different songs, including a number of fiddle breakdowns played by Smith with strong backing by Sam and Kirk. Smith also played some banjo on this album. (Smith was an interesting claw-hammer banjo player—no one seems to know where he picked this up—but had earlier recorded only one example of it, "I'm Bound to Ride," for Bluebird.) He backed Kirk's fiddling on an old Civil War tune, "Lafayette," and played an interesting solo he called "Uncle Buddy." He also recorded his famous version of "Whistling Rufus," where he played the middle chorus with the bow right on the bridge, giving the fiddle a strange, hollow, distant sound.

But the folk festival tours and the record albums were now becoming few and far between, and Smith spent a lot of his time playing with old pals around the middle Tennessee area. Smith traveled a lot during the last several years, and a lot of his friends, sensing perhaps that his days were numbered, made home recordings of his playing. Walter Bailes recalled one such home session:

> About 1970, Arthur went down to see Zeke Phillips in Birmingham. This was after Zeke had joined Country Boy Eddie. Arthur worked a few dates, did a few guest shots on Eddie's show. I was there one day and Arthur was staying at his daughter's home in Centertown, and we went out there, went in the study, closed the door, took out our instruments, and we played. Man, we played. He played like he was in his prime: he was every bit as good. But I didn't have a recorder. I've wished many a time since that I had had a recorder for that afternoon. Johnny Wright, he had more sense. When Arthur visited him next week, Johnny got it all on tape.

He continued to wander restlessly. We get confused glimpses of him here and there. He played for a couple of years at Terrytown in Loretta, for square dances. ("It was the only time I've ever known my daddy to play with a electric pick-up," recalled Lavonne.) He went into the hospital in 1968, and shortly after he got out, he attended one of the first fiddling conventions of the Tennessee Valley Old Time Fiddlers Association. Shortly thereafter, he moved to Louisville, and in 1969 made his last appearance at Bean Blossom, with Sleepy Marlin and Tommy Riggs. He got sick again in January 1971, went into a hospital again, and the end finally came on February 28, 1971.

The services were held in Dickson. His old friends from the Opry, the old-timers from Dickson and Humphreys counties, and many friends and fans of all sorts braved the cold weather to pay their final respects. He was buried in James Cemetery, near McEwen, just a few miles from where Smith had first learned to scrape out a tune on a fiddle. The music, and the man, had come full circle. Five days later Roy Acuff announced Smith's death to the vast radio audience of the Grand Ole Opry. "He was the king of the fiddlers," Acuff said, and thousands across the country nodded.

THE MUSIC OF ARTHUR SMITH

When anyone begins talking about Arthur Smith's most important legacy, his music, the talk always gets around to one thing: his fiddling style. What was it about Smith's playing that allowed him to attract such large audiences when old-time fiddling in general was in decline? What was it about his playing that caused other fiddlers who heard him only casually to remember for years afterwards his skill? What was it that enabled him to be a looming influence over fiddlers at today's conventions, even while nearly all of his records were out of print?

In a very real sense, Smith was one of the first "modern" fiddlers. His 1935 recordings bore very little relationship to the fiddle music that had preceded them on record. The fiddling of the late 1920s that dominated the records was heavily influenced by the north Georgia shuffle style of people like Earl Johnson and Gid Tanner. Suddenly, five years later, we have Smith, with a fiddling style that is somehow, in some way, radically different. And somehow Smith's style sounds, to modern ears, like "contest fiddling," whereas none of the other old-time fiddlers remind us of this.

Smith himself apparently never talked much about his style. He simply called what he did "country fiddling." His children call the style simply "rolling notes" or "long bowing" or "continuous bowing." I asked Howdy Forrester what he thought was different about Smith's style, and he said: "The thing I remember is that Arthur did more with the fingering than with the bow. He did a lot of accents with his fingers, where the rest of us at that time—Clayton McMichen, myself, and others—we did it with more bow work. Arthur also tended to leave a lot of the rhythm to his back-up men, to the guitar." This emphasis on finger action reminds us of what Grady Stringer—Smith's alleged mentor—said ("I used my fingers mostly") about developing his style. Walter Bailes also emphasized that Smith's style was very important, that his success didn't come simply from being a good technician. "His style was different; his finger action was the difference. He could get two notes to a normal fiddler's one." Kirk McGee said: "It was the way, I think, he held his hands. His action was so fast, he'd get disgusted, wanting to play so fast. He'd put in all those little grace notes."

Many of the musicians who played with Smith stress over and over again that he had a good knowledge of his fingerboard, and that his accents were clean and sharp. This especially comes out in the way Smith controlled his E string. Such clear noting is one of the benchmarks of modern contest fiddling. But Smith was an aggressive fiddler as well, especially when compared to other clean-noting technicians of his day, like Kessinger or McMichen. On many records Smith seems to be charging into a tune, deliberately setting a blistering tempo. Perhaps one of the reasons he played and wrote so many rags was because they gave him a chance to do a lot of fast, sharp noting. Part of his style must also be his "blues" influence, usually apparent in his use of sliding notes. And part of his style must also be found in his waltzes, all too often underemphasized in Smith's work. As far as I can tell, he was one of the first Southern fiddlers to make use of the kind of daring octave jumps so much in favor in today's contests (as in his "Paris Waltz"), and his fondness for double stops apparently influenced many a fiddler ("Love Letters in the Sand").

To be sure, Smith did his share of trick fiddling. Walter Bailes recalled, "We had to talk him into doing trick stuff. It wasn't his favorite type of fiddling." Yet this obviously pleased audiences. One of Smith's most famous publicity poses for WSM shows him playing the fiddle while holding the bow under on crossed leg. His clean noting made his version of "Mocking Bird" a thing to remember. Dick Burnett, the great old Kentucky minstrel who heard most of Kentucky's best fiddlers, recalled that Smith "played the 'Mocking Bird' so clear you could see the feathers." His trick version of "Whistling Rufus," in which he played high up on the bridge, attracted attention, as did his version of "Green Valley Waltz," in which he sang the last chorus in wordless harmony with his own fiddle. (Mike Seeger reports, incidentally, that Smith was the only fiddler he had ever seen do that.) In songs like "Louise" and "Had a Big Time Tonight" he has his fiddle echo the vocal line, much in the way a blues guitarist echoes a line with his guitar. In "Orange Blossom Special" he goes through most of the usual histrionics that have come to characterize that song (and get it banned from most serious fiddling contests).

Nor should we overlook Smith's songwriting in assessing his overall importance. Smith took this part of his career very seriously, and he produced a number of fine vocal songs. He published three or four songbooks during his career, and all the songs in these books were songs Smith customarily sang on the radio and on tour. "Once we got him to singing, we couldn't get him to stop," recalled Kirk McGee. Indeed, Smith was a good singer. He had a warm, flexible voice and knew his range very well. Walter Bailes said: "I would say that if Arthur, with his singing, had stayed on the Opry, he could have given any of them competition. People say Acuff was the Opry's first good solo singer, but Arthur was doing fine singing way before Roy Acuff came on the show." Perhaps not everyone would agree with Walter Bailes's enthusiasm for Smith's singing, but no one can argue with the quality of Smith's songs. He composed constantly, usually playing a number over and over on the fiddle until he got it right. "He would lay in bed on his back with that fiddle and work on songs, moving his foot in time," said Walter Bailes.

In the 1930s, Smith wrote many of his vocal songs with the Delmore Brothers and recorded with the Delmores many of his finest songs. In some cases, there appears to have been a genuine collaboration; in others, Alton Delmore seems to have merely acted as a transcriber and editor for the songs. (And, in fact, Alton admits as much in his "Preface" to Smith's folio *Arthur Smith's Original Folk Songs*: "Arthur plays by ear and doesn't read music, so I helped him get these songs ready for our publishers.") The folio lists such songs as "I've Had a Big Time Today" and "There's More Pretty Girls Than One" as coauthored by Alton and Smith, but lists other songs like "Pig at Home in the Pen," "Walking in My Sleep," "The Farmer's Daughter," and "Why Should I Wonder" as solely Smith's songs.

Everybody has his or her own favorite Smith fiddle tune. Many of the classics have already been mentioned in the history of Smith's career. Perhaps his most single famous tune was "Blackberry Blossom." His daughter Lavonne recalled how Smith composed this song. "In 1931 we were living down at Bruceton and Daddy began working on this song, but he didn't have a name for it. So later on that next year he began to play it over the air at WSM, still didn't have a name for it. So the station decided to have a contest to name it, and offered a $5 prize to the person who submitted the best name. He had the letters sent to the post office down there, and it got to where we had to go get the mail with a cardboard box, we got so many letters. The winning title was 'Blackberry Blossom,' and it came from a woman in Arkansas. She named it because it was the time of the year—March—when the blackberry blossoms come out."

There are several different older fiddle tunes with the name "Blackberry Blossom," and Smith's version should not be confused with any of these older ones. It does bear some resemblance, in the A part, to a Kentucky tune played by Dick Burnett, and recorded in 1930, though it is possible that Burnett picked up his tune from hearing Smith play over the radio. Smith's B part is quite different from Burnett's.

Most of the rest of Smith's fiddle tunes fall into three categories: tunes that Smith composed himself, tunes that are solidly in tradition (such as "Bill Cheatham," "Katy Hill," and "Bonaparte's Retreat"), and tunes that are borrowed from jazz, blues, or pop sources (such as "Goofus," "Chittlin' Cookin' Time in Cheatham County"—a variant of "St. James Infirmary"—and "House of David Blues"). Of these, by far the most interesting are the former category, the originals, which must include most of the real Smith classics: "Peacock Rag, Tree Stomp," "Fiddler's Dream," "Red Apple Rag," "Dickson County Blues," "Florida Blues" (picked up widely by bluegrass fiddlers), and "Smith's Rag."

ARTHUR SMITH THE MAN

After all is said and done, though, we are left with the puzzling enigma of Arthur Smith as a human being, as a personality. What kind of a man produced this great music and these important changes? We apparently don't have any direct evidence about this: nothing survives in which Smith really speaks for himself, and explains who he thought he was, and what he was trying to do, what his music meant to him, and what it cost him. Though it seems everybody's brother has home tapes of Smith fiddling, apparently no one thought to sit down with him and interview him, or let him talk about himself for posterity. What we have left are scattered insights into Smith by his friends and family, and the hints they provide about the kind of man Smith was.

First off, Smith was a serious man, and he approached most of what he did with a certain amount of directness and purposefulness. He took his fiddling very seriously, for instance, and believed in the dignity of his calling. In 1933, for instance, Judge Hay decided to have publicity photos of the Opry bands made, and, in order to enhance the "rustic" or "hayseed" image he was building for the show, he dressed the musicians in old clothes and put them in rural settings. Sam McGee told me (before he died) that when the Dixieliners session with the photographer came up, Smith showed up on time wearing his best suit, ready for the picture. But the photographers insisted that he take off the suit, don old clothes, and pose with the McGees in, of all places, a pig pen. "Arthur was furious," Sam recalled. "He first threatened not to go through with it, but he finally came around. But if you look at that picture, you can tell he's mad." The picture, ironically, became one of the Dixieliners' most popular publicity shots, and is still used widely today. If you look closely on good copies of it, you can still see a pig over to the left.

Smith didn't approve of trick fiddling, either, and didn't believe in showing off before an audience when he played at contests. (One feels he would fully approve of the kind of rules enforced at many modern fiddling contests, rules designed to reflect the dignity of fiddling as a folk art.) Kirk McGee: "When he played it didn't look like he was puttin' on a show. He just got in a world by himself." Smith disliked fellow Opry fiddler Sid Harkreader, for example, because he felt Harkreader played too much to the audience. Smith strived for perfection in his performance, on occasion at the expense of showmanship. "I've been on the stage with him many a time," recalled Lavonne, "when he'd stop playing, find out whoever was playing out of tune. If it was himself, he'd tune it, if it was Sam he'd tune it, or Kirk. I've even seen him take the fiddle—sometimes Kirk played the fiddle—he'd take the fiddle out of Kirk's hand and he'd tune it."

In the course of his career, Smith had to play a lot of modern country music to survive, but he never left his commitment to old-time music. "He always preferred just a simple stringband, fiddle, banjo, and guitar," said Lavonne. Kirk recalled that he and Smith were once watching Gene Autry's fine fiddler, Carl Cotner. "Cotner was playing 'Stardust,' using a lot of harmony all the way through, and I said, 'Arthur, why don't you learn that,' and Arthur said, 'Huh. I wouldn't play it if I knew it.'" Yet many of the songs Smith chose to sing (as opposed to fiddle pieces) were newer, more popular songs, though they were performed in a semi-traditional style. Blythe Poteet went so far as to say, "Arthur was not what you call a folk musician at all, except for his old fiddle tunes." Smith was a composer and an innovator, but he worked within the confines of a tradition, and many of the songs he even composed had their roots in folk balladry. "Give me old time music," he sang in one of his songs, and it seems apparent that he saw "old-time" as a living musical genre.

Smith's single-minded purposefulness showed up in areas other than his music. Fishing, for instance. Smith went at it with a vengeance, as this story by Kirk McGee indicates:

> Arthur liked to fish, and down close to Waverly, why, the railroad ran along close to the river there. There was this special hole, he knew the fish were in there. Well, he was gonna dynamite the river and get the fish. Well, you can't just go dynamitin' a river, even back then. So Arthur, he knew the train schedules, 'cause he used to work for the railroad. He decided he would time the dynamite to go off just as the train passed, and no one would hear the blast, it would be covered up by the train, you know. So fixin' up his dynamite, he cut the fuse too long, and when this freight was comin' by, he lit it. And—well, it didn't go off till the freight had got way around the hill. All the country heard the blast. But he got the fish. Boy, he got 'em.

In contrast to the lively McGees, Smith was a little quieter and more conservative in public. Sam recalled that Arthur didn't exactly approve of some of their cutting up. A favorite stunt of Sam's, when the band needed to get through a crowd in a hurry, was to throw a "fit"; he would scream, jerk, bug his eyes, and Kirk and Arthur would have to "restrain him." "We got through the crowd," recalled Sam, "but Arthur felt it was a little foolish." On another occasion, Smith found out that one of his fans had referred to him as having a big nose. The man had said, on being directed to Smith, "My goodness, what a big nose. No wonder he can play the fiddle so well." The McGees thought this was great fun, but Smith worried over it and brooded about it for several days.

Smith was blunt and direct in his dealings with people, and he had a temper. "He was fractious," said Kirk. "He was high-tempered. We'd have our little differences, and Arthur would take off. Then after a while we'd get back together." For the most part, Smith knew exactly where he was at, and he didn't mince words with people. This lack of diplomacy probably cost him a few jobs, but it also earned him the respect of a lot of his friends. Everyone knew that Smith had a drinking problem, and it would be a distortion of this account to minimize it. Nor does it help much to point out that, in the rough, hard musical work of the 1930s, heavy drinking was all too common. It helped relieve the long, hard drives over hundreds of miles of single-lane roads, the grind of hundreds of one-nighters in local schoolhouses, the poor pay. I can think of very few musicians who played during this time—who played on a professional, full-time basis—who did not drink heavily. In spite of this consideration, we must admit that Smith's drinking seriously influenced his career and his music. Worse yet, even when Smith wasn't drinking, he had a reputation for drinking that haunted him. This was why, in later years, Smith could not get back on the Opry. Walter Bailes said: "They say Arthur was such a drunk. But that's not quite true. In some ways, he was a scapegoat for the Opry. Often Arthur was judged by the look in his eyes more than anything else; he could take one drink and he would show as much as if he had had three or four. He looked drunker than he was a lot of the time."

As with most cases, the drinking was only a symptom, not a cause. Another symptom was Smith's incessant wandering. Looking at his career after 1938, one is struck with how restlessly he moved from place to place, a year here, six months here, a few weeks here. His family would lose track of him for months at a time, and then he would show up one day. "He had nothing against it, he just wouldn't come home," said Blythe Poteet. Most of his later years he wandered around by himself, playing with whatever pick-up bands he could find. He would show up at recording sessions with just his fiddle, and hope he could find some boys to back him. In too many ways he fit aptly the stereotyped image of the "Luke the Drifter" character that we find in so much honky-tonk music. But he was also like one of the old Irish minstrels, wandering endlessly around the country, making a little money here or there with his fiddle, never settling down for long. Was what drove him to drink the same thing that drove him to wander?

One thing that emerges always was his absolute love for his music. Kirk McGee: "He was the kind who would go out in the country and stay with some old man and fiddle for weeks on end, not get anything out of it. And this when he needed to be out playing, making some money." Maybe it was the need to professionalize, to commercialize the thing he loved so much, his music, that bothered him. A psychologist might make a lot of the fact that, as long as Smith continued to work on the railroad and make his music a full-time career, his troubles continued as well.

In spite of the fact that Smith was not an ideal family man, he earned the respect of his thirteen children and passed onto several of them some of his musical talent. Eldest daughter Lavonne played piano and organ (though not professionally) and for years was a frequent judge for fiddling contests around the Chattanooga area before her death in the 1990s. Son Earnest, with whom Smith recorded and broadcasted, still plays in Detroit and has himself made several records there. Bobby Smith is a modern country singer who recorded in Nashville for Caprice Records, and Douglas Smith is a full-time musician currently playing with his modern country band around the Ft. Knox area in Kentucky. Another daughter, Pat Slatton, of Haleyville, Alabama, is a successful songwriter who has had numbers recorded by the Mills Brothers.

We keep coming back, in the end, to the essence of Arthur Smith's music, his fiddling style, and how it was a reflection of the man. We have offered several explanations of this style, and there are several theories as to where it came from. Kirk McGee felt it was an outgrowth of a regional Humphreys-Dickson County style that seemed new mainly because people around the country had never heard it. Others feel that it grew out of Smith's own considerable technical skill, a skill which made him impatient with traditional fiddling techniques. But Smith's own explanation of his style is perhaps the most apt, and the most poetic. He told Ernest Tucker, simply, that he dreamed his style one night, and that the next morning, without ever playing this new style on his fiddle, he went to work on the railroad, announcing casually to his fellow workers that he had invented a new style. I like this explanation as well as any, and I think it gives special meaning to one of Smith's first and best fiddle records: "Fiddler's Dream."

Sources

Much of this chapter has been based on personal interviews with friends and family of Arthur Smith. These included Sam McGee (interviewed near Franklin, Tennessee, April 9,

1975; June 27, 1973; and June 8, 1974) and his brother Kirk (interviewed at Franklin, August 29, 1974 and June 17, 1977), as well as personal interviews in the summer of 1977 with Grady Stringer (Dickson, Tennessee), Howdy Forrester (Nashville, Tennessee), Walter Bailes (Gatlinburg, Tennessee), Floyd Pruett (Dickson, Tennessee), Ernest Tucker (Fayetteville, Tennessee), Jimmy Wakely (Hollywood, California), Bill Wesbrooks (Nashville, Tennessee), Roy Acuff (Nashville, Tennessee). Especially helpful was the late Lavonne Brown, Smith's daughter, who shared photos and family documents (Hixson, Tennessee). Blythe Poteet, who played guitar with Smith and other early Opry greats, talked at length about Smith's fiddling style and music.

Some of the research in this chapter was developed for liner notes to a two-LP retrospective of Arthur Smith's vintage recordings issued by County Records in 1978 (County 546 and 547). I am also indebted to the co-author of those notes, Barry Poss, for his own insights and for generously sharing his own interviews with Lavonne Brown and Kirk McGee. Quotes from Alton Delmore come from his autobiography, *Truth Is Stranger Than Publicity*, originally published in 1978 and in 1995 reissued in a new edition by the Country Music Foundation Press and distributed by Vanderbilt University Press.

General suggestions and contributions were made by Bill Harrison, Neil Rosenberg, Doug Green, Les Leverett, and Ivan Tribe. Frank Driggs, then with RCA Records, made available the original session sheets for Smith's Bluebird recordings. Mike Seeger shared his memories of the Folkways albums he produced by the Dixieliners in the late 1950s. Bob Pinson of the CMF also helped with the discography. Our thanks also to other members of the Smith family, including sons Earnest Smith, William C. Smith, and Robert Smith. Much of this material originally appeared in a special tribute to Arthur Smith in *The Devil's Box*, Volume 11, No. 4.

Bob Wills, Fiddler

THE LEGENDS ABOUT BOB WILLS ARE SOMETIMES MORE
revealing than the facts of his biography. There was a night in the
late thirties or early forties when the distinguished classical violinist Jascha Heifetz found himself appearing in a town in Texas. After
a splendid performance at a local hall, the violinist and his manager
checked into the local hotel. Tired from traveling, the great musician
let his manager tend to the registration and paperwork. Taking his key,
he tucked his instrument case under his arm and wearily started up the
stairs to his room. Suddenly the desk clerk looked up. "I'm sorry," he
said, "you can't take that violin up to your room. We have a rule against
having musical instruments in the rooms." "Good heavens, man," said
the manager. "Don't you know who that is? That's the great Heifetz!
The great violin player!" The clerk was not impressed. "I don't care if
he's Bob Wills. Nobody takes a musical instrument up to any of our
rooms."

When you cross the Red River, Waylon Jennings explains in his
1974 hit song, "Bob Wills is still the king." His music is still very much
a part of the live music scene in the Southwest, and his fiddle tunes still
dominate most contests in the South. Though he died in 1975, and was
virtually inactive for a decade before that, Bob Wills still looms over
fiddling like no other figure. His tunes like "San Antonio Rose," "Maid-
en's Prayer," "Faded love," and others are still very much a part of the
active repertoire of thousands of modern fiddlers, from contests to
bluegrass to western swing. Wills records, dating as far back as 1932,

have remained in print through the LP age and into the CD age, and continue to attract new listeners. In 1996 plans were begun for a comprehensive reissue of the entire corpus of Wills recordings for major companies, a tribute accorded no other fiddler. A major biography, Charles Townsend's *San Antonio Rose: The Life and Music of Bob Wills* (University of Illinois) appeared in 1976, and in 1995 an earlier biography, Ruth Sheldon's *Hubbin' It*, appeared in a new edition (Country Music Foundation Press). Wills has been widely hailed as a founder of the dynamic musical hybrid called western swing, but he also has emerged as perhaps the most potent single influence on modern contest fiddling.

This is a fact that is too often overlooked in the continuing attention being given to Wills and his music. Historians have shown a disturbing tendency to dwell far too much on the popular side of the Bob Wills music. There are constant assertions that Wills himself was really interested in jazz, or big band music, or pop music, that his heart was not really in the folk and old-time music of his native Texas plains. Charles Townsend himself emphasizes this in his biography, possibly because many of the best informants for the Wills story are people who remember the middle and late periods, when Wills was indeed carrying with him a band of as many as twenty-two pieces and a battery of amplifiers and electric instruments. And while some of the 1940s Wills bands were as slick and impressive as real swing era bands, the 1930s bands were far from good swing bands. With their chomping tenor banjo, their slap-tongued sax solos, and their archaic repertoire, they were light years away from the hot new 1930s bands like Benny Goodman or Count Basie; they more resembled pop bands of the 1920s. Rather than copying the real swing era classics from Basie or Goodman, these bands focused on the various hokum and jug bands of the early 1930s, the sources of pieces like "Nancy Jane" and "Osage Stomp." The real hits that made Wills's reputation were not especially jazz records, but ones derived from fiddling and fiddle tunes. Though he started out as a more or less typical Southwestern fiddler, and made records that don't sound all that different from dozens of other Texas records of the time, Bob Wills soon found out how to make fiddle music appealing to the new audiences that were flocking into his 1930s dance halls. He learned what compromises he had to make to put fiddle music in this new setting and figured out a formula that allowed him to create this new synthesis. Like many of the other great synthesizers, from Bessie Smith to Elvis Presley, he figured out how to preserve the best of the older traditional music, and yet put it in a framework that would make it palatable to a more general audience. He was a musical translator, and fiddle music was his Rosetta stone.

One way to understand just how pervasive this influence was is to look at the direct quotes from Wills or his brothers. There is actually quite a lot of taped interview material with Wills, but writers about him have sometimes not used this testimony all that fully. Even in the late 1940s, after he had become a national star and a popular success with his big band, Wills told a radio interviewer: "It still thrills me for 'em to want to hear these fiddle tunes. We do a lot of singing, but when a guy comes up as asks for one of those old-timers like 'Beaumont Rag,' 'Lone Star Rag,' 'Twinkle, Twinkle Little Star,' or 'Brownskin Gal,' it always gives you a wonderful feeling. Because that fiddle is my life."

And, indeed, it was. Few men inherited the kind of fiddling tradition Bob Wills did. Both grandfathers, nine uncles, and five aunts all played the fiddle, and Bob's father, John Tompkins Wills, was a well-known Texas contest fiddler who on occasion even defeated the legendary Eck Robertson. It is generally known that Bob's father and family were into fiddling, but what isn't so widely known is just how pervasive this tradition was or how influential Bob's father himself was. "They knew him as Uncle John Wills all over the state of Texas," recalled Bob's brother Johnnie Lee. "And both of our granddads, from over in east Texas, they were both fiddlers. They were different types, but they were really good." On top of this, the family that John married into, the Foleys, were full of good traditional musicians.

All this musical interest provided the setting for the arrival of the newest Wills—Bob, born at one minute before midnight on March 6, 1905, in Limestone County, south of Dallas. As he inspected his first-born son, Uncle John said, "I'll make a fiddler out of YOU, son!" His brother-in-law, standing by his side, looked at the baby's hand and added, "He'll make a better fiddler than you, Johnnie. Look at them long fingers."

Uncle John won his reputation playing at ranch dances and later at fiddling contests. Johnnie Lee recalled what it was like back in the 1920s at some of these Texas fiddling contests:

Dad went to a lot of fiddling contests back in those days, and they often gave away fiddles to the winners. There were a few he went to where money was given. I remember some of the names of the ones he always went up against: Eck Robertson, Lefty Franklin, Copeland. I remember one particular contest in Munday, Texas. Papa, when he got to play a contest, he'd raise his bridge higher than usual, and instead of tuning his fiddle to a natural A, he would tune it to a C on a piano. That would make it higher, and make it more brilliant and louder. There wasn't any microphone back then, and his old fiddle was loud, with its steel strings. And they had this thing they called the "Lone Indian" and he could holler the thing in high C—that's pretty high. The audience couldn't see if the fiddle was doing that or if he was hollering. They would allow some trick fiddling back then, and he had three or four that he would holler in, right in the same key. One time when Papa had won a contest, this old man came up to him and said Wills didn't out-fiddle him, he out-hollered him.

One time we drove into a little town in Texas where they were having a contest, and we noticed a gang of people there at the corner of the square. We got in closer and saw it was a fiddle and guitar playing; it was Copeland. We drove up another block and Eck Robertson, he was out playing that evening before the deal. Well, Eck Robertson won first that night, and Papa won second, and Copeland third. Copeland got mad, and he went over there and rented a cafe, to stay open and let them play, them three, they was gonna contest. Papa wouldn't play a bad tune on a fiddle—it had to have a lot of fiddling to it—so Copeland lasted about four tunes, and he run out. And Eck Robertson, he played seven or eight tunes. Him and Pop was good friends; he wasn't mad at father. Pop, they left him playing and he played on for another hour or two, never playing the same tune. In other words, he wasn't a contest fiddler, some one who knew only three good ones. All of the ones he played, he made them good.

When he was eight, Bob's family moved (by covered wagon) to Hall County in western Texas, where he shortly learned his first fiddle tune. As Wills recalled it on his 1964 *Keepsake Album* (Longhorn), one afternoon his thirty-five-year old cousin Olford Sanders was trying to learn to play a simple little tune which old-time music fans today know as

"Goodbye, Miss Liza Jane." Wills finally had enough of the noise and told his cousin that he thought he, Bob, all of nine years old, could play it better. His cousin said, "Son, if you can, I'll take this fiddle and bust it over the foot of the bed." Wills picked the tune out with a fair amount of ease and handed the instrument back to his cousin. "He must have thought I'd beat him," Wills recalled. "We went in the house, his mother was in the kitchen, and he said, 'Ma, come here.' Just as she walked to the door of the bedroom, he taken that beautiful little fiddle, hit it over the bed, and busted it in one thousand pieces."

More formal instruction was not long in coming. Wills's granddad, Tom Wills, had moved to west Texas with the clan, and one day he determined to instruct young Bob in bowing styles. Johnnie Lee Wills recalled the scene vividly: "We were always taught to pull the long bow. My granddad taught Bob that. He took the bow away from Bob one time when he was just a kid. Bob was in there playing it and using just a little bit of the bow, and Granddad took the bow away from him and put it up, and said, 'Till you learn how to use it, don't pick it up anymore.' Of course, then he explained to him, he said, 'If that bow wasn't meant to be used, it wouldn't have been made that long.' And so from then on, Bob pulled a long bow."

At about this same time young Bob was accompanying his father when the elder Wills went to play at ranch dances in the area. He often played mandolin behind his father's fiddle, and in later years Bob recollected the hard work and sheer drudgery that came from such work. "Used to, my dad would tell me in the cottonpatch, chopping cotton or whatever we was doing, 'Go and unhook [the mules] and clean up and rest a bit, we're going over and play at so-and-so's headquarters, some ranch or another.' And I knew it was for all night. We'd stop [at] midnight and have supper, but I knew it was all night. Well, you know, that's pretty hard on a kid—I mean a little kid—and I used to go in crying and tell my mother, 'When I grow up to be boss of my own, I'll never step my foot in a dance hall as long as I live.' So I'm gonna say to everybody, it don't pay to say what you won't do, 'cause you're liable to wind up doing that very thing. But I used to do that, because it was so hard on me. I used to drop the pick—and that finger's still got scars on it from that—I'd keep playing, you know, with blood running down on that little mandolin. It was tough."

Besides a legacy of hard work and discipline, though, these ranch dances gave Wills some other elements of his music that were to show up in later years. One of these was Wills's famous cry, "Ah ha," that became such a trademark. About 1948 Wills recalled the origin of that little cry. "That come by accident. Back to the old ranch dances, years ago, me and my dad used to get in a buggy and drive thirty or forty miles, and I played a little mandolin, and Papa the fiddle. Well, we'd get pretty peppy along through the night. Those old cowboys, you know, had a lot of spunk. And it was accidental with me. Papa used to have a word years ago in a square dance: once in a while he'd yell, 'UP BOYS!'—in other words, give 'em more pep. . . ." Years later, when Wills was performing on radio with W. Lee O'Daniel, O'Daniel stopped Wills from giving that cry during band numbers on the radio show, thinking it was undignified and distracting. "He stopped me from doing that for about six months. And we got better than 250,000 letters wanting to know what became of the little animal that was on the show. They said, 'Put him back on.'"

Other parts of the Wills legend also had their origins in these early days of family fiddling, ranch dances, and contests. The song that was eventually to become "Faded Love" had been played for years by both of Wills's grandfathers, though it was always thought of as an instrumental. "Maiden's Prayer" was favorite of Wills's dad, John Wills, who would get up early in the morning, around 4 A.M., sit out in the front yard to the Wills farm as the dawn crept up on the plains, and play the melody to himself. "An old fiddle out at that time in the morning would sound awful lonesome," recalled Johnnie Lee. Other tunes came to Wills from contests, and in fact his first real fiddle, the one he eventually donated to the Country Music Hall of Fame, was an old fiddle his father had won in a contest. "It was a cheap fiddle," Wills recalled, "but it happened to be a great cheap fiddle. It was easy to play. I got a little hand, and the neck [of that fiddle] was a fraction shorter than standard fiddle, and it just fit me."

As Wills developed his fiddling, he developed as a person: he went through a stage of preaching; did a stint in a medicine show, doing blackface routines and even singing; and attended Amarillo barber college. For a time he had a band in New Mexico that included some Mexican-American musicians, and developed for them a tune to be later known as "Spanish Two-Step." He also became a fan of the great blues singer Bessie Smith, and traveled miles to hear her in concert.

In late October 1929, about the time the stock market was crashing, the Brunswick Record Company set up a field recording session in Dallas. For several days they recorded acts like the East Texas Serenaders, the Red Headed Fiddlers, the Stamps Quartet, and cowboy singer Marc Williams. Shortly after the engineers finished with Williams, they made a couple of test recordings by a pair identifying themselves as "Jim Rob Wills and Herman Arnspiger." It was Bob Wills, of course, and he was making his first records. One of them was a version of Bessie Smith's "Gulf Coast Blues"; the other was a piece called "Wills Breakdown." We shall never know what they sounded like, for neither was ever released, and the metal parts for the masters were apparently destroyed in 1956. Both, however, were almost surely fiddle instrumentals, and they probably sounded very much like the other Texas fiddle band music recorded at that same session.

By 1930 Wills and his guitar player Arnspiger, a cotton worker whom he had met while doing time in a medicine show, were calling themselves the Wills Fiddle Band, and playing around the Ft. Worth area. The possibilities of making a full-time living out of ranch dances, though, were not good, and getting worse; once Wills was given a doped drink at a dance by other jealous musicians present. Joining forces with a young singer named Milton Brown, they found jobs on the new medium of radio and began playing over KFJZ in Ft. Worth. Radio work appealed to Wills, and he was successful at it. He helped form the Light Crust Doughboys, but left in late summer of 1933 to form his own band, which soon became known as the Texas Playboys. They debuted over WACO in Waco, Texas, but soon moved to the powerful 25,000-watt station at Tulsa, KVOO. It was there that they established their real reputation.

As Wills began recording, first with the Light Crust Doughboys in 1932, and then with his own group starting in September 1935, he continued to emphasize his fiddle tunes and continued to remember his old ranch house dances. His first recording session included a band of some thirteen pieces, with no less than four fiddlers. It included Wills classics like "Maiden's Prayer" and "Spanish Two Step," but also included a lot of pop material. Significantly, at the end of the session, Wills went back into the empty studio with Sleepy Johnson and did four fine fiddle-guitar pieces: "Smith's Reel," "Harmony," and two waltzes. Over the next several years, Wills would continue to do a few fiddle specialties at various sessions; he later recalled that these records were intended for home square dancing.

Unlike the other great commercial fiddlers of the 1930s, Bob Wills did not feature traditional fiddle tunes on the majority of his records, though he did craft arrangements of pop and blues tunes in which the fiddle often took the lead. Between 1929, when he made his first unissued session for Brunswick, and 1942, when the war and a musicians' strike closed down most recording studios, Bob Wills & the Texas Playboys recorded some 197 sides. The lion's share of these were done for the old American Recording Company, a conglomerate which released product on a dozen different labels, including Sears's Conqueror imprint, Vocalion, Columbia, Okeh, and others. Of these, not more than twenty-five were classic fiddle tunes of the sort that his father played, and that showed up in Texas fiddling contests (see table 4).

Among these twenty-five sides, though—and some of them were not even released until decades later—were some that had an amazing influence on grassroots fiddlers. They included the original or most popular versions of standards like "Maiden's Prayer" (1935), "Spanish Two-Step" (1935), "Silver Bells" (1938), "Beaumont Rag" (1938), "Twinkle, Twinkle Little Star" (1938), "The Waltz You Saved For Me" (1938), and "Don't Let Your Deal Go Down" (1938). Most of these were actual hits and were issued on numerous 78 labels, and then on a rich variety of LPs. In addition to these generally popular tunes, though, were Wills's versions of many tunes specifically from the classic Texas repertoire: "Crippled Turkey," "Brownskin Gal" (the Eck Robertson favorite that Wills dubbed "That Brownskin Gal"), "Done Gone" (another Eck favorite, which Wills called "Done and Gone"), and "I Don't Lov'a Nobody" (which Wills forged into a medley with the old dance hall favorite "Big Ball in Cowtown").

Wills embraced two quite distinct Texas traditions—the squaredance style that was a strictly functional way of playing for the ranch and dance hall parties, as well as the more ornate contest style, with its "fancy fiddling" that often included subtle variation and improvisation, a more deliberate tempo, and complex bow work. Uncle John Wills knew both traditions, though he had moved more into the contest style in his later life. Wills's own fiddling on these records, though, is surprisingly straightforward, and suggests he was more at home with the dance style. When asked in later years about these traditional fiddle records, Wills admitted that they were aimed at the home square dance market—at people who wanted simple, straightforward music to dance by. "I don't think it worked out," he noted, thinking of their low sales and unreleased sides. "I don't think anybody ever bought one of them." In these early years of recording, the mid-1930s, he was at once

Table 4 Bob Wills Recordings of Familiar Fiddle Tunes, 1929–1942

Wills Breakdown (composer unknown)	Dallas, 1929, Brunswick (unissued)
Spanish Two-Step (original)	Dallas, 1935, ARC
Maiden's Prayer (original)	Dallas, 1935, ARC
Smith's Reel (traditional)	Dallas, 1935, ARC
Get Along Home, Cindy (traditional)	Chicago, 1936, ARC
Crippled Turkey (traditional)	Chicago, 1936, ARC (not released until 1987)
Silver Bells (19th century)	Dallas, 1938, ARC
Beaumont Rag (traditional)	Dallas, 1938, ARC
Twinkle, Twinkle Little Star	Dallas, 1938, ARC
Ida Red	Dallas, 1938, ARC
Prosperity Special (aka Rat Cheese Under the Hill, Pike's Peak)	Dallas, 1938, ARC
Waltz You Saved For Me (1920s pop)	Dallas, 1938, ARC
Don't Let Your Deal Go Down	Dallas, 1938, ARC
Lone Star Rag (traditional, aka Stone's Rag)	Saginaw, Texas, 1940, ARC
That Brownskin Gal (traditional)	Saginaw, Texas, 1940, ARC (not released until 1987)
Corrine Corinna (traditional)	Saginaw, Texas, 1940, ARC
Let Me Call You Sweetheart	Saginaw, Texas, 1940, ARC
Blue Bonnet Rag (original)	Saginaw, Texas, 1940, ARC
I Don't Lov'a Nobody (traditional, incorporates Big Ball's in Cowtown)	Saginaw, Texas, 1940, ARC
Done and Gone (traditional)	Dallas, 1941, Conqueror
Girl I Left Behind (traditional)	Dallas, 1941, ARC (unissued)
Little Liza Jane (traditional)	Hollywood, 1941, Columbia
Bob Wills Stomp (traditional?)	Hollywood, 1941, Columbia
Liberty (traditional)	Hollywood, 1942, Columbia
Good-bye Liza Jane (traditional)	Hollywood, 1942, Columbia

uneasy about his own fiddling and yet determined to keep his fiddle "up front" at the sessions. "I was a little afraid of my fiddle all through there," he said. "I couldn't navigate with it very good. Listening to the fiddle records—after hearing what Texas fiddling became in the hands of Texas Shorty, Benny Thomasson, and others—one is struck by how straightforward Wills's playing is. His first released fiddle solo, "Smith's Reel," has him playing the tune through four times, cleanly and neatly, but with no purposeful variation; it sounds like dozens of other competent fiddle records from the Southeast in the 1920s. "Crippled Turkey," a far more interesting piece with some fine playing and unexpected timing and harmonics, shows Wills's interest in complex pieces. Unfortunately, it influenced nobody at the time, since it remained unissued until the Country Music Foundation found it and put it on their excellent LP, *Bob Wills Fiddle*, in 1987.

What begins to get interesting to modern ears are the fiddle tunes he began to arrange for his full band starting in 1938. Here Wills develops a formula that allowed him to mix the sound of the western fiddle with the more modern sound of the electric steel; the piano; the heavy rhythm section of bass, drums, and tenor banjo; and the hot "take-off" solo. It was what would later be called "western swing," but Wills seldom used that term. When Hank Penny asked him in 1948 what he called his music, Wills responded: "Texas fiddle band music." One of the first uses of this formula came in the 1938 Dallas session when he recorded "Twinkle, Twinkle Little Star." The first two choruses feature Wills's solo fiddle, backed by brother Johnnie Lee's prominent tenor banjo and the rhythm section; next comes a take-off chorus by pianist Al Strickland, who totally departs from the melody; next comes another hot take-off solo by second fiddle player Jesse Ashlock; then, right on the heels of Ashlock's solo, Wills returns to play the melody straight for a final chorus. This general formula seemed to work, for Wills used it again and again in numbers like "Prosperity Special," "Don't Let Your Deal Go Down," "Lone Star Rag," "That Brownskin Gal," "I Don't Lov'a Nobody," and even "Liberty," the latter done as late as 1942 in Hollywood. The formula includes Wills starting off playing a chorus or two of the tune himself in a straightforward way, letting two or three of his better improvisers take solos (including, always, a hot fiddle soloist like Ashlock or Joe Holley), and then returning to a final chorus of Wills's lead. "Done and Gone," dating from February 1941, begins with Wills playing the odd, unbalanced melody, followed by a chorus on the steel by Leon McAuliffe, a hot fiddle chorus by Louis Tierney, and one by Al Stricklin on piano. Wills then returns for a final chorus on his solo fiddle. None of the main melody instruments are ever heard playing together. But at this same session, a hour or so later, the band recorded a number called "Oh, You Pretty Woman," with a brass and sax section that sounded like a big band. (Wills by now had thirteen pieces in his recording band.) And even in his Hollywood days, with his big band sound in full cry, Wills always insisted in adding to the sessions one or two of his old fiddle tunes—presented in these new "hot sandwich" arrangements.

There were other ways Bob Wills effected this compromise between old and new music, fiddle music and swing. Though he no longer entered many contests after he became nationally famous, Wills did continue to play numerous concerts and dances in the Southwest. One of his fans was a fiddler from the Tucson area named Edd Smith, who recalls that in the late 1930s Wills and his band would come into a local town for a dance/concert. "They would play a set," he recalls, "and then he would let some of his band members off the stand to chase girls, and Bob would invite the local fiddlers to come up and play as guests." The local fiddlers got to expect this, and each would always make sure his fiddle was in his truck. Wills enjoyed listening to the local talent, and the local musicians could come away with bragging rights that they had "played with Bob Wills." And for a time in 1940, when his main band was full of saxophones and trumpets and fancy arrangements, Wills, backed only by Eldon Shamblin and Tommy Duncan, started an early morning radio show over KVOO, "Bob Wills's Fiddle Time." He enjoyed it, but his burgeoning fame soon meant he had to give it up.

In later years, as Wills moved from record label to record label, he continued to manage to record fiddle tunes and pieces featuring his fiddle. His most famous, of course, was "San Antonio Rose." As Wills admitted, years later, the "Rose" was "a steal from 'Spanish Two-Step.'" Art Satherley, the famous A&R man who worked for Wills during his stint with the American Recording Company in the 1930s, asked Bob at a 1938 session, "Bob, give me another 'Spanish Two-Step.' Got one?" As Wills recalled it, he said, "We sure have."

> And the boys began to look at each other, and they were saying, "We haven't got one." And I said, "Oh yeah, we'll just play 'Spanish Two-Step' backwards." What I meant was, see, I started "Spanish Two-Step" in A, and throwed it to Leon McAuliffe, and he went to D on the bridge part of it. Well, what I had in mind was starting in D and let him go to A. And do you know how much time was spent on the music part of "San Antonio Rose"? I doubt very seriously if there was five minutes. 'Cause we ran over it about the second time. And he [Satherley] said, "That sounds good, Bob." We wasn't ready, but I said, "OK, let's catch it." And Satherley named it. He came out—and I thought, how silly can a man be? To call what is more or less a breakdown "San Antonio Rose," but he wanted to call it that, and I didn't argue with him.

In later years, Wills often left a lot of the fiddling to men like Joe Holley and Johnny Gimble and Louis Tierney—specialists in hot take-off solos and complex twin or triple fiddling. Often on records with these men, Wills confined himself to playing the "straight" part of the tune, and letting the youngsters do the variations on the melody. Yet as late as 1964, when Wills broke up the Texas Playboys, he went back into the studio with his old sideman Sleepy Johnson, who had joined him on his first fiddle solos some twenty-nine years before, and cut a whole album of the old fiddle classics he knew and loved: "Big Taters in the Sandy Land," "Billy in the Low Ground," "Beaumont Rag," "Done Gone," and "Gone Indian." The album, called *Bob Wills Keepsake*, was issued on a small independent label, Longhorn.

In the end, which came with Wills's death on May 13, 1975, fiddlers of all sorts paid homage to the person who had probably had more commercial success with the art than anyone else in history. At Wills's funeral in Tulsa, Johnny Gimble, Keith Coleman, and Curly Lewis, accompanied by Eldon Shamblin on guitar, fiddled Wills's favorite tunes, and closed the book on a grand era of American fiddle music.

Sources

The quotations from Johnnie Lee Wills come from a series of interviews with the author in Murfreesboro, Tennessee, October 1974. Some of these interviews were reprinted in "Making Western Swing," *Old Time Music*, No. 15 (Winter 1974/75), 11–21. Many of the quotes from Bob Wills are drawn from a radio interview done by Hank Penny for KGIL (San Fernando), 1948. Other quotations are from Charles R. Townsend, *San Antonio Rose* (Urbana: University of Illinois Press, 1976), and from Rich Kienzle's monograph-liner notes to Bob Wills in Time-Life's *Country & Western Classics* (Alexandria, Virginia, 1982). The quotation Edd Smith is taken from a video produced by Jim Griffith in 1995. Also useful is an album entitled *Bob Wills Fiddle*, produced by the Country Music Foundation (CMF 010-L), with programming by Bob Pinson and annotations by Charlie Seemann.

Slim Miller of Renfro Valley

Y OU CAN GO OVER IN EASTERN KENTUCKY OR NORTHERN Tennessee and talk to old-timers about some of their favorite fiddlers of ages past, and they'll tell you a lot of names that you haven't heard, and they'll mention a lot of tunes that nobody plays anymore, but over and over again they'll talk about a man named Slim Miller. They'll use this name as an almost legendary standard of excellence. "He was almost as good as Slim Miller," they'll say, or "He finally got to where he sounded a lot like Slim Miller." Very few fiddlers get to where they have such status, where their art defines the standards of the region. In Georgia, probably, the standard was Clayton McMichen; in North Carolina, Tommy Magness; in Texas, Eck Robertson; in Tennessee, Arthur Smith or Tommy Jackson. In eastern Kentucky, it was an ungainly, comic man who held forth at Renfro Valley for over twenty years, and who answered to the name of Slim Miller. This is a stab at putting together his story.

I never got to interview Slim Miller, nor as far as I know did anyone else. He died August 27, 1962, before anyone cared very much about putting together the history of old-time music. His story has to be pieced together from memories of others, from earlier writings, and from occasional facts that surface here and there. Especially useful have been the writings of Miller's long-time friend and mentor, John Lair, the man who spent most of his career with Miller and who built the Renfro Valley Barn Dance that Miller helped so much to popularize. When Miller is mentioned in any formal histories of country music (he seldom is), he is described as a comedian and a master of ceremonies;

all too often overlooked is what most of Miller's fans knew him for best, a superb old-time fiddler.

Miller is often thought of as a native of eastern Kentucky, but in fact, he was born in Indiana. His full name was Homer Edgar Miller, and he was born March 8, 1898, in Lizton, Indiana, about twenty-five miles northwest of Indianapolis. He was adopted and reared by a neighbor, and this foster father happened to be an old-time fiddler himself. By the time young Homer was twelve, he was a skilled fiddler and posed proudly with his first instrument for an anonymous photographer. He was also growing into a tall lanky lad of six-foot-three inches, and by the time he got out of high school he was good enough to take a job with a local orchestra in Indianapolis. For a time he even traveled with theater stock companies in the area, playing all kinds of popular music and learning lessons about stage technique, timing, and presence that would help him later on.

In 1930 Homer and another Indianapolis native, tenor banjo player Ray Gully, made their way down to Knoxville, Tennessee, where they joined a new band being formed by Hugh Cross, a tenor singer from Oliver Springs, Tennessee. Cross had recorded widely in the late 1920s with Riley Puckett, McMichen, the Skillet Lickers, and Cumberland plateau fiddler Luther McCartt. In 1930 he was putting together a band to play on the radio for a local dentist named Hamilton, who was try-ing to use country music to advertise his new "painless" methods of tooth-pulling. The band was called the Smoky Mountain Ramblers, and included Henry ("Heavy") Martin on guitar and Walt McKinney on Hawaiian guitar in addition to Homer and Gully. This may have been Homer's first real job with a Southern-styled stringband.

It also led to his first recordings. In March 1930 the Brunswick-Balke-Collender company moved their portable recording equip-ment—1,600 pounds and $28,000 worth of it—into the old St. James Hotel in Knoxville to record everybody from Uncle Dave Macon to fid-dler Uncle Jimmy Thompson to McFarland & Gardner. Included were six sides by the Smoky Mountain Ramblers, featuring Cross's singing and Homer's fiddle. He is featured on one solo side, "Bear Mountain Rage" on Vocalion 5437, one of the rarest of old-time records. The rag sounds like a genuine ragtime composition, replete with breaks and different melodic strains. It certainly doesn't appear to be from South-ern tradition and may reflect some of Homer's vaudeville troupe background. Other songs the Ramblers did were Western styled, including an early (maybe a first) recording of the later Gene Autry favorite, "Back to the Old Smoky Mountains." At the same session, Homer and the boys got to engage in a little acting, as they were featured in a four-part skit called "The Great Hatfield-McCoy Feud," directed by A&R man Bill Brown and also featuring fiddler Lowe Stokes. It was a miserably unfunny skit and richly deserves the oblivion into which it has sunk.

These records, coming as they did in the midst of the Depression, did little to enhance Homer Miller's reputation with the general public, nor did they inspire the Smoky Mountain Ramblers. That unfortunate band soon dissolved, leaving the painless dentist Hamilton to find another stringband to attract his customers. Nor can one say that "Bear Mountain Rag" is deathless fiddling. Miller sounds cautious, nervous, and uncertain of what's going on. Rushed by his guitarists, and distracted by Bill Brown's idiotic yammering about how wild the women in Knox County were, Miller does little except define his style: a thin, liquid tone coupled with a smooth-flowing sense of ornamentation and a remarkably loose wrist. His tendency to use graceful, even cascades of eighth or sixteenth notes suggests the mandolin playing of Karl Davis or the Prairie Ramblers' Chick Hurt.

As Herbert Hoover and Franklin D. Roosevelt fought out the 1932 presidential election, Homer beat it back to Indianapolis to look for work. He didn't know it, but the next chapter of his career was being outlined by a brash young Kentuckian named John Lair, who had recently moved to Chicago from Louisville and was busy persuading WLS program director Steve Cissler to let him start a new stringband over the station. The "WLS Barn Dance" had started in 1924 and had featured a number of traditional musicians from Kentucky: Chubby Parker, Walter Peterson, and Bradley Kincaid had emerged as stars by 1930. On a vacation trip home that year, Lair invited two singers from near Berea, Karl Davis and Harty Taylor, to come up to Chicago and try their luck singing on WLS. Lair helped the boys join the union and helped manage them (for fifteen dollars per radio show), calling the act the Renfro Valley Boys. Within a few months, Lair had added two other musicians, singer-guitarist Doc Hopkins and a fiddler named Gene Ruppe, and began calling this larger unit the Cumberland Ridge Runners. As the band prospered, WLS gave Lair permission to add more members, and by 1932 Hugh Cross had also joined the team, as a replacement for Doc Hopkins.

This is where Slim Miller re-enters the picture. As Lair recalled, "Hugh hadn't been with us long before he began singing the praises of a fiddler he had once worked with, a boy he described as 'a long tall drink of water that could turn a fiddle every way but loose.' He was living at the time in Indianapolis, Indiana, and when we went down there to play for the state fair, Hugh had him come in for an audition. I hired him, though, even before he got his fiddle out of the case. We put Slim on fiddle and let Ruppe drop back to his first love, the five-string banjo."

Ruppe didn't stay around long, though, and Red Foley was brought into replace him, as well as a Chicago night club singer named Jean Muenich, "The Red-Headed Bluebird," whose name Lair changed to Linda Parker, the "Sunbonnet Girl." With this team in place, the cumbersome band made its first recordings, on April 11 and 12, 1933, for the American Record Company in Chicago. Ten sides resulted: one featuring a Lair vocal, two featuring Rambling Red Foley, two featuring Linda Parker, three featuring group singing, and two instrumentals featuring Miller's fiddle: "Roundin' Up the Yearlings" and "Goofus." Both are masterpieces.

"Yearlings" is a tour de force of Miller's fiddle licks, with new, subtle variations in almost every stanza. (In 1978 it was reissued on the Rounder LP *Kentucky Country*.) "Goofus" was more popular, though. It was Miller's version of an old novelty song from the 1920s that had become a favorite of hokum jazz bands. Miller speeded it up, geared it to Karl Davis's exciting mandolin, and almost singlehandedly made it a fiddlers' favorite. Two years later, Arthur Smith was to think enough of it to do a "cover" version of it for RCA's Bluebird records. The ARC session was also notable for producing a recording of the first "modern" version of "Old Rattler," later to be made a favorite by Grandpa Jones. (Tennessee singer George Reneau had also recorded an early version of the song, but without the chorus.)

While the original Cumberland Ridge Runners began to break up in 1935—Linda Parker died of a ruptured appendix in 1935, and Doc Hopkins, Red Foley, and Karl & Harty left to pursue separate careers—Miller remained a favorite on the WLS Barn Dance. His fiddling was heard widely across the country, and many of the tunes he played on the air but never recorded are still well known today. An example is "Miller's Blues" that Luke Smathers of North Carolina still plays. When John Lair decided to move back to Kentucky, and establish a new barn dance show out of Renfro Valley in 1939, Miller eagerly joined him and became an early favorite on that program.

While he continued to hold forth as a premier fiddler, he also began developing a second important talent, comedy. Lair recalled:

> His natural flair for comedy . . . in time came to be his biggest asset and he had few equals as a sure laugh getter. Slim could convulse any audience with his pantomiming, without ever opening his mouth. A play of quick-changing expressions on his face told the whole story without spoken words. The vice president of the nation's most important talent and booking agency was once visiting me from New York on matters pertaining to our network radio show and stayed over to witness a barn dance performance. He stood in the wings and watched Slim work. He told me later that Slim had the most perfect "timing" for his comedy he had ever seen and properly belonged in the "big time." He went so far to say that with a little coaching he could be the equal of Jackie Gleason, at that time the new comedy sensation of the country. I talked to Slim about it, but he was not much excited about it.

Throughout the forties and into the fifties, Miller reigned over Renfro Valley like a clown prince. In the early days, his name headlined the Renfro Valley tent shows, and he often led the back-up band at Renfro Valley as well. Typically dressed in baggy pants, a checkered shirt, and bright bandanna, stooping over with that lanky six-foot-three-inch frame and smiling when he played a breakdown for Granny Harper to buck dance to, he cut quite a comic figure. (Several older musicians have told me that the late Stringbean modeled his costume in part on that of Slim Miller.) Some of his comedy bits became trademarks: the crossing and uncrossing of his long legs, the loss of a banana he had just peeled, or simply a long, steady stare into the audience—a trick done by countless rube comics in country music today. For years, whenever Miller was at a cafe, he would leave an autographed picture of himself on the table in addition to a tip.

Unfortunately, he did not record as much as his fame would seem to warrant. After the 1933 session, he did help out on several Karl &

Harty records (including their bouncing, favorite version of "I'm S-A-V-E-D"). Though he played a character on the air named "Uncle Doody," he apparently does not appear on the recording of that name by the Coon Creek Girls. He did appear in the television series "The Renfro Valley Folks" for Pillsbury's Best Flour in 1956 and must have made dozens of radio transcriptions, though these have not to my knowledge been catalogued or indexed so as to tell us what fiddle tunes he might have preserved.

In later years, Miller and his wife Clara leased and operated the Scenic View Motel in Renfro Valley. Miller's health, never the best, began to really fail in 1960, and he had to retire from regular participation in the Barn Dance. Off and on for eighteen months he fought cancer, but at last, in September 1962, the fight became too bitter. John Lair wrote in Miller's obituary: "He sleeps the last long sleep beneath the shade of a few tall trees near the top of a hill overlooking Travelers Rest, in a remote and beautiful spot in the Kentucky hills he had learned to love. A lonesome spot, perhaps, for a man who loved crowds . . . but a quiet and restful place." His legacy: a lot of fine memories, and all too little music.

Sources

My portrait of Slim Miller is drawn from a series of telephone interviews with his widow, Clara, as well as various published writings of John Lair, especially those in the *Renfro Valley Bugle*. Many of these were made available to me by the late Reuben Powell, the master historian of Renfro Valley. Data on the Knoxville sessions comes from my own research, and from my long article about the sessions in *Old Time Music*, No. 12.

III

Staying the Course

The Mystery of
"The Black Mountain Rag"

A LONG WITH "LISTEN TO THE MOCKINGBIRD," "Orange Blossom Special," and "Over the Waves," "The Black Mountain Rag" is one of the most popular fiddle tunes in modern history. Every young bluegrass band has to take a shot at it, it is a favorite at bluegrass festivals, and it has become so pervasive at fiddling contests that many judges totally prohibit its playing in the fiddling competition. The other three tunes all have fairly cut-and-dried histories. We know pretty much who wrote them and how they got into circulation. With "The Black Mountain Rag," though, there is a good deal of controversy and confusion, made even more odd by the fact that this piece is by far the most modern of the four. As most fiddlers and fans know, this piece became popular in the 1940s and, through several key recordings, entered the repertoires of thousands of musicians across the country. Exactly who originated the tune, though, and exactly who made the first and most influential recording of it, have remained a mystery. The extent of this confusion—as well as the popularity of the song—can be seen when one examines a printout of the copyrighted versions of the song on file at the BMI (Broadcast Music Incorporated) offices in Nashville. BMI shows no less than thirty-two different arrangement copyrights or composer copyrights for "Black Mountain Rag." And this in spite of the fact that most record labels, including the ones on the biggest hits of the song, still show it as "Traditional."

The cast of characters in the mystery is rich and varied. It includes five main suspects:

1. *Pleaz Carroll*, an obscure fiddler from west Alabama who flourished from 1910–1925;
2. *Charlie Stripling*, old-time fiddle great who recorded with his brother in the 1920s as the Stripling Brothers;
3. *Leslie Keith*, a legendary bluegrass fiddler who worked in east Tennessee with the Stanley Brothers, Curly King, and others in the late 1940s;
4. *Curly Fox*, nationally known fiddler and radio star who encountered the "Black Mountain Piece" in the 1940s; and
5. *Tommy Magness*, influential north Georgia fiddler who worked with Roy Hall and later with Roy Acuff on the stage of the Grand Ole Opry in the 1940s.

So much for the characters, and more of them later. Now for the victim. The tune itself usually, but not always, consists of three parts, with the B or C parts often involving some sort of plucking of the strings or strumming of the strings by hand. The tune itself probably originates from the so-called "Lost Indian" family of fiddle tunes, which have been found all over the South from Texas to Virginia. The tune family is more associated with a special tuning (A–E–A–C#) than with any melodic contours. Fiddlers usually describe "Black Mountain Rag" as being played in "cross tuning," which can mean several variations from the standard E–A–D–G, such as E–A–E–A or D–G–D–G.

Without doubt, the central figure in the controversy about the tune is Leslie Keith, who is generally credited with composing the tune under the title "The Black Mountain Blues." Indeed, Keith's claim to the tune was so well known that in 1947 and 1948, when he was on the radio in Bristol, Tennessee, he was billed as "Leslie Keith with his Black Mountain Blues Fiddle." A songbook he put out during this time contained an entire page in which he explained the history of the tune (see below). In 1976 Bob Sayers published an interview with Keith in *Bluegrass Unlimited*, in which the editors described Keith as "a rather solitary and enigmatic figure in the history of bluegrass" who moved from the mainstream of bluegrass in the late 1940s to total obscurity a few years later. By 1976 Keith had moved to Arizona, where music scholar Jim Griffith, along with Bob Sayers, had rediscovered him and were documenting his career.

It was a fascinating career, and deserves a recap here. Keith was born March 30, 1906, in Pulaski County Virginia, the son of a banjo-playing father who died when Keith was three. His mother, a musician herself, moved him to Birmingham, Alabama, in 1923 when he was seventeen, and he began playing fiddle at local square dances and swapping tunes with other local musicians. He spent a lot of time with a road show in Alabama—some kind of outfit similar to a medicine show—where he perfected trick fiddling and spent two years as a prison guard in 1928–29 where he "learned a lot of blues stuff." He also listened to fiddlers on the radio: at first, records by John Carson, Fiddlin' (Cowan) Powers, and Doc Roberts. Later he heard the Grand Ole Opry and Arthur Smith: "There has never been a man born or done died that could play old-time fiddle like Arthur Smith," Keith maintained.

In the early 1930s, Keith and his mother moved to Crossville, Tennessee, where he and a cousin named Dallas Hughes would go "busking"—they played on the courthouse steps for nickels and dimes. His mother died in 1935, and while visiting an aunt in West Virginia he was approached by some local musicians about whether he could play the fiddle. He told them he had come in second to Clayton McMichen at a contest in Birmingham, and they were impressed enough to invite him for a tryout. Soon he was playing with Joe Woods & His Harmony Band over WHIS in Bluefield, doing trick fiddling (standing on his head and fiddling behind his back). He also did tricks with a bullwhip. Not long afterward he was appearing all over the South, often billing himself as "Tennessee Champion Trick Fiddler." He worked for a time with the Stafford Brothers, the Stepp Brothers, and the Holden Brothers, who recorded for Decca. He often appeared on the same program as Bill and Charlie Monroe, and for a time played with Charlie Monroe. One memorable night he actually competed against his idol Arthur Smith, and using "Black Mountain Blues" to counter Smith's "Mockingbird" and "Bonaparte's Retreat," he succeeded in tying him on three playoffs. Just how Keith developed the "Black Mountain Blues" during this time is best described in his own words, from his 1948 songbook, a very rare little folio put out while he was working at Bristol:

HISTORY OF "THE BLACK MOUNTAIN BLUES"
by
Leslie Keith

I was born in 1906 in the mountains of Old Virginia. When I was a very small boy my greatest ambition was to become a fiddler. Every time I was where there was a fiddle, I would try to play it. In fact, I would walk for miles to be around one, hoping that I would get a chance to play it. When I was 20 years old my mother bought for me the fiddle I now have. We had a Victrola, so I managed to get a few records that were old-time fiddle tunes.

Well, after I played those records and learned them, it wasn't so hard for me to fiddle most anything I wanted. When a stage show would come through our little town, most of them would let me do a number on their show as a guest artist. The people seemed to like it very well.

Then I decided to get down to business and learn everything I possibly could about old-time fiddling, so I could get on radio. Then a little later I tried out at WBRC in Birmingham, Alabama, passing the audition with the fiddle. I played there a while.

Then my mother and I moved to Tennessee. Where we lived in Tennessee we could see the "Black Mountains," and so one Sunday afternoon while I was sitting out on the front porch, I decided to make a tune and call it the "Black Mountain Blues." I had learned a tune from a real old fiddler down in Alabama which he had called "The Lost Child."

So I took a little bit of this tune, and a little of two or three of the Carter Family's tunes, and put them all together and made "The Black Mountain Blues."

The first time I played "The Black Mountain Blues" on the radio, I began to get lots of requests saying they liked the tune very much. Then in a few weeks I had gotten so much mail for "The Black Mountain Blues" that I had to play it almost every day to answer the requests. I've received more mail for "The Black Mountain Blues" than any five other tunes I play.

During my radio career I have won several big fiddler's contests, and the tune that won all the contests for me was "The Black Mountain Blues," and you radio friends are responsible for making "The Black Mountain Blues" the most popular fiddle tune I play.

I had to quit radio to go into the service in 1942. I was in the army three years. I was overseas for seventeen months and saw service in the North African Campaign. Fourteen months of that time I was entertaining the soldiers playing "The Black Mountain Blues," which seemed to be the favorite for thousands of soldiers I played it for over there. I am very thankful to be back in the United States playing for my radio friends once again.

So anytime you friends would like to hear "The Black Mountain Blues," or any other tune, just drop me a card or letter to any radio station I may be on and I'll be glad to play it for you.

I also play a five-string banjo and guitar, and try to sing. So here is hoping that each and every one will enjoy the pictures and history of "The Black Mountain Blues."

There is indeed a Black Mountain near Crossville, in Cumberland County; it is located on state sector maps on Grassy Cove 117 SW, and is near the Cumberland County line in the south central section of the county, near Burke and Big Lick. People have often mistakenly assumed that the Black Mountain of the tune is the more famous Black Mountain in North Carolina, and, in fact, one claimant to the origin of the tune lives in the North Carolina town. Keith's testimony, though, pretty much proves the name of the tune came from this Tennessee site, and no evidence whatsoever has been found of an earlier reference to the tune under the "Black Mountain" title.

More interesting and complex is Keith's admission that he adapted the tune from a "real old" Alabama fiddler's version of "The Lost Child." In a later interview with John Delgatto, Keith specified that this fiddler was a man named Jim Montgomery, a neighboring farmer whom Keith knew from Birmingham. He also recalled that another Alabama duo, the Stripling Brothers, recorded a version of "The Lost Child" in Birmingham in 1928. This version was quite popular and influential and was kept in print on various labels throughout the 1930s.

Charles and Ira Stripling (their names, coincidentally, were to be echoed in a later famous Alabama duo, the Louvin Brothers) were from Kennedy, Alabama, in Pickens County, just due west from Birmingham on the Alabama-Mississippi line. (One of their best tunes was "Kennedy Rag" which is still played by Norman Blake, among others.) They learned many of their tunes from local west Alabama fiddlers, including "Big Footed Nigger in the Sandy Land." They played a number of cross-tuned, bluesy pieces, including "Wolves Howling," another of their most famous. (It and others are included in County 401, *The Stripling Brothers: Old Time Fiddle Tunes*.) The brothers played fiddling contests all over the South until 1939, and recorded until 1936. In later years Ira ran a business in Birmingham and Charlie became a deacon in the Baptist church. They were recorded a final time in 1952 for the Library of Congress, but few of these tapes have been circulated.

There is no way of knowing exactly how "Lost Child" moved through the Stripling Brothers' repertoire. They admitted they had learned their version from another old-time west Alabama fiddler named Pleaz Carroll, about whom little is known. There is no evidence to connect the Striplings or Pleaz Carroll with the Jim Montgomery who taught the tune to Leslie Keith. However, there is evidence that the tune was well known in central Alabama in the 1930s, even apart from the Striplings' recording of it. For instance, in Carl Carmer's portrait of Alabama folklife, *Stars Fell on Alabama*, published in 1934 but based on trips around the state several years before, "Lost Child" appears in a list of fiddle tune titles he gathered from area fiddlers. The tune may well have been in folk tradition before the Striplings got it.

One thing is certain: without doubt, the Striplings' recording of "Lost Child" is the basic melody for "The Black Mountain Blues" as Keith played it. Anyone who listens to the County reissue can determine this for himself. When Keith claimed he took "a little bit of this tune" ("Lost Child"), he was not entirely accurate: he took quite a bit of it. In fact, the B and C sections of the Striplings' "Lost Child" are virtually identical to Keith's version; these are the sections that involve pizzicato effects. The A part of the Stripling version differs from Keith's in the last phrase only; Keith here uses a minor blues run and sliding notes which differ from the Striplings'. Both Keith and the Striplings use a version in the C section that later musicians were to change: they both play a version of "Bile 'Em Cabbage Down" by strumming the fiddle strings.

To complicate matters more, in 1952 the Striplings recorded their version of "The Black Mountain Rag" for Ray Browne and the Library of Congress. We have no records of what the Striplings might have said about this tune, or whether they considered it related to "Lost Child," but their 1952 recording is quite different from the 1928 version of "Lost

Child." Their A and B parts are pretty much normal, but their C strain is a dramatic departure from the Keith "Lost Child"-"Cabbage"-strumming business. Charlie instead builds a phrase around a dramatic F# note repeated in sharp staccato bursts, very much like a jazz trumpet soloist. By this time, it is quite possible that the Striplings had been exposed to the popular records of the "Black Mountain Blues" and were basing their version on those rather than on any earlier form. It is also possible that they were reflecting yet a third family of tunes that didn't get documented.

Whatever the case, as the Stripling Brothers' star descended, Keith's began to rise. By 1939, when the Striplings stopped going to fiddlers' contests, Keith was in custody of the tune. When he first played the tune over WHIS Bluefield, he recalled, "I went up there and did that tune and the phone didn't stop ringing all that day. By the fourth day, I had between 380 and 400 pieces of mail calling for that piece!" He played his tune overseas, as he mentioned in his account, and then in 1946 he got a call from Lee Stanley, who asked him to play the fiddle with and teach the business to Stanley's two sons Carter and Ralph. Keith joined the Stanleys, along with Pee Wee Lambert, on a new radio station, WCYB, in Bristol. The show was called "Farm and Fun Time." Dates get vague in here, and people's memories get fuzzy when you talk to them, but it is very important to establish exactly what happens next and when it happens.

We know Keith was on board with the band by March 22, 1947, for that week's issue of *Billboard* reported: "Leslie Keith is at WCYB, Bristol, Va., with Carter Stanley and the Clinch Mountain Boys." We also know, from old WCYB radio transcriptions that are dated, that he left the Stanleys and was with Curly King & the Tennessee Hilltoppers, a rival Bristol band which was more country than bluegrass, by Christmas of 1948. Keith recalls that he was with King "less than a year." Transcriptions show him gone by June 1949, and Bill Bolick, of the Blue Sky Boys, remembers that Keith joined them in June of 1949. Thus it would seem that, assuming he stayed with King nine or ten months, that Keith left the Stanleys sometime in September or October 1948.

This date is confirmed by other sources. Jim Shumate, his replacement, only stayed with the Stanleys a short time before he left to join Flatt & Scruggs in late summer 1948, and it was after this that Keith joined Curly King's band. This is important, because sometime during this period Keith made his original recording of "Black Mountain Blues" for Jim Stanton's Rich-R-Tone label in Johnson City, Tennessee. Stanton recalled: "Leslie came to me with this 'Black Mountain Blues.' I remember he had just left the Stanley Brothers and was working with Curly King, and that it was a sort of a comedown for a man like Leslie. He did a session with Curly, and then wanted to do his 'Black Mountain Blues.' His wife did a vocal act then as Little Maggie, and she recorded some piece on the other side [this was "Two Finger Rag"], and we recorded 'Black Mountain Blues' for the main side. Don Campbell played steel, Shorty Marshall on bass, Maggie played rhythm guitar, and Leslie fiddle." Without doubt, Keith had left the Stanleys and was with King when he made this important recording of the tune that had become so associated with him.

The two tunes were scheduled for release on Rich-R-Tone 428, and while we have release dates for some Rich-R-Tones (427, for instance, was released April 16, 1949, and 431 was issued July 21, 1948), these dates don't seem to follow any chronological order, and are not very useful in determining recording dates. However, the fact that the released number 428 had been *assigned* before 431, and thus, July 21, 1948, suggests that the tune had been recorded by then. Most of the original Rich-R-Tone files were destroyed in a fire years later, and the master numbers seem to have been assigned by the pressing plant and make no chronological sense at all. Yet our chronology of Keith's movements make it unlikely that he recorded the piece before July 1948, since he didn't join King's band (which included Don Campbell, who played on the record) until September or October 1948. There is also the problem that an American Federation of Musicians union ban on all recording extended from January 1948 throughout most of the year. Assuming that country artists and independent labels heeded this ban (a somewhat questionable assumption, to be sure), this would mean that Keith probably recorded the piece in the fall of 1948.

Recording and releasing are two quite different things, though. When was Rich-R-Tone 428 released to the public? A list sent to Jim Stanton from his pressing plant in 1950 shows that 428 had still not been released at that time, and record collectors have not been able to turn up any copies of 428. Still, Jim Stanton recalled that 500 copies were pressed, but they were "not promoted very well." Why? There was apparently some disharmony between Carter Stanley and Leslie

Keith over his leaving the Clinch Mountain Boys. Keith mentions in his *Bluegrass Unlimited* account that when he met his replacement, Jim Shumate, Shumate asked him, "Did they give you a dirty deal in any way— if they did I'm just going home," to which Keith replied, "It's perfectly all right, Jimmy, they're good boys." He also said that the Stanleys wanted a faster, more bluegrass-styled fiddler, and asked him to leave. Yet Jim Stanton recalled that Carter Stanley didn't want the record of Keith's promoted. "Carter got mad at me for doing it," he recalled. "I lost interest in it because I didn't want to rock the boat. I used to let Carter tell me what to do too much." The Stanleys were still the big stars of the Rich-R-Tone label, and Stanton couldn't afford to alienate them. Also, he was by no means sure Keith had written the tune. "Every fiddler I've met claims to have written 'Black Mountain Rag,'" he recalled. "Every one of them does that finger picking part in a slightly different way, and that's where they get the idea that they wrote it. Leslie Keith had a special way of doing that where he would pluck and fiddle at the same time—it was a cute deal and nobody else could do it." So in the end, possibly due to pressure from Carter Stanley, Keith's first recording of "Black Mountain Blues" was not distributed to the public.

Perhaps it wouldn't have made much difference anyway. For before Keith did his recording, the piece had been recorded by the man who was to play probably the biggest role in popularizing it, Curly Fox. On June 5, 1948, while Keith was still playing with the Stanleys, *Billboard* announced the release of King 710, "Black Mountain Rag" backed with "Come Here Son," as played by Curly Fox.

This piece had been recorded back in 1947, before the recording ban, but when? The King logbooks for 1947 show master numbers but no exact dates, and the *Billboard* news columns for 1947 show no news of the Curly Fox–Texas Ruby session that produced "Black Mountain Rag." Yet the *Billboard* files do describe a Homer & Jethro session that took place in October 1947, and by comparing those master numbers with Fox's, we can estimate that the recording session took place in November 1947. (Even this, though, is not the first known recording of this piece under the name "Black Mountain Blues" or "Black Mountain Rag." That honor goes to a fiddler named Sam Leslie, who, accompanied by guitarist Palmer Crisp, recorded a version for the Library of Congress in 1946. It was recorded by Margaret Mayo, Stu Jamieson, and

Freyda Simons on a field trip to Allen, Kentucky, and was later issued on AAFS LP No. 20. This was not a commercial recording, though, and was not made public for some years; Sam Leslie seems to have gotten the piece from Keith's version.)

Curly Fox's November 1947 recording of the tune marks its first commercial appearance on disc. It was one of eighteen songs he and Texas Ruby and their band did at a marathon session, probably called because record companies wanted to stockpile recordings in anticipation of the looming American Federation of Musicians strike. The band members at that time were Red Phillips (guitar and bass), Ozzie Middleton (steel), and Mose Rager, who takes a brilliant electric guitar solo on the C part of Fox's recording of "Black Mountain Rag." (The legendary Kentucky guitar player who taught Merle Travis how to play the finger picking "Kentucky choke" style, Rager spent only a few years as a professional, and his work with Curly Fox yielded some of his only known vintage recordings.)

Fox recalled how he came by the tune:

> Part of it I made up. But I can tell you where I got the idea from. In 1935 I played a fiddler's contest at the auditorium in Charleston, West Virginia, and I met a guy there named Leslie Keith who played this piece with his fiddle tuned up in this crazy key. I heard him and thought it was the quaintest sound I had ever heard on a fiddle. Well, back then you didn't want to go up to a guy and ask him how he played a tune, so I finally figured it out for myself. I finally worked out my own bass part, different from his, with the double string work. It took me about six months, but I finally got it into my own syncopated style, where you play on top of the beat. I didn't use it for a while, though, and when I did I changed the name from "Black Mountain Blues" to "Black Mountain Rag" because it was too fast for a blues. Jimmy McCarroll and I had earlier done a thing called "Home Town Blues" that was too fast and which we changed to "Home Town Rag." I got to playing it on the Grand Ole Opry, and then when we went up to do this session for King, we were doing eighteen sides, and Ruby was getting as hoarse as a horse. To give her a break Syd Nathan [the owner of King] said, "Curly, haven't you got a fiddle tune to throw in," and I said, "Hell, I got a hundred of them." Then Red Phillips, my bass

player for fifteen years said, "Hey, Curly, let's do that 'Black Mountain Rag.'" So we throwed it in, not thinking much about it. They were bettin' on singers in those days and didn't do anything special to promote the record.

Nevertheless, the pairing of fiddle tunes was the second record issued from the session, and became the decade's biggest selling instrumental country record—and probably the biggest selling fiddle record of all time. Fox recalled that total sales eventually topped out at 600,000 copies. Yet the piece never got onto the *Billboard* best-selling charts. Why? Fox said he sold most of his copies at personal appearances and thus they weren't reflected in the *Billboard* charts, drawn from jukebox plays and radio station plays.

Hundreds of young fiddlers had experiences with Fox's record that were like those described by Gordon Terry. "Ain't no telling how many nickels I put in the jukebox when Curly's record of 'Black Mountain Rag' came out. And I played it for six months on the jukebox before I found out he had it cross-tuned. And don't you know I had a problem trying to play it? I wanted to play it and I did day and night until I learned it."

Comparing Fox's version to others, one first notices the breakneck tempo he sets—twice as fast as many of the others, including Keith's 1974 remake of it on his Briar LP. The double stops and shuffle rhythm are prominent, and Mose Rager takes the C part on the guitar; Fox does try on one verse to pluck the C part, not too successfully. By the third verse, Rager's guitar parts have become independent take-off solos, with little relationship to the melody line. Unlike many modern fiddlers, Fox does not double-time the tempo on the last verse, and unlike many other fiddlers he embroiders the melody with daring jazz-like frills and runs. It is a splendid performance and deserves its fame.

Since King 710 was released in the middle of the recording ban, other companies couldn't get cover versions of the song out to take advantage of Curly Fox's sales. When the ban ended, the race was on. On January 15, 1949, Roy Acuff's fiddler Tommy Magness recorded a version with Acuff's band for Columbia in Nashville. This excellent version, however, was never issued as a single and came out in May of 1949 as part of an album of square dance tunes issued by Roy's band. Magness copyrighted the tune with the Acuff-Rose publishing company in

February 1949, and his family continues to feel that he had a hand in writing it, but there is no real evidence to suggest this. Magness's version is not really any different from others, except that it is taken at a slower tempo and is backed only by acoustic instruments. Leslie Keith told John Delgatto that Magness "was never able to do the 'pickin' part,'" but in fact he does so quite well on the Acuff record.

Other cover recordings soon followed. Jim Stanton himself got one by Glen Neaves which he issued on his subsidiary Folk-Star label, and Tommy Jackson used the piece for one of his first Mercury recordings in 1949. In later years other performers continued to revitalize interest in the "Rag." Tex Logan almost started a riot at the old Newport Folk Festival in the 1960s when he did the tune with the Lilly Brothers, and Doc Watson copied Curly Fox's record and made the "Rag" into a guitar picking showcase. Chet Atkins even recorded a version with the Boston Pops Orchestra.

A list of fiddlers who have recorded the "Black Mountain Rag" would take pages, but it would be highly instructive to compile a tape of different versions and examine it for stylistic differences. It would be a great litmus paper for the nuances of American fiddling. But, in spite of all its popularity, the "Rag" still is a mystery tune, coming from the misty farmland background in the western Alabama fields of the 1920s to the glittering show palaces of Las Vegas in the 1980s. How did the "Lost Child" become the "Rag" and who were the musicians who preserved it until Leslie Keith and Curly Fox could bring it before the American public? Many answers are gone forever: the Stripling Brothers, Leslie Keith, Tommy Magness, Carter Stanley, and Tommy Jackson have passed away, and the valuable record company files are missing or destroyed. What we have left is a case of circumstantial evidence that can only partly suggest the full pedigree of one of the most exciting tunes in American music history.

"Over the Waves":
Notes toward a History

SOMEONE ONCE SAID, "NO ONE REALLY LISTENS TO WALTZES—
except fiddlers." There may be some truth to that: certainly the
average fan at a fiddling contest gets tired of hearing a procession
of waltzes, some of which drone on for five or six minutes. But most
fiddlers know that a good waltz is the ultimate test of many features of
fiddling, such as tone and bow control. That's why waltzes have always
been a part of fiddling contests. But there's been very, very little written about the country waltz. I can recall one brief article in *John Edwards
Memorial Foundation Quarterly* a few years ago. There are a few record
albums devoted to the waltz, by Chubby Wise and (an early) Vassar
Clements. But for as great a role as it has played in old-time fiddling,
the waltz has been sadly neglected.

Perhaps the most popular current waltz among Southeastern fiddlers (and most most Tennessee Valley Old-Time Fiddlers Association
members) is "Over the Waves." I recall hearing this tune no less than
twenty-six times at the annual Athens, Alabama, convention in 1974
during the eliminations. "Over the Waves" has always been a popular
country waltz and is one of the most enduring tunes to have entered
the folk fiddling tradition. A fascinating study could be made on the
ways in which the tune itself has changed over the years, or even how
different fiddlers play the tune now in different styles. Folklorists are
forever collecting and studying the texts of vocal songs: when are we
going to get the same treatment for instrumental tunes? A brief history of "Over the Waves" reveals the kind of things such an instrumental
"family tree" can yield.

Most people think that "Over the Waves" was written by Strauss,
the famous German "waltz king." The tune did have a light classical ori-

gin, but not with Strauss. The tune's composer was in reality a Mexican native named Juventino Rosas (1868–1894). Rosas is listed today as a "serious" composer, but he spent much of his life involved with the folk fiddling of his native Mexico. Rosas was a pure-blooded Otomi Indian, and by the time he was eight years old he was playing a small fiddle in his father's band in Mexico City. This band, apparently an itinerant stringband, roamed the streets playing on corners for coins. Juventino's brother, the guitarist in the band, was killed in a lover's quarrel, and Juventino got a job as a violinist in a church (where he doubled as bell ringer). By the time he was fifteen, the young violinist was good enough to land a job as first violinist in a touring opera company.

But it was hard to make a living doing opera throughout the Mexican countryside, and the company soon disbanded. Juventino was forced to join the army to keep on eating. He was an army bandsman, and he gained a working knowledge of band music during this time. But he wasn't cut out for the army life, and he returned to Mexico City. Here he decided to try to make it as a composer, and began doing drawing-room pieces for a Mexican publishing company. In 1891 he wrote a set of waltzes entitled "Sobre las olas," which translated into English as "Over the Waves." The waltz became popular at once in Mexican orchestras, especially as a dance tune. But Juventino was not really too worried about it. During this time he had suffered through a frustrating love affair, and finally, in disgust, he joined a traveling *zarzuela* company and took off for Havana. (The *zarzuela* was a sort of combination of a folk opera and a minstrel show and featured very lively tunes and music.) In Havana, Juventino caught a fever and in 1894, at the young age of twenty-six, he died.

It is by no means clear how Juventino Rosas's popular Mexican hit of 1891 made its way north into the United States and into nearly every aspect of American folk and even popular music. For the song was by no means known only to country fiddlers. Early New Orleans jazz men played the tune (and still do); it was known as a standard for concert bands and was recorded by a formal concert orchestra for Victor Records in 1926. Mario Perry recorded an Italian accordion solo of the piece in New York in 1926. The Italian connection to the tune was emphasized even more in 1951 when it was used in the Hollywood film *The Great Caruso*, a musical biography of the greatest of the Italian singers. Here the song was rearranged and fitted with words by Paul Webster and Francis Aaronson and was called "The Loveliest Night of the Year." It was sung by the star of the film, Mario Lanza, and became a big popular hit of 1951.

But the tune was also being recorded by old-time fiddlers during this time. The tune was apparently part of the Northeastern fiddler's repertoire, for it was recorded by Henry Ford's Old Time Dance Orchestra (fiddle, dulcimer, cembalo, and tuba) in 1925, and Ford probably published the music to it in his series on old-time dances he ran in *The Dearborn Independent*, his weekly magazine. But an important Southern version of the song was recorded in Dallas in 1925 by Jimmy Wilson's Catfish Band, an outfit that influenced countless musicians in the Southwest, including Bob Wills. Uncle Steve Hubbard recorded an early version for Gennett, and Doc Roberts recorded later 1931 versions for the same label. Roberts was one of the most influential Southern fiddlers, and his version might well have been the prime source for many Southern fiddlers. Other early versions included those of the Stripling Brothers (Decca), the Humphries Brothers (Okeh), and the Perry Brothers (Decca); there are probably a dozen other ones lurking under assumed names. Mississippi duo Narmour & Smith called their unusual version "Winona Echoes," and Doc Roberts called his (in one version) "Farewell Waltz." Later versions were recorded by Bob Wills and Arkansas bandleader Hugh Ashley. Oddly, the Library of Congress catalogues only list two pre-1940 recordings of this song: a harmonica solo recorded in Calumet Michigan in 1938 and a version by the Mitchell (South Dakota) Old Time Orchestra in 1939—which shows the tune was still nationwide in its folk appeal. (I would appreciate further contributions from readers knowing of other early Southern fiddle versions of "Over the Waves.")

Often we see folk melodies go into classical music: the works of Dvořák, Ives, and Copland are but three examples. But it's rarer to find a classical melody going into folk tradition, as "Over the Waves" did. When the full history of the melody is traced, it will be a fascinating account of how all facets of American music can work together.

Tommy Jackson:
Portrait of a Nashville Session Fiddler

T OMMY JACKSON'S NAME STILL COMES UP A LOT WHENEVER
fiddlers get together to talk about their art, even though he died
in 1979, was virtually inactive for ten years before that, and none
of his records have been in print for years. Fiddlers who are in their
prime today remember Tommy Jackson as "the old man," their major
influence when they were starting out. Very few fiddlers around today
learned directly from the early masters like Doc Roberts and Clayton
McMichen, and it's getting harder to find musicians who learned
directly from such "middle generation" stalwarts such as Arthur Smith
or Georgia Slim. But Tommy Jackson hit his stride in the 1950s and
1960s, and for a decade or so his records were about the only fiddle
records on the market.

There are odd signs of just how influential Jackson's music was. An
excellent instrument maker in Tennessee recently received an order
from Sweden for a fiddle. Along with it was a dog-eared copy of a
Tommy Jackson LP. The customer wanted a fiddle with the same kind
of tone as the one heard on the record. Young musicians have to borrow some old Jackson albums to tape and invariably find them well
worn. "One of them was flat worn out," said one such borrower. "I had
never seen an LP that was literally worn out, but this one about was."

What can account for this popularity? Tommy Jackson didn't play a
lot of rare tunes, and he was certainly no virtuoso fiddler on his
albums. Art Galbraith, veteran Ozarks fiddler and student of Jackson's,
has explained: "There's no better way to learn a tune than from a
Tommy Jackson album. He plays the melodies absolutely straight and

true with almost no embroidery, and you can really hear what the melody is supposed to sound like." Others like Jackson's drive and his timing (he always used a full Nashville studio rhythm section), while others liked his tone.

Still others admired his versatility. He could play any kind of music, and do it well. He was a master studio musician, and those who somehow never heard his fiddle LPs heard him on countless country records by every major singer. He created back-up styles used today by country bands, and, when the chips were down, could jam with the best of them, playing chorus after chorus of jazzy take-off solos.

During his life Tommy Jackson played his share of music. For over twenty years, he was the premier Nashville studio fiddler, and he probably played on more records than any fiddler in history. His back-up work ranged all the way from Hank Williams to acid rock, from the western swing of Bob Wills to the bluegrass of Bill Monroe, from the banjo picking of Grandpa Jones to the smooth stylings of Tammy Wynette. In addition to countless sessions backing up other stars, Jackson emerged as a star in his own right in the mid-1950s, when his long series of fiddle albums became popular with square dancers around the country. Fiddlers and bluegrass musicians listened too, for during the 1950s Tommy Jackson was about the only fiddler you could hear on records and on radio, and a strong case could be made for Jackson's keeping fiddling alive in Nashville during those lean years when rock & roll threatened to engulf country and bluegrass. It was difficult for any fiddler growing up in the late 1950s and early 1960s to avoid coming under Jackson's influence to at least some extent.

Lovers of classic bluegrass have listened to Jackson's fiddling more times than they realize. He was the fiddler on Bill Monroe's 1951 version of "Kentucky Waltz" and was twin fiddling with Gordon Terry on several 1957 songs, including "Fallen Star." He recorded with Charlie Monroe on his 1956 session for Decca. He was on the first great Capitol session with Jim & Jesse, at Nashville's old Tulane Hotel in the early 1950s, and he backed his pal Mac Wiseman on some of Mac's best Dot records, including his 1960 version of "Two Different Worlds," with the Osborne Brothers. (Mac himself once went out of his way to play back-up guitar for one of Jackson's solo fiddle LPs on Dot.) Jackson himself recorded an LP of *Greatest Bluegrass Hits* which included his unique fiddle versions of "Uncle Pen," "Cabin in the Hills," and "Blue

Moon of Kentucky." Red Rector was an unsung sideman on one of
Jackson's albums, and Oscar Sullivan (of Lonzo & Oscar) played on
another. There are probably dozens of other examples of Jackson playing bluegrass, even though he didn't really consider himself a bluegrass
fiddler. He recalled: "I've always played enough of it to get by because
with the stuff, you have to play it pretty much all the time just to stay
with it. I've always concentrated on having a variety of things to do.
When you're making a living at it, you don't know till you get into a
studio what you're going to be asked to play."

Since Jackson won a place in history as one of the first Nashville
studio stars—one of the original "Nashville Cats"—it is perhaps sym-
bolic that Jackson was a complete product of the Nashville music
scene. Though he was born in Birmingham (March 31, 1926), his family
moved to Nashville when he was barely one, and he grew up listening
to the Grand Ole Opry of the early 1930s. He recalled that he was fascinated with the two leading fiddlers on the Opry then: "Grandpappy"
George Wilkerson, the original head of the Fruit Jar Drinkers, and
Arthur Smith, then with the Dixieliners. (Jackson later recorded many
of Smith's tunes on his fiddle LPs and made them available to new generations of fiddlers.) There was a little music in Jackson's immediate
family: his grandfather had been an old-time fiddler, and his uncles, but
there was apparently not much contact with their music. His own
father was a barber, and when young Tommy started showing an early
interest in the fiddle, he encouraged him. Some of Jackson's earliest
memories are of his father taking him at the tender age of seven into
local Nashville bars and letting him sit up on the bar and saw out "Back
Up and Push" for nickels and dimes.

"I've been a professional since I was ten years old," Jackson was
fond of telling reporters. He was indeed a passable fiddler when he was
ten and formed a local band with a neighbor kid named Russell Handy,
who played guitar. A couple of cousins, a bit older, joined, and the
band had a mandolin and bass fiddle. "Those were pretty hard times
back then, and the four of us would go down and play on street corners in downtown Nashville. We'd stop on a street corner, start playing, pass the hat—you'd be surprised at how much money we'd get. Of
course, the cops would run us off, but we'd just move to another corner, pass the hat, start all over again. We called the group the Tennessee Mountaineers. I did a lot of fiddle tunes, and Russell knew a

bunch of old songs. I remember especially 'Greenback Dollar'—I guess that's one of the first songs I learned to play with him."

Before long the boys began to play regularly at Nashville radio station WSIX, on a Saturday program called "The Old Country Store." It was an hour show, sort of a mini-Grand Ole Opry, with a variety of local semi-professional acts on it. The boys got $1.50 for doing the show—good money, perhaps, for 1936, but still not as lucrative as "busking" on street corners. They found out they could hit the streets in early evening—around six—and play while Nashvillians shopped up and down Church Street. "We got to where we would make $40 to $50 a week doing that. The money helped out, and it sure helped out at home too, because money was pretty tight then." Later, movie houses would hire Tommy and Russell to stand outside the box office and play fiddle tunes. Curious onlookers would gather, watch the boys, look over the movie posters, and get hooked. Anybody that liked good fiddling, it would seem, could also appreciate the Marx Brothers.

After Russell Handy left town in 1938, Jackson got plenty of work with other groups in the area. Before he was out of high school, he was working up to five days a week for an early morning radio show and was playing square dances and beer taverns at night. For a time he was with Goober & the Kentuckians in the early 1940s, broadcasting over WSIX, and by the time he had graduated from high school in early 1944 he was a seasoned musician. In the war years, when able-bodied men were hard to come by, he could get work with a number of name bands.

Thus he found himself, at age seventeen, playing regularly on the Grand Ole Opry. Curly Williams, the leader and fiddler of the Georgia Peach Pickers, went back to the farm and Jackson replaced him in the band. He worked with Jimmy Selph in the band, which was not really a classic stringband so much as a more modern, western-style band featuring a smooth vocal trio, steel guitar, and the lot. A few months later he joined Paul Howard's Arkansas Cottonpickers and learned even more about western swing. It was a short apprenticeship, though. The draft was staring Jackson in the face, and on April 17, in order to get into the Army Air Corps, he enlisted.

Unlike a lot of musicians, Jackson didn't play all that much music during his military service. Most of the time he was crouched in the tail gunner's turret of a B-29 making reconnaissance flights over the Pacific. He loved flying, and in later life had a pilot's license for a time. Once he and his B-29 crew flew north from their base in Arizona and flew the huge bomber down into the Grand Canyon: "That's something very few people's ever done," he told a reporter. By the end of the war, he had made sergeant, turned down an offer to attend Officer Candidate School, and collected four bronze stars, the Air Medal, and a few other honors. When the war was winding down, he did find some pickers on the remote Pacific island of Tinian and got up a weekly jam session. There were fringe benefits in the fact that two of the jammers worked daytime in the officers' mess and managed to keep the little stringband very well fed.

He was discharged on April 3, 1946, and as soon as he got back to Nashville he resumed work as a free-lance, full-time professional musician. He toured for a while with Whitey Ford, the Duke of Paducah, along with a road show that included Annie Lou & Danny, the York Brothers (a nice brother duet from Kentucky who recorded a lot for King), and Jimmy Selph. Jackson quickly found out, though, that he didn't like road work: he was uneasy driving and hated traveling. In those days, it was virtually impossible for a country musician to be a professional unless he toured constantly, but Jackson was young and didn't know that. He hooked up with Milton Estes & His Musical Millers, who were just starting a new program on WSM for Martha White Flour. (This was the early morning program that would later feature Flatt & Scruggs, and which was still aired decades later at 5:45 A.M. over WSM.) "I was able to stay in town pretty much then," Jackson recalled. "We worked short dates, couldn't get very far with that early morning show." After a year or so at this, Red Foley came to town and started another early morning show, aired about two hours later. "Red offered me a job, and I didn't have to get up so early, so I took it." It was a good move.

In 1948–49 Red Foley was emerging as one of the leading singers in the nation, and in addition to his morning show, he soon was handling "The Prince Albert Show," the part of the Opry that was carried coast-to-coast on the network. Regulars on the show included comedy stars Rod Brasfield and Minnie Pearl, the Jordanaires (later to become back-up group for Elvis Presley), and banjoist Stringbean. Jackson, part of Foley's regular band, the Cumberland Valley Boys, usually had a fiddle solo somewhere in the show. Even so, there was not much money in it. Jackson remembered, "Road scale back then was $10 a day. That Prince Albert Show paid $22 or $24, and there were 600 or 700 stations that carried it." Jackson began to look for other sources of income.

One was recording. Jackson had been working closely with other members of Foley's band, including Zeke Turner, a lead guitar player; Jerry Byrd, a steel guitarist; and Louis Innis, a rhythm guitarist. The four of them began to get a reputation as a solid, versatile band adept at playing all sorts of music. Record producers like Capitol's Ken Nelson and Decca's Paul Cohen (who recorded Foley) were coming into Nashville to use the new studios that were slowly developing and were wanting to use pickup bands to back their singers. "Since we were the only band that stayed in town all the time, they started using us on most of the recordings by other artists." Through this odd combination of circumstances, the Jackson-Innis-Turner-Byrd band became the first real Nashville studio band, and Tommy Jackson found himself defining a new type of music profession.

Jackson's first record was a momentous one: The second session was by a new Alabama singer named Hank Williams, four sides recorded in the old WSM studios on February 13, 1947, for the old Sterling label. Jackson's fiddling pleased Hank and Fred Rose, and later Williams sessions followed. In April 1947 Jackson created the famous fiddle intro to "I Saw the Light," and played on "Move It on Over," Hank's first big hit. In 1948 he backed Hank on "Lovesick Blues," in a rare session recorded in Cincinnati.

The studio band, of course, backed Red Foley on his recordings as well, including classics like "Satisfied Mind" and "Never Trust a Woman." The problem in working with Red, though, was that Foley would periodically get tired of his radio show and dissolve the band. A few weeks later, he would call up and re-form. "It was a little nerve-wracking; you didn't know from day to day whether you had a job." Because of this the band moved, in November 1948, to Cincinnati and struck out on its own as the Pleasant Valley Boys. Soon they were making $200 a week from WLW and appearing on "Everybody's Farm Hour" with Farmer Roy Battles. They also found that the record producers they had worked for in Nashville thought enough of their work to move many of their sessions to Cincinnati. In addition, they became a regular studio band for King Records, headquartered in Cincinnati, and did sessions with the likes of Cowboy Copas, Hawkshaw Hawkins, Grandpa Jones, the Delmore Brothers, and the York Brothers. Occasionally guitarist Billy Grammar was flown in from Washington to augment their studio band.

It was while he was in Cincinnati that Jackson made his first solo records. He was doing a back-up session for Rex Allen, the cowboy singer then under contract to Mercury. In charge of the session was Murray Nash, then gaining fame as the producer for the first Flatt & Scruggs records. Allen's father was a fiddler, and he liked fiddling. He asked Jackson to make a couple of custom discs of "Black Mountain Rag" and "Fire on the Mountain." Jackson obliged, and Nash liked the songs enough to release them as singles.

Sales were surprisingly strong, and between 1949 and 1953 Jackson cut twelve fiddle standards on the Mercury label. In 1953 he signed a contract with the newly formed Dot record company of Gallatin, Tennessee, and continued to record successful singles. His first Dot release was "Arkansas Traveler" / "Soldier's Joy," one of the first Dot records to be issued on both 45 and 78 formats. But the real innovation came a few months later, when Dot got the idea of combining twelve of Jackson's singles onto an LP format and aimed it at the square-dance audience. Square dancing was becoming a big middle-class social fad in the early 1950s, and clubs were springing up everywhere. There was a need for canned square dance music that a local caller could use when calling a dance, and a need for fiddle tunes that went on longer than the customary three minute limit of the 45 or 78. Jackson's LPs filled this need, and they were lapped up. *Popular Square Dance Music—Without Calls* (1953) was quickly followed by *Square Dance Tonight* (1957) and *Do Si Do*, which offered detailed dance instructions on the back of the album. Before it was all over, Jackson had piled up eleven LPs for Dot and around thirty singles.

Jackson's square-dance sales made him the most heard, and the most imitated, fiddler of his generation. "I always kept the tunes as simple as possible, 'cause I was selling a beat," he explained. He broke with tradition after his first few records, and added a full rhythm section: piano, bass, drums, guitar, and mandolin. His favorite back-up man was Hank Garland, the legendary Nashville guitarist, who played some lead guitar and often even mandolin on Jackson's sessions. The

Dot engineers also played games with the sound of Jackson's fiddle. His son Mychael told me, "A lot of fiddlers wonder how Tommy got that special tone to his fiddling. Some of it was done in the studio. Dad used to try to explain it. He said that instead of putting a slap-back on the bass, they would put a slap-back on his fiddle." For whatever reason, Jackson's clean, driving, straightforward style won a lot of admirers. And some of the tunes he wrote or popularized—such as "Crazy Creek," "Cherokee Shuffle," "Acorn Hill" (named after a little town where his wife's folks came from), and "Bitter Creek Breakdown"—are still standards among fiddlers today. A few of his records, such as his Decca version of Arthur Smith's "Fiddler's Dream," sold over 40,000 copies in the 1960s.

Meanwhile, he continued to make a name for himself in session and radio work. He, along with the rest of the Pleasant Valley Boys, had returned to Nashville after a year or so at WLW. He broke with Red Foley shortly after Foley left Nashville to go to the Ozark Jubilee in Springfield, Missouri, about 1954. He realized, perhaps with a start, that he could now make more staying in Nashville studios than going on the road, even with a headliner like Foley. He soon found dates with everyone from Roy Acuff to Ernest Tubb, and recorded with most in between. Among his favorites were Faron Young, on whose recordings Jackson popularized a double stop back-up technique, and Ray Price, with whom Jackson invented what Bob Wills later called a "walking fiddle" style and which became vastly popular among back-up men. Soon Jackson was doing so much studio work that he became known as "the fiddle man" to the studio producers, and, as Buddy Spicher recalled, if Jackson couldn't handle all the work, he would broker the overflow to other young fiddlers like Spicher or Johnny Tona.

During the fifties, Jackson also became associated with the Grand Ole Opry. He rejoined the network segment of the Opry, and for some thirteen years he was to have a featured fiddle solo on coast-to-coast radio: another key to his influence on other fiddlers. "This was before the days when they had a staff band," his son recalled, "and Tommy would be there and people would come up to him and say, 'Hey, I've got to go on in ten minutes and I don't have a fiddler. Can you back me up?'—and he'd get out there." Jackson played the famous 1961 Carnegie Hall concert featuring the Opry cast. In fact he opened the show, and he and the Stoney Mountain Cloggers (referred to as "Tommy Jackson's

Square Dance group") were singled out for special praise by the New York reviews. But Jackson left the Opry in 1962 after an argument (a silly one) with Opry manager Ott Devine, and in 1963 embarked on a new career of producer. He became the "Nashville rep" and chief assistant to Texas producer H. W. "Pappy" Daily. Jackson set up important sessions with George Jones, Melba Montgomery, Judy Lynn, Gene Pitney, and others. This lasted about five years, though, and he went back to studio work.

Like many Nashville studio men, Jackson's personal musical preferences went far beyond country. "He liked jazz," said his son, "and a lot of those guys in Ray Price's band did, especially swing." Even before the war, Jackson had collected all the Bob Wills records he could, and liked the hot swing fiddle he heard there. Later he and Wills became close friends—Wills always wanted Jackson for his Nashville sessions, and in the 1960s asked Jackson if he would consider teaming up on the road—and remained an influence on Jackson's music. Another love was the music of French violinist Stephane Grappelli, who worked with Django Reinhardt & the Hot Club of France, a 1930s jazz quintet featuring acoustic guitar and fiddle. Jackson never met Grappelli, but he somehow acquired a complete set of his records on tape and generously shared them with other interested Nashville studio men. In more recent years, Jackson became fascinated with what Vassar Clements was doing on his solo albums and spoke several times of making an album of "commercial jazz" in which he could stretch out and experiment to his heart's content. A slight step in this direction was an album he did with Buddy Spicher, *Country Pops*, for the Somerset label.

And this was part of the problem that dogged him during the last years. His son Mychael, then a successful rock musician performing under the single name Mychael (his real full name, Mychael Jackson, having been usurped), explained some of it: "If I could sum up anything he ever tried to stress to me about music, it was to be an artist. He was definitely an artist. He felt that he was creating an art form. He felt confined to this hoedown style, but that was his bread and butter. He tried to get the record companies to take something besides hoedowns, but they wouldn't. And in a sense, he understood why. He was practical; as much as he loved jazz, he knew he couldn't get too far above people's heads, or it wouldn't sell. When I started out, I was into

Brubeck, and he kept saying, get into simple melodies instead of com-
plicated ones."

It was ironically, a trap Jackson himself had helped build twenty
years before, when he forged his square-dance style and developed the
back-up style for the studios. It was an economic trap and an aesthet-
ic trap, and he grew increasingly bitter and more alienated from the
music scene—especially the newer musicians and producers. The
drinking got worse and worse. "He was pretty well frustrated with the
music business by the time he died," recalled Mychael. "He felt he had
been sort of forgotten. Even in the Nashville papers, he used to say, he
got more publicity on the sports pages for his fishing catch off Center
Hill Lake than he did for his music. It was really sad toward the end. He
wouldn't even talk about the music business, and I couldn't even get
him to pick up his fiddle and jam around the house."

Health problems for Jackson got increasingly worse as well, but
there was still time for a few last good moments. There was a fine 1976
album with Hank Thompson, and Jackson played on his son Mychael's
first RCA album, *Mychael*, a heavy experimental rock album that used a
lot of studio overdubbing. (It was a testament to Jackson's versatility
that he was able to fit into a 1970s rock band.) Apparently Jackson's last
country album was a Columbia set that reunited Ray Price's Cherokee
Cowboys. Jackson never got to do the experimental, free-form fiddle
album he always dreamed of, though Mychael found some studio tapes
in Jackson's files that he hopes some day may make an album.

Jackson died on December 9, 1979, and only a sharp-eyed reader
looking through the death notices in the Nashville papers would have
read about it. Word spread through the grapevine, though, and the
people who picked and fiddled learned about it soon enough. "Tommy
was only fifty-three years old," one friend remarked. "He had a lot
more music to play."

Sources

I did not have an opportunity to interview Tommy Jackson personally, but I did do
extensive interviews with his widow, as well as his son Mychael (Antioch, Tennessee,

February 1982). I also made use of an interview with Jackson by Doug Green, done in Nashville in February 1976. I also drew upon a large collection of personal correspondence, business papers, and photographs in Mychael Jackson's possession. Discographical data were drawn from Dot files at the Country Music Foundation and from the author's personal files.

Ernie Hodges:
From Coal Creek to Bach

IN THE EARLY 1970S, THERE WAS A GOOD DEAL OF discussion in *The Devil's Box* about a famous series of fiddling contests that were held annually at LaFollette, Tennessee, a small town up near the Kentucky state line which had little other claim to fame. Many fiddlers recalled going to LaFollette when younger, and many wrote in to recall some of the impressive musicians they had heard there. One of the repeated winners of the contests in the 1930s was a young man named Ernest Hodges. The name rang a bell with a lot of people, and soon soon readers were writing in saying, "What ever happened to Ernie Hodges?" Somebody suggested in print that he had heard that Hodges had died, and for a time it looked like it was a case of another important fiddler going to his grave without having a chance to tell his story. Then a letter arrived, addressed in a bold, forceful hand, to say that we were wrong in announcing the demise of Ernest Hodges. The writer could speak with a certain authority here, since his name was Ernest Hodges. Like Jonathan Swift's Bickerstaff, he wrote to assert that accounts of his demise were premature, and that he was alive and well and living in Waynesboro, North Carolina.

Ernie Hodges was a letter writer of the old school, and after several months' correspondence, it seemed obvious that he had a remarkable story to tell. Eventually it was told in a series of personal interviews at the Hodges home overlooking Waynesville, a set of visits that eventually led to my producing Ernest's first and only LP album. Though he had not made many commercial records, Hodges had been performing professionally for decades, on radio, on tours, at fiddling contests, and as a teacher. His career path had brought him into contact with almost all of the classic fiddlers from the 1920s and 1930s, and he had stories and opinions about most of them. He was a veritable Boswell of old-time music. He had a keen sense of history, a sharp memory, and an eye for detail. Yet he himself was a superb fiddler who could have been a recording artist as big as Kessinger or Smith, had he chosen to take that route. He didn't, though, and remained an observer of the entire Southern fiddling scene as it developed in the "golden age." His story—presented primarily in the form of an interview—seems an appropriate way to sum up the Southern fiddling scene during the time covered by this book. It is an overall look at the fiddling scene, and lets us see how the different musicians appeared in context.

Ernest Hodges was born on December 26, 1907, at the foot of Beech Mountain, North Carolina, but moved with his family to Kentucky when he was seven. Around 1914 the family settled in Lincoln County, about fifty miles south of Lexington, not too far from Dabville, and not too far from Somerset, home town of fiddling great Leonard Rutherford. Young Ernie grew up listening to many of the area's leading fiddlers, such as Rutherford, Doc Roberts, and Clark Kessinger. In 1926 when he was nineteen, Hodges had started playing and was good enough to enter the fiddlers' contest at the State Fair in Louisville. He didn't win first, but he kept a letter he received from an official, Thomas Basham, explaining why. The letter, dated September 18, 1926, read in part: "I want to compliment you on your splendid playing at the State Fair. But for the fact that the contest had been arranged especially for old fiddlers, you undoubtedly would have won the grand prize. Your being so young, you were handicapped twenty points to start with. . . . As a man who has devoted some twelve years of his life to music, from country dance music to the managing of big orchestras, I want to say that you certainly can play the fiddle."

Hodges soon teamed up with the famous banjo team of Frank Lewis & Bailey Briscoe and traveled throughout the South with them, learning their vast repertoire of traditional and vaudeville tunes, and picking up some of the classical banjo styles of Fred Van Eps and Vess Ossman. Lewis & Briscoe helped to spread this banjo style throughout the South and their influence on playing styles or the region is just now being appreciated. They too never recorded, but through their travels and popularity influenced as many people as most recording artists. Even today Hodges remembers his tenure with these two banjoists as a high point in his life.

By 1928 Hodges had joined with his brother Ralph, a guitarist, and tenor banjoist Johnny Blainer, to form the Hodges Brothers Band. They played around Kentucky and finally on the radio in Cincinnati. There they became the Dixie Vagabonds and were soon heard nationwide on NBC. In the fall of 1934, Hodges went to Atlanta where he performed on WSB, again over an NBC hook-up. At one point, Hodges's fiddling and banjo playing was heard on seventy-two stations nationwide. But Hodges was not satisfied with simply making traditional music. He wanted to learn proper techniques and formal musical methods. Thus from 1934 to 1942 he studied at the Leffinwell Violin School in Atlanta and later became an instructor there. He learned to play and appreciate classical music as well as old-time music. But he continued to play on WSB with major well-known figures from old-time music. There were the Rice Brothers, Paul and Hoke, who played occasionally with the old Skillet Lickers gang and in the 1930s had a string of successful records for Decca. There was also Charlie Bowman, the Johnson City fiddler who played with the original Hill Billies in the late 1920s, and Riley Puckett himself the great blind guitarist, who achieved fame with the Skillet Lickers. There was Dwight Butcher, famous as a vocalist and songwriter. The list goes on and on.

But by about 1940 Hodges began to play less and less traditional music, and in fact did not play much of it for the next twenty years. He remained in Georgia, first at Five Points near Atlanta. He began to repair and make instruments and moved to Gainesville, where he said he "could fiddle a little, teach a little, fix fiddles, farm, and grow broilers." But fans continued to seek him out, wanting to hear him play, and by 1960 he was active again.

In 1968 Ernest married his star pupil, Darlene Collins from North Carolina. Darlene's family knew many of the famous old-time performers from the western North Carolina area, including Aunt Samantha Bumgarner, whose banjo was heard on some of the very first old-time records. A few years later the couple moved back to North Carolina, to a beautiful home high on a bluff overlooking Waynesville. There Ernest continued to teach, make and repair violins, and accept occasional lecture and concert engagements. He was the subject of a thirty-minute documentary filmed in 1967 by Georgia Educational Television, a show which has been run on fifty stations from Texas to Maryland. He has represented North Carolina at the national folk festivals in Washington and was active in the Smoky Mountain Folk Festival. His wife, an accomplished guitarist, often played back-up for Ernie's fiddling.

On my way up to see Ernie Hodges, I had been doing some research on Uncle Am Stuart, the old champion Tennessee fiddler who had made some interesting 1924 records for Vocalion and who had also traveled with the Hill Billies on their tours. It was natural, then, that our talk turned to Uncle Am:

Q: Ever play with Uncle Am Stuart?

A: Never played with him. All I got from him was through Charlie Bowman. Charlie played with him. He told me he was a right testy old fellow. The boys were all great on playing tricks after the show. So one night, Charlie told me, they all went out having a good time. Some of them had imbibed a little too much. Anyway one came back, and Uncle Am had gone to bed. Uncle Am was absolutely terrified by snakes, especially rattlesnakes, so one of the boys came in and found a stuffed rattlesnake downstairs. It was a good idea, so he—Uncle Am hadn't quite gone to bed—he slipped it under his bed and lay the cover down on it. They said they almost had to leave town when Uncle Am pulled that cover back and found that stuffed snake in there. They never would tell him who it was because they were afraid he'd kill him. . . . But Uncle Am was a good old fiddler, old-timey way.

Q: We were talking earlier about Uncle Am preserving one of the oldest fiddling styles on record, and you mentioned that you had some turn-of-the century cylinders by fiddlers like Charles D'almaine. Do you find an appreciable difference of style on these very early records?

A: Yes, the style seemed to change when commercialism began getting bigger, say 1940 or so. Western-style fiddling, pop fiddling, entered into it. Fiddlers wanted to make a bigger show, and they didn't play from then on so much the old-time way. Now the best old-time fiddlers, or the better fiddlers, musically speaking, that I've ever known, and I've known lots of them, they could read music well enough to learn real hornpipes, and some of them can play schottisches. One of the finest fiddlers I ever heard was Henry Ford's fiddler about 1930–1935, an old man in Indiana. We were putting on a fiddlers' contest in a theater in Dayton, Ohio, and this old fellow came. And I saw he had a fine-looking fiddle— fiddle strung up with the old-time strings, the guts strings—and when he played he set the fiddle on his lap, down, and had the bow as you'd play a cello. I believe he was left-handed. I'm not certain of his name—whether or not it was Mellie Dunham. A marvelous player, authentic, Scotch-Irish—he knew his fiddling, just as the music was written. He played professionally, beautiful, and the crowd didn't catch it, they did not appreciate him at all. They wanted something more flashy. And once in Louisville there were two fiddlers that played, competed against each other, used "Devil's Dream" as their tune. They were both fine fiddlers, but the one who played it with a little more abandon got it, the prize. And another fiddler in the South, you can't overlook if you don't know about him, is Fiddlin' Doc Roberts. He made many records, over 100. I think he died two or three years ago. My wife and I hunted him up in Richmond, Kentucky, about three years ago, and we all played some—I think he was seventy-nine or eighty—and we played awhile. And the next year they came through and stopped over at Camp Nelson to see an old friend. He told us Doc had died, and then someone else told us that, so we never went by there no more. I didn't tape the session. Doc wouldn't have played a tune for tape under any circumstances. He got a raw deal. Somebody from New York came down, these searchers, and talked him out of all his letters and everything he had. He trusted them enough and they took it all to New York, and it's never been heard of and he never got it. He was bitter. All those fiddlers up there now, they've heard about it and been gyped and everyone will tell you no tape. That's the first thing they'll tell you.

Q: How accurate do you think the phonograph record—the old ones—is in representing the quality of music available in the South in the 1920s? Do you think the best got recorded, or were there some good old-time musicians who simply refused to record?

A: Well, some of them had the same experience I had, or something similar, and would never record again for the small sum they would get for it. For instance, the Blue Sky Boys, as popular as they were, just got $50 a record. You know they sold in the millions. Well, in 1928 there was a music dealer in Corbin, Kentucky, that claimed he was selling thousands of records for Columbia, and he asked all the fiddlers and players, he took them all to Johnson City to record. I wanted to make a recording. My brothers sang and we had a good outfit—oh yes, we wanted to go. My father had an old-time gospel quartet [he was a music teacher]. So I talked with a friend of mine, Bailey Briscoe, a fine banjoist, of Lewis & Briscoe fame. I played with them all over the country, and he went with us. We didn't understand it until a little later, but this music dealer, he was gonna crowd us all into big cattle trucks and drive over those mountains that long way. Well, we all had cars, and we said, "No, we'll drive." So we drove, and it made him mad. He told the company that if they ever put out any of our records he wouldn't ever buy any more records from the company. So they didn't put ours out. We put on several good ones, two or three original things [see table 5]. They wouldn't release anything from our quartet. There was Dick Parman singing—he was a member of Dad's quartet. We called ourselves the Hodges Brothers, the Hodges Quartet. And Bailey Briscoe recorded under his own name. If they still have those masters,

Table 5

The Columbia files for the 1928 Johnson City sessions that Ernie Hodges remembered show the following unissued sides:

Wed, Oct.17

147216	Dog-Gone Mule	Hodgers (sic) Brothers
147217	What Are You Going to Do with the Baby?	Hodgers (sic) Brothers
147218	I'll Go Flipping Through the Pearly Gates	Hodgers (sic) Quartet
147219	You Can't Make a Monkey Out of Me	Hodgers (sic) Quartet
147220	The Joke Song	Bailey Briscoe
147221	Times Are Getting Hard	Bailey Briscoe

that would be interesting to get. One of the songs we recorded, we were always hunting something different, so we found that old song "What Are You Going to Do with the Baby-On" and put it on and sang it. Maybe "Golden Slippers—I don't recall.

What they wanted then was that "Moonshine Still in Georgia" kind of stuff. I remember one of the session men was a man named Bill Brown. He told me what was making the big hit then, the Skillet Lickers and Fiddlin' John [Carson].

Q: Remember anything about Brown? [Bill Brown was a well-known A&R man for Columbia and later for Brunswick-Vocalion. He was an Atlanta native who later went into the bakery business there.]

A: Just went about doing his job, that's all. He was about thirty to thirty-five at the time. He'd be getting some age on him now. I feel sure he was from New York. He certainly wasn't like any Southerner I'd ever seen. He was quiet, never said much. Seemed to be strictly business. I later did write Columbia a time or two and asked them, at least let us have the masters, but I never got any response.

Q: You remember any of the other artists at this session?

A: Charlie Bowman was there. I didn't know him till later, but he was there with his daughters. From around Corbin there were fifteen or twenty went down; I think John Walker went. But it was a disappointment to us, and we came on back after it was over and we had been informed it would not come out. This man's name was Golden, he had a music store there in Corbin, and he had actually got trucks to haul the people over there. I couldn't say for sure if he was getting money per head, but if he wasn't I can't see why he would get angry.

Q.: Did you play a lot in Kentucky?

A: I played in sixty-five counties in Kentucky, met a lot of people, but I didn't get to the extreme western part. . . . Mostly around Lincoln County, near Stanford, stayed with my grandfather after I was eight or nine years old. My father went to Corbin and became a railroad man there. So I played around a lot there and met just about everybody.

Q: Did you ever play with Leonard Rutherford?

A: Yes, many times. He was a very good and smooth old-time fiddler. The last time I saw him was at a friend's house in

Kentucky. We were playing there, and he came in one afternoon with some other people, Gene Ruppe, I think. Gene was an ingenious fiddler and a banjo player—had a wooden leg that he had made himself. Lived down there around the Sunbright section. We all played that afternoon five or six of us, and that was the last I seen or heard from Rutherford. But there's another fellow you should know about, and you may know him—he put out a good many recordings—is Grayson, another blind fellow, a fiddler. I think he was from Mountain City when I knew him.

Q: How about backing up a bit now and outlining your own life?

A: I've been planning for several years to do an autobiography, I've had such an interesting life. I was born at the foot of Beech Mountain in Avery County, North Carolina, where the ski slopes are, near Boone, at Banner Elk, December 26, 1907. I have a tape recording of an interview with my father about how he got his musical education by walking forty miles over those mountains to learn how to sing gospel music, to teach theory, harmony, and so on. So I attended his singing school, of course, as a boy, and I don't recall when I couldn't read music because of that—it was an immense help to me later. We moved to Kentucky when I was about seven, to Lincoln County, a long way back in the hills, in uncleared land. We cut trees, about three families, after a burn-out up there. They wanted to gather up in that rough country, and it was so difficult to farm. They concurred it would be better—had an uncle out there. So three families of us settled there on that ridge known as Shakerag and joined Kick Ridge on one side, I don't know what on the other. Anyway, there's where I grew up.

I always wanted to play; it was just in me. And string music, I never heard but a little. I heard my father play once. . . . He was a fiddler and a good one, but he quit. He quit and he somehow seemed to think that it was a little bit anti-religious. Anyway, I had to have a fiddle, a banjo, or something. So one day I told my dad, "I've just got to have a fiddle." And he said, "Oh, that's more difficult than you think." Oh, I know I could learn it. Well, I started digging ginseng, fetching possum skins, anything I could get working, making 50¢ a day, until I got $25.95, and I sent to Sears

Roebuck for a fiddle, bow, case, and instruction book. Two weeks before that I went back to my dad's house—I was with my grandfather then—and I saw Dad had a fiddle on the bed. I asked him if it was in tune; he said it was. So I strummed it. He said, "Yeah, it's in tune," so I kept that in mind, and when my fiddle came in, in about two weeks, I knew how to tune it up. We had one of the old-fashioned telephone lines to cover that end of the county, the old Lum 'n' Abner kind, and I got the fiddle about noon and called my mother up about 4 o'clock and played "My Old Kentucky Home" all the way through.

My first banjo, my grandfather helped me make that out of a gourd, with horsehair strings. Then I borrowed a better banjo, homemade with groundhog hide stretched on it, tacked on it—practiced on it until I got a better banjo, an old-timer. It was just a matter of going from one thing to the other, and I knew several of the old tunes, and I heard Fiddlin' John [Carson] play a tune or two on the record. I learned everything quickly and practiced all the time.

So the first fiddler's contest was when I first started to high school. I learned they were going to have one at Stanford. And I just had to go in order to hear fiddlers. I knew a blind man, had heard him play "Cluck Old Hen" and "Mississippi Sawyer," and that was about all he could play, and I'd learned all that, so I had to go to this contest. There were nineteen fiddlers there. Fiddlin' Doc Roberts was there from Richmond—I'd heard about him, and so of course he got the first prize. They gave the second prize to an old fellow who lived there, and he was a good old-time fiddler in his style—Breedlove. But I got the third money. I was just starting in high school, fourteen, maybe fifteen. I'd ride horseback to high school, twenty miles a day, walking if the weather's too bad. Ride a horse up and down that little mountain there. That was the first contest. That was about 1920.

The next one was that same year. I went to Louisville, I was on the stock judging team, took my fiddle, and won a contest. First prize, and lost in the finals because I was handicapped twenty points because I was so young. I got a letter from the judges about that.

After that, now, they had many contests in Kentucky. And

during the Depression days that was one of the ways of making a few dollars. You could nearly always get $10 for a contest, up to $30 or $40 sometimes.

Q: How were these early contests conducted? Did you, for instance have to play solo without any back-up? Did all contestants have to play the same tune? What criteria did they use to evaluate you?

A: They didn't put down many rules. Except that it should be old-time music. They let you play it solo, alone, or with one accompaniment. They didn't allow a band to help you out. Most people I recall generally used a back-up man, though there were some times that they didn't. Both ways. Usually guitar, sometimes just a banjo. I remember one interesting contest in Richmond, Kentucky, at a theater. Now this is funny, and if any of them are still living, they'd still joke with me about it. Al Sampson, a player and a machinist, and a gang of us, maybe Gene Ruppe, I don't remember how many, heard about this contest up in the country not far out of Richmond. There was a fiddler who lived up there who played just like Kessinger, couldn't tell the difference. I don't think it was Kessinger, but just like him, I've heard the records. He was famous around there as a fiddler, and I knew by that that they'd lean pretty strong to him. It was in a high school auditorium. Well, we all played without any accompaniment—that was one of the rules. So they got down to us. The judges were confused, because the crowd was liking my part, so much they'd made us play another piece again. We had a play-off. There was only $10 in it. We played a waltz. Then finally we'd play a hornpipe each. Then another one. The crowd was on my side and they kept hesitating. Finally he said, "You've got to give it to somebody," and I said, "Yes, give it to one of us." So they said, "We'll let you play one more piece." So I went out and did "Pop Goes the Weasel" as a juggle trick. I was angry by that time with the way it went, and he played. They gave it to me, and we gave him $5.

The other thing that they laughed at me about was at Richmond, Kentucky—no, it was a town down south of Louisville, Nicholasville. They had a contest and the prizes were for first fiddle, a fiddle unaccompanied, fiddle with banjo, and best-looking fiddler. I got [number] three. Of course, you can imagine what an ugly bunch of fiddlers there must have been there, and they've been kidding me about it for years.

Q: You earlier talked a little about Charlie Bowman. Did he learn much from Uncle Am? Do you think Uncle Am was much of an influence on other fiddlers in this part of the country.

A: Charlie never mentioned him in that respect to me. One fiddler playing with another is likely to pick up a few things. That's how they learn it. But Charlie couldn't be described as a student of Uncle Am. Charlie was very musical, and he heard other fiddlers and he never had any special heroes among them. I lived with Charlie for years and got him a job in Atlanta and he stayed down there, and he had I believe ten children by his first wife. Later he married a girl in Atlanta and had another child. He died when he was about sixty-eight, sixty-nine. . . . Good many years ago. He lost a leg, and they honored him in Washington— had a big show in his honor and he went up there. But Charlie's spirit was broken after that, he didn't live very long. But Charlie was pretty original; he played the old-timey way. I've got a record or two here that he did with Hopkins. He also made some with his brothers, and his daughters made some as the Bowman Sisters.

Q: What do you think of the so-called "super style," the careful, deliberate contest style that some fiddlers are cultivating today? Do you think it is a movement away from the original Southeastern style, or an improvement on it?

A: Well, there's been some of it all the way back. When Fiddlin' Doc Roberts played that first contest that I'd ever seen him or heard him in, he played "Turkey in the Straw" . . . and he played it very slowly, and each note distinct, not fast at all. And he played it brilliantly, I allowed, loud and strong and very well. Clayton McMichen used to play a fairly slow style, and it was effective. After all, they were more interested in getting the prize than they were in any special style. They'd develop whatever style they wanted to win the prize. But I haven't noticed too much in the fine playing, in the finest playing such as these Scotch fiddlers like McAndrew and those. They're musicians. They don't play anything too fast or too slow. The Scotch are very particular about their trills, where they go in. Especially bagpipes, they make you play that one stem there for several years before they'll let you play anything else. And fiddlers used to be pretty much that way in the early days, but they started breaking out of that long about the time they started making these Southern records, to a great extent. You can hear some recordings of mine made about 1910 or earlier, where they had an orchestra or several pieces, with them.

Q: Did most of the fiddlers you grew up with in Kentucky use the long bow or shorter bow?

A: Very few people among the country fiddlers that didn't know anything about music or had much background in it. They used too small or too little bow, not enough bow to bring out a full tone. Too short strokes, not enough to pull that tone out, and a lot of them would hold the bow way up beyond the frog, and just all different positions. You can't even say that that represents good fiddling of that style—it doesn't. In good fiddling, they used their bow quite a lot. Now you don't use from one end to the other on a hornpipe or a reel, but you do on some things, and those who bow best play best. Now Charlie Bowman used a fairly good amount of bow, he fingered well, he had a good sense of harmony, he could back-up fiddle, he could do most anything. He could play guitar some, banjo some. Play a balloon, play a washtub—he was very versatile.

Q: What did they think of trick fiddling in the contests of the 1920s and 1930s? Would a good trick fiddler tend to win a contest?

A: No, no, you had to be legitimate usually. Now the reason I used "Mocking Bird" successfully, it was accepted as an old-time piece, and my variations were my own, and while I did do some bird whistling and things like that, I kept it in the context of time, and made a musical thing out of it. What I was doing was trying to develop a piece that would have mass appeal and yet have enough class to be appreciated by the musicians. I finally arrived at that point in between. Many a musician has asked me, "My goodness, why don't you record it or get it written?" And I never did. But though the common person can understand it, it's full of difficult passages. I even have some pizzicato passages in it.

Q: Was a pizzicato passage common back then?

A: Not too much. I innovated a great deal. Before I quit playing contests I was playing classical music. I studied violin about eight years with a master after I went to Atlanta and played standard repertoire. But even before I went to Atlanta, I could read and had developed the correct way of bowing and fingering.

Once when I was playing "Speed the Plow" there at Atlanta at WSB, there was a WPA orchestra there. The conductor had played seven years with Victor Herbert, and I saw him while I was playing call the whole orchestra out there to watch me. When I got through playing it, he walked up and shook hands and said, "I see you've had some marvelous training. Where did you study?" "Never had a private lesson in my life." He couldn't understand it. I worked hard, though, for seven to eight years, under an old master who had himself studied under five world-famous masters. So I've got a classical background now, and it's been worth lots. In fact, I've recently had the music published for a composition for five-string banjo that I play. It's based on Bach. It's been published by the American Banjo Fraternity. We are keeping alive the old classic style of playing the banjo, and it's been going on for many years. Based on the old classical style of players like Van Eps and Ossman and MacFarland. A scientific way of playing. I've heard of a man from here in Asheville, Aligood, who played the classical style, but I never met him. But the banjo at the turn-of-the-century did play some ragtime, some marches, two-steps, and clogs. And breakdowns. Fact is, in my show-business days in the 1930s, I would play Van Eps as some of my featured numbers, his marches, "Poppies and Wheat." It's a technical thing that takes from one of the banjos to the other. Always made a big hit with them. But when the Jazz Age came on they wanted a tenor sound, and they cut the fifth string off, and made a tenor and a plectrum. I never cared for Eddie Peabody because he just strummed it.

But you have to admire the country players. They kept the banjo before the public. But the classical style is coming back, and bluegrass has gone as far classical as it can go. Unless they learn to read and get better stuff. Today in my programs I find young people are wild about my banjo section. I will play this Bach presto, and a caprice based on Paganini, and they've never heard anything like this on the banjo. Then I play some country pieces, like the "Coal Creek March"—that's a pretty good piece of music.

Q: Back in Kentucky, do you recall the old-time musicians on the banjo employing strange or unusual tunings?

A: Oh yes. They'd tune a banjo anyway they wanted to. There was a B tuning—the "Sebastopol March" is usually played in a D tuning—then they used several minor tunings. I never employed but two tunings, the C string up to G, like the bluegrass tuning, or the C string down. That's where I know about all my other keys, with the C string down. Except where I have to use that in a harmonic, such as bugle calls. I don't run the bass up, very few of the classical banjo players ever do, except for what it's written for.

Q: When you were growing up, who were the most widely admired banjo players?

A: Lewis & Briscoe. When I was a kid, I'd never heard anything but "Turkey in the Straw" or "Cripple Creek" rapped off just like grandpappy did it. I knew how to do it, only I always liked to use my fingers and I'd never heard a fine banjo player. I did hear Fred van Eps on something. I thought that didn't even sound like a banjo to me. It was the hole in the head banjo that made the difference.

One day in the one-room school house, in came a couple of fellows, and I didn't have a good banjo, just a cheap banjo, and I saw that that was a real case. And the teacher said, "They're going to put on a show here tomorrow night. This is Frank Lewis and Bailey Briscoe." So they got out and played "Cincinnati Clog." Had got a little S. S. Stewart, short neck, and tuned up one tuning—I'd never heard anything like it—and ended up with a breakdown. I just had, absolutely *had* to see 'em. I was up in the air twenty feet, told my grandpappy he just had to go up there. On the way up, I said, "Grandpa, they've got to stay somewhere tonight—let 'em come down and stay with us." He agreed, and I told 'em when the show was over. Lewis did a blackface act. I later was with 'em, worked in the same show for years, two or three years. I ask 'em, said, "I play the fiddle, play the banjo a little bit and the fiddle." "Oh, so you do, huh?" And they said they would come spend the night. So we all went down there, as soon as we got in lit the lamp, and Briscoe, he was a character: "So you can play the fiddle?" "Yes." "Get your fiddle. Maybe we'll play a tune with you." So I got the fiddle and cut loose on something. I saw him wink at

Frank, and they took out their banjos, and we just had a time. It just tickled him to death. Said, "I got a brother-in-law, Virgil Lewis, great fiddler, lives in Louisville. He's a jewelryman up there. You're the only ever play equal him. I want you to come over and spend a week or two with me at Sparta." So I went over there just to learn the banjo. Now they played the correct chords, they played the banjo well. They got it right. They called it scientific playing. They'd heard some classical players in the past I think. While they didn't read, they did play good music—so far ahead of the ordinary playing around through the bluegrass section there. I later joined them, played with them, had 1,001 experiences with them—almost killed a few times. But that's another story.

Q: Neither of them ever recorded?

A: Bailey went with us and recorded at Johnson City—"Coal Creek," maybe "Cincinnati Clog," I don't know. *One* record, and it never came out. Bailey to his dying day, said, "Honey, you must write and see if they will just send us that test record." But I was never able to get it.

Q: Did you know Lowe Stokes?

A: I knew Lowe well. He's still alive out there in Oklahoma someplace. But at the time I heard him, he wasn't better than Mac. He couldn't possibly be, because he had lost his right arm by then. He had a contraption he'd made to fit the bow. This was in the thirties. I knew him in Cincinnati. We put on several big fiddler's contests there—Music Hall, Taft Auditorium, several groups of us would organize it. He was there.

Now McMichen in his last days was a much improved fiddler over most of his records. After he left Georgia and settled around Cincinnati and Louisville, and played there. We took his spot in Cincinnati when we went there. We had been at Louisville, this was the Hodges Brothers. However, we did get together with Mac and play a lot, and Mac could read music enough to learn, say, "Durang's Hornpipe" how it ought to be. He did do good solid, clean fiddling, and he was much better at the last. In the early days Stokes and he played very much the same. Now another thing, speaking of Georgia fiddlers, I knew 'em all: Gid Tanner, John Carson there at the last, played with 'em. Now Gid's son,

Gordon, is a fiddle maker himself, and he told me that he done the fiddling on some of those last records, like "Down Yonder." Gid Tanner wasn't a good fiddler—didn't pretend to be. Neither was Fiddlin' John. But Gid Tanner was as ugly as homemade sin, and he was the funniest fellow you ever saw on stage. Big red faced fellow, and he just looked so country, you just fell in love with him. He was a character, just like Junior Samples on "Hee Haw," only more so, 'cause Gid was funnier.

Q: What was Gid's function in a stage performance by the Skillet Lickers?

A: He'd saw with 'em and do a lot of talking—he was the comic. It was mostly a musical show. Riley did about all of the singing. They had different ones with 'em at different times.

Q: I sometimes wonder how many of the old-time fiddling contests were really contests and how many were more or less staged events designed as entertainment.

A: Well, I've had a lot of experience with fiddling contests. You know, you hear a fellow say, "I'm the United States Champion," or "I'm the World's Champion." Well, all you have to do to have a world's champion is go into a town, put you on a show, and advertise it as world's champion, and let somebody win it by popular applause. Or rig it. All right: he becomes the world's champion. He uses that. Those are just show tricks. Most of them started after 1940. Most of them were honest. However, many of them let the audience do the judging. Other times they'd have three judges. Fiddlers or those knowledgeable in fiddling. And they'd be as honest as they could—sometimes they might have preferences. A lot of time the Skillet Lickers would do a concert and use the name fiddling contest just to draw a crowd. Now they used to have some big fiddling contests in Atlanta. There was a fellow there called Alec Smart, little old fellow, and he'd stage contests back in the Skillet Lickers' days. I knew Alec. He had a contest or two back in 1934 after I went down there. But it sort of faded out by then. They used to have a lot of contests during the late 1920s.

Q: Who were the leading fiddlers around Atlanta in the early 1930s?

A: There were some nobody's ever heard of. There was a

physician, Dr. Powell, originally from North Carolina, and he moved back there just before he died—a good old-time fiddle player, he could read music, but he could play the old-time music. And Two Manning was an old-timer—I've got a hand-written piece or two or music that he did for me. He'd been a telegrapher and a piano tuner, and he was a good old-time fiddler. Had an unorthodox style—claimed he had telegrapher's cramp, but he did play those old tunes, hornpipes correctly, slowly and methodically. Then the Rice Brothers, Paul and Hoke—one of 'em's dead now—had a father-in-law, Bud Silvey, who was a good fiddler. Hoke is dead now, went to Nashville after we broke up.

Q: Some people have said that Hoke Rice was actually a better guitar player than Riley Puckett. Would you agree?

A: Oh well, he may have played better in some ways. He wasn't famous as a guitar player. They sang mostly. Charlie Bowman played with 'em a good while, went to Shreveport and played with them down there a while.

Q: Then you went to Atlanta in the fall of 1934?

A: Yes. We had been the Hodges Brothers playing around throughout Kentucky and into Cincinnati. They had promised us a spot on WCKY, and we knew it would go out everywhere better, in Covington then, Wilson's station, and they promised us that the moment McMichen moved. If he quit, we would have his spot. They were running over with outfits there: Guy Blakeman, a fine fiddler playing around up there—you may not have heard of him—later committed suicide. So we went up there when we heard that Mac was going to leave. We were the Hodges Brothers then, and then we became the Dixie Vagabonds and took on a larger show. I was sick then, for several months, and my brother Ralph was running it then. I went back and we got on the NBC program. We were very popular, one of the most popular musical outfits in the United States, according to one music magazine. I finally got tired of it all, and went back, and from there we had a chance to go to WSB in Atlanta. My brother still plays some. He's out in California. The other day he sent me a guitar record he did. He and his wife did nightclub work for years.

We had a good musical outfit. Everybody could read music. We had anything you could want from a sixteen- to twenty-piece orchestra for dances or for country or for anything. On the network it was known as "Happy Days in Dixie."

Q: Did you know Earl Johnson?

A: Oh yes. He died just two–three years ago. He was at my house just before he died. He had learned to play the banjo. That's when I was living in Georgia. There was another Johnson that used to play the fiddle, Laurel Johnson—dead now too. He copied a lot from Arthur Smith. He played well, but not professionally, except for an occasional radio show.

Q: What did you think of Arthur Smith?

A: I played on a show with him, East Point, at the edge of Atlanta there, somewhere in the 1940s. I was interested in his fiddle and wanted to see it and found it was just about a $50 fiddle. It sounded different in those days from other fiddles. But of the old-type fiddling, he was just about as good as anyone. He's been copied, and his influence has spread around. His influence is in [Howdy] Forrester's playing, and that of several others. He really wasn't that good—he was limited, but he sounded good, and in that day people were just as interested in hearing him fiddle as they were to hear anybody else sing. In that day people wanted to hear instrumental music, occasionally songs, but they didn't want it commercialized, as they have done in Nashville now. They've ruined Nashville. I quit listening to the Opry in the 1940s, and I hardly ever listen but a little while anymore. It's nothing but commercialism, and it's all the same. They don't want it, 'cause they can't sell fiddling, and they can sell songs. Even when the fiddle was losing popularity, I never found an audience I couldn't excite with the fiddling. So I know what the people want, and do appreciate: good stuff.

Q: A lot of people today say that modern fiddling is a lot more technically proficient than it was in the old days. What would you say about that?

A: If you take your general fiddlers, it would be very surprising if they're not better. In the old days, a fiddler could just hear another fiddler—that was the only way. If he couldn't read music, he had a limited chance of learning anything. Today there are records running out your ears. Every day you can hear it, and you can study the best and the poorest; you can hear fiddling from Sweden, or Scotland, or Canada. You can hear the best, and if you can't get it today—well, they ought to be twice as good today. And generally they are better today, certainly [better] than those who didn't read music in the old days. *But,* they're certainly not better than the old originals who could read music and play it according to the violin rules.

Q: If you had to make out a list or the top three fiddlers before 1940, who would be on it?

A: Well, I didn't hear enough of them. I would have to put that old man, I forgot his name, Henry Ford's fiddler [possibly Mellie Dunham]. He was by far the best musician among the fiddlers who played old-time music, technique and all, even though he held it funny. But there was a fiddler in Kentucky that I met—now he wasn't the best, but he was good, and he was lively. I don't know whether his name is old man Clausen or what. But Frank Lewis and I were on our way from a show trip and stopped at this little place, and these fellows recognized us and insisted that we go out in the country and hear a fiddler play. So we finally did—it was way up on a side of a hill, yard grown up, big old country house. He came out and had a beard down to his waist. They said, "These men want to hear you play a piece." "Gimme a fiddle." So I handed him my fiddle, glanced at it, and he cut loose on "Buck Creek" and two or three pieces, and he used one end of that bow as well as the other. He was a little rough—of course he was old—but he could play. I'd heard of him, but I don't remember his name. This was the central part of Kentucky, down close to Loretta [Marion County]. And Guy Blakeman was a good fiddler in his day. He was from somewhere around Cincinnati, northern Kentucky. He played WCKY when I did. There was a good little fiddler down at Lexington, Charlie Linville. He's a little on the modern style.

Q: You are a fiddle-maker too; how did you get into that line?

A: I began repairing violins when I was at the Leffinwell Violin School in Atlanta. In 1936 I made my first violin. Made it because I couldn't afford one as good as I wanted. As a boy, I met up with quite a few fiddle-makers and fiddle players. That's how I learned how the ribs of a good fiddle ought to be curved and how a well-made fiddle ought to sound. But, now, I learned how to make fiddles by practice. I feel it takes ten to fifteen years to really learn the art.

Q: How long does it take you to make a fiddle?

A: At least a year, but it takes years and years of experience to get even a passable instrument, And you've got to be careful of the wood you choose. Usually I use curly maple for the back and sides and spruce for the top. And it's got to be wood that has a voice, a musical tone of its own. Then you've got to carve the wood of the back and top exactly—and I mean exactly—to the right thickness. If the wood is too thick, the fiddle will sound thin and squeaky. If you whittle it too thin, the tone will be hard and coarse, have these overtones, what we call wolftones.

Then you've got to set your bass-bar in a certain way so that it gives great body to your G. You must set the sound post of pine that joins the top and back inside, and then you thump it and listen. Then you blow through the F-holes and listen. You keep making these very minute adjustments until the tone you get when you tap the back and top, these tones should be exactly a step apart. The vibration of your breath when you blow through the F-holes tells you if the air space is vibrating as it should. Then you set the neck, just so. I use this fine ebony on the fingerboard. Apply the varnish—it has to be special too, has to let the fiddle breathe so it can sing.

You know, fiddle-making has been passed over as an art. It's a real art, like painting or drawing. But it is a real art. You can see it and you can hear it in the music.

Acknowledgment

Special thanks to Mr. and Mrs. Hodges for their time in answering questions and sharing their scrapbooks and record collection.

Discography

NOTE: The albums listed below contain material by artists discussed in the text. Although many of the vintage recordings listed have been reissued on LP, far fewer have made the transition to compact disc.

Anthology: Bob Wills. 1935–1973. Rhino 2-CD set, 70744. Contains original versions of "Faded Love," "Maiden's Prayer," et al.

Appalachian Waltz. Mark O'Connor, Yo Yo Ma, Edgar Meyer. Sony SK 68460. Current recordings that have been described as O'Connor's tribute to Texas-style fiddling.

Championship Years. Mark O'Connor. Country Music Foundation CMF-0150. On-stage recordings of the fiddler when he was active on the contest circuit; superb examples of standard contest tunes.

Decca Country Classics, 1934–1973. Various artists. 3 CD set. MCAD3-11069. Among many vintage cuts are ones by Curly Fox and Clayton McMichen's Georgia Wildcats.

Hank Garland and His Sugar Footers. Bear Family 15551. 1950-era sides that feature Tommy Jackson playing "hillbilly jazz" items like "Seventh and Union" and "Hillbilly Express."

Legend of Clark Kessinger. County 2713. A repackaging of some of the finest Kanawha sides from the 1960s.

Music of Kentucky, Vol. 2. Various artists. Yazoo 2014. Anthology of old-time vintage recordings, including those of Bill Shepherd and others.

Old Time Songs and Tunes. The Skillet Lickers. County CD 3509. A complete CD devoted to vintage 1926–1931 sides by the Skillet Lickers, though the emphasis is on the later, three-fiddle sides.

Possum Up a Gum Stump. Various artists. Alabama Traditions 103. Field and commercial recordings of Alabama fiddlers, including Charlie Stripling.

Roots 'n' Blues: The Retrospective. Various artists. 4 CD set. Columbia Legacy CK4 47911. Original 1920s recordings by Fiddlin' John Carson, Charley Bowman, Narmour & Smith, and the Skillet Lickers.

Rural String Bands of Tennessee. Various artists. County CD (forthcoming). Includes Grayson & Whitter's "Train 45" among others.

Rural String Bands of Virginia. Various artists. County CD 3502. Includes Fiddlin' Powers's "Old Virginia Reel, Parts 1 and 2."

White Country Blues, 1926–1938: A Lighter Shade of Blue. Various artists. 4 CD set. Sony Legacy C2K 47466. Included among the selections is "Carroll County Blues" by Narmour & Smith.

Index